Folk Religion of
the Pennsylvania Dutch

T0197962

Folk Religion of
the Pennsylvania Dutch

Witchcraft, Faith Healing
and Related Practices

RICHARD L.T. ORTH

McFarland & Company, Inc., Publishers
Jefferson, North Carolina

LIBRARY OF CONGRESS CATALOGUING-IN-PUBLICATION DATA

Names: Orth, Richard L. T., 1976– author.
Title: Folk religion of the Pennsylvania Dutch : witchcraft, faith healing
    and related practices / Richard L. T. Orth.
Description: Jefferson, North Carolina : McFarland & Company, Inc.,
    Publishers, 2018. | Includes bibliographical references and index.
Identifiers: LCCN 2017055017 | ISBN 9781476672267 (softcover : acid
    free paper) ∞
Subjects: LCSH: Magic—Pennsylvania. | Pennsylvania Dutch—Religion. |
    Pennsylvania—Religious life and customs. | Folklore—Pennsylvania.
Classification: LCC BF1622.U6 O78 2018 | DDC 133.4/3097481—dc23
LC record available at https://lccn.loc.gov/2017055017

BRITISH LIBRARY CATALOGUING DATA ARE AVAILABLE

ISBN (print) 978-1-4766-7226-7
ISBN (ebook) 978-1-4766-3074-8

Front cover: a barn (avowed to be the "Most Beautifully Decorated
in America," with hex signs; a Pennsylvania Dutch farmwife pouring
milk at a stove; 11½-inch hand carved figure (circa 1900) used in a
Powwow cure to break a Hexerei spell (photographs from a private
collection used with permission)

Printed in the United States of America

McFarland & Company, Inc., Publishers
  Box 611, Jefferson, North Carolina 28640
  www.mcfarlandpub.com

This book is dedicated
to my longtime mentor, Richard H. Shaner.
Thank you for being my friend and remaining by my side
all these years even in the most tumultuous of times.
I hope you can accept my departure
and thank you!

Table of Contents

Preface

Among *Auslanders* (outsiders) observing the Pennsylvania Dutch Country, and even some who are part of the Pennsylvania Dutch folk culture through its descended community, the practice of Powwowing is often confused with Hexerei. As in most of Western civilization, there has long existed (and still exists) among the Germanic "Dutch" people a belief in white and black magic. The art of white magic in the Dutch Country is referred to as Braucherei or, more popularly, Powwowing. Hexerei, of course, is the art of black magic. Powers used to heal in the art of Braucherei are derived from God (the Holy Trinity), but the powers employed in Hexerei are derived from the Devil, in the simplest explanation. Therefore, one who engages in this sort of dark magic has bartered or "sold his soul to the Devil" and is destined for Hell, so practitioners beware!

For nearly three centuries, the Pennsylvania Dutch have not hesitated to use Braucherei in the healing of their sick and afflicted, and, regionally, the culture has canonized early 19th-century faith healer Mountain Mary (of the Oley Hills) as a saint for her healing powers. But we will get more into her remarkable story later (as well as that of her contemporary, John George Hohman, who published numerous early 19th-century books on the matter). This form of faith healing has many counterparts in our civilization; however, the subset of Hexerei, witchcraft, or black magic was always considered the utmost form of evil in the region, and only desperate people (and those with devious intentions) have resorted to its equally powerful and secret powers.

Yet dating back even earlier than the widespread use of Braucherei and Hexerei in the Pennsylvania Dutch Country, among the oldtime traditions of the Pennsylvania Dutch people, are the 18th-century broadside amulets that have been handed down since colonial times. These amulets evolved into iconic good luck charms among devout Christian families who lived in southeastern Pennsylvania, which included French Huguenot pioneers, also grouped as Pennsylvania Dutch, along with some who lived in New York State with the Holland Dutch, a distantly different group/heritage (I will elaborate below). Always written in the German Pennsylvania Dutch dialect, these "Himmelsbriefs," published in German, were amulets of religious folk beliefs and a reminder of native Christian folklife in that they protected each family from evil, house fire, and unfortunate health hazards as long as members practiced a Christian lifestyle.

"Pennsylvania Dutch" is the original term used by William Penn's English colonists here and abroad to describe these immigrants from Rhineland Germany, and it refers to this Rhenish German civilization of native Palatines covered throughout this book. This "cultural group" includes not just Germans but also French Huguenots, Swiss Amish and Mennonites, Holland Dutch Mennonites, and Moravians. Collectively, these people shared a German vernacular and, in arriving in America in large waves from the same geographic region, they sought farms in Pennsylvania (Penn's Woods) and nearly outnumbered William Penn's English immigrants.

This early American cultural melting pot, located in southeastern Pennsylvania, included these naturalized Rhineland citizens who swore allegiance to the United States but also assimilated with English laws and standards. However, in terms of everyday work habits and living customs (folk religion included), they followed in their native Rhineland fashion and continued their unique German dialect in America, which soon became known as "Pennsylvania Dutch" rather than formal High German. "Pennsylvania Dutch," as a colonial English-created colloquialism, was a more precise Americanism, indicating a broader group of individuals from Europe's Rhine Valley with pre–Revolutionary roots, as opposed to, say, "Pennsylvania Germans" or "German Americans." Many scholars interchange the terms (Pennsylvania Dutch with Pennsylvania Germans), and some use the latter exclusively; however, neither option is the preference of this author.

A Hexerei Vocabulary

The word "hex" (witch) is but one of several terms from the Pennsylvania Dutch dialect that have been assimilated into American English. It has been accepted by American lexicographers and is recognized in most standard dictionaries. The following is a simple vocabulary list of variations on "hex" as it was used in the Dutch Country.

FERHEXT: bewitched

HEXA-BRIEF: a piece of paper with Hexerei formulae written on it

HEXA-FOO: witch star or foot

HEXA-HEWWEL: witch stick with a mysterious moving propeller

HEXBALLA: witch ball; a ball of hair found in a cow's stomach at butchering time

HEX BOOK: witch book; a book containing occult knowledge

HEX DOCTOR: witch doctor

HEXESCHUSS: a shot fired to kill or drive out a witch

HEXING: bewitching

HEX-RING: a circular spot of ground where nothing will grow

HEX-SIGN: a geometric design painted on the forebay or front of a barn in certain parts of the Dutch Country

HEX-SPELL: witch spell

WAFFLE-HEX: a circular waffle produced from a rosette-type iron

Part I

*White and Black Magic
of the Pennsylvania
Dutch Country*

Hexerei
An Introduction

A Practice of Witchcraft

The occult practice of witchcraft among the Pennsylvania Dutch, despite its longevity, has rarely been accurately presented to the public. There is undoubtedly no other field in which the Pennsylvania Dutch folkways have been more misunderstood than the practice of Hexerei. From the earliest years of the 18th century to the present day, Hexerei has remained an underground belief and practice, and only in the last 40 years has enough evidence been collected to present a detailed study on the subject.

Pennsylvania Dutch witchcraft has been traced to Europe, and is similar to that which was popular in medieval times, but its persistence among the "Dutch" in America is due in part to the publication of various occult books and the efforts of several people to make a living from this practice. In almost every community, existing side by side with the practice of Braucherei was the cautious belief in Hexerei. The most astonishing fact about black and white magic among the Pennsylvania Dutch is that they did exist prevalently, and they actually worked. Cases upon cases are recorded from all parts of the Pennsylvania Dutch Country in which the powers of black and white magic have been successful. It is this success, more than anything else, that has kept these two supernatural forces alive in the culture even in today's world.

In parts of the Dutch Country today, Powwow and hex doctors who once derived a livelihood from performing services for the believers in these arts are now mere hobbyists, but effective nonetheless. However, it is much easier to find a percentage of these Germanic people who will be alarmed by any reference to the "cursed" *Sixth and Seventh Books of Moses*. The subject of witchcraft is a sensational one in any civilized culture, but among the Pennsylvania Dutch its former commonplaceness and unchallenged realism have been so interwoven in the culture that there are still some older folk in the backcountry prone to believe that Hexerei (witchcraft) is a normal phenomenon. In almost every phase of Pennsylvania Dutch folkways, there is recorded influence of this ancient art, from incantations to exorcising a witch from a butter churn to the more romantic love potion.

Furthermore, the religious nature of the Pennsylvania Dutch has sustained these beliefs up to the present day more so than among any other people in America. One folk practice most confused with Hexerei is Braucherei, also known as Powwowing. The art of Powwowing is a form of faith healing practiced popularly by laymen in the culture who derive their power from God. Although most Powwowing is performed for domestic ills, occasionally a Powwow doctor will break the spell over a ferhext (bewitched) person. The hex (either man or woman) who cast the spell is usually a neighbor in a community who wishes to make trouble for another person for a variety of reasons.

Within the Pennsylvania Dutch culture, there are various occult books that constitute a body of knowledge for those wishing to practice the art. One such book is the infamous *Sixth and Seventh Books of Moses*, a volume so powerful that mere possession of it will bring the owner good fortune. The most circulated book in this field, however, was John George Hohman's *The Long Lost Friend*, printed in Reading as early as 1820. Next in popularity to this volume was the three-book set compiled by Albertus Magnus titled *Egyptian Secrets*, printed in Allentown in 1869.

As witchcraft is not considered a pleasant subject, and since much of this knowledge is kept secret, one rarely encounters any reference to Hexerei in

Only after my great aunt Naomi suddenly passed away, and no one else volunteered, did I find her copy of the dreaded *Sixth and Seventh Books of Moses*.

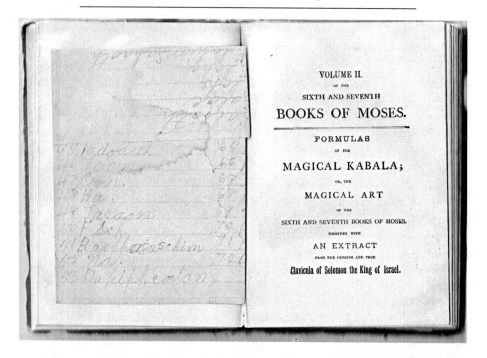

Title page of Volume II of the *Sixth and Seventh Books of Moses*, which claims to instruct readers in the spells used to create the miracles portrayed in the Bible.

a typical conversation. People who wish to learn about the occult must acquire the confidence of their informant before ever thinking to casually inquire about it. Although there is no historical truth to colorful "hex signs" warding off evil, any individual interested in the occult will find the real practice far more exciting than these colorful decorations.

As a young man, I was astonished to learn that my great aunt and uncle had the dreaded *Sixth and Seventh Books of Moses* and that my great aunt was able to do more than *Brod essa* (eat bread), a popular phrase used by the Dutch to describe a mysterious person suspected of being a witch. Later in life, I became familiar with their neighbors and was fortunate enough to learn of my great aunt's practice of Hexerei mostly through their interactions, although preferably indirect.

This collection of hill folk lived well outside of town when the area (like many other small farming communities at the time) had forested hills, contained a one-room school house, and boasted a few one-horse farms. Perhaps this was the common tie that bonded me with my long-time mentor and colleague, Richard H. Shaner, as we both had nearby mysterious members of the family practicing Hexerei, as I'm sure others did. His experiences with his well-known, notorious aunt are covered in chapter 6, "Secrets of a Pennsylvania Dutch Witch in the Oley Hills."

One of the first questions ever posed to me concerning my aunt, who at the time was in her 80s, while I had established relations with her neighbors, centered on whether I had ever seen her wood-stove plates pop. After replying "No" to the inquiring neighbor, I was told that if you had visited too long, she would make the iron plates pop high in the air. Although I never witnessed the popping plates for myself, my great aunt Naomi's stove was a very peculiar type, as I recall. The stove, easily dating to the latter half of the 1800s, had its fire box on the opposite side from all other stoves of its kind. Additionally, behind the cast iron flue, which supported a shelf in the rear of the stove, was a series of Xs with ambiguous symbols similar to hieroglyphics in Magnus's book—quite unusual.

My great aunt and uncle were rather mysterious, even to me (as I'm

An 1840 copy of *Egyptische Geheimnisse* (*Egyptian Secrets*) by Albertus Magnus. My grandmother, a churchgoing Christian, was embarrassed by her kin and other hill folk who pursued German-language occult books in the backwoods of Berks County.

sure they were to their neighbors), and their home was visited infrequently. Aunt Naomi was not at all like my other relations, being suspicious and crafty, and I thought her unpleasantness might have come from her debilitating arthritis and old injuries when she either fell or was pushed around early in life.

Despite her chronic issues, Aunt Naomi could walk with the aid of a stick or cane and would huckster her garden crops on foot among the hill folk. One of her former customers told me as I gathered field research that "old Naomi" had cast a spell on her newborn infant. The result of the spell was that the child would not eat, which would eventually lead to death. "Doc" M., the local hex doctor, told the woman that Naomi was the hex, and if she wished to break the spell, she had to make a path of salt around the perimeter

My great aunt's Sixth and Seventh Books of Moses's stove was very peculiar in that its fire box was on the opposite side from all other stoves of its kind, easily dating to the Civil War. A series of Xs was later discovered behind the cast iron flue.

of the house. The following Saturday morning, the mother, having performed this simple task days prior, waited eagerly for when it was time for Naomi to call with her produce. In the distance, the mother saw Naomi as she approached the house on foot. However, as soon as she reached the spot where the circle of salt crossed the path, without any ado, Naomi turned around and never returned again. The following day the child regained its appetite.

Probably the most unusual or devious episode was that related to me by Earl H., who lived across from "Old Naomi." As it happened, Earl admitted that he had experienced the same problem many years ago: his child would not eat. Upon consulting the same hex doctor, he learned that Naomi had "ferhext" his child. The wise doctor told Earl that, upon returning home, he should take the next diaper that the baby messed, wrap it up, and hide it under a crock (redware pot or container) in the attic. After doing this, the "Doc" cautioned him, the witch would come to see him and wish to borrow something—"do not lend her anything." That night, after Earl had attended to the instructions, my great aunt Naomi came to call. As she approached Earl at his house, she said, "I have a terrible taste in my mouth; will you lend me some bread?" Earl stoutly replied, "No." The next day his infant was well.

Since my great uncle and aunt never had any kids, I often wondered if Naomi resented others being able to have children, and if my uncle had married her under some strange spell. Even when my aunt was single, she was known to be peculiar, but, then again, my uncle wasn't typical, either. Sometimes considered just as peculiar as my aunt, his life revolved around fishing and drinking, sometimes bartering "shine" (moonshine) as a last resort.

After the death of my great aunt, I was summoned by my family, as no other member had volunteered to check on him and very reluctantly offered my assistance "only if needed!" (most likely cautious of what Naomi might have left behind of the non-physical type). In assisting my great uncle I began clearing out their modest backcountry abode. Overly curious, always cautious, and other times perhaps too eager, my eyes were open for a glimpse of their copy of the *Sixth and Seventh Books of Moses*, but instead I found two small envelopes hidden in the attic marked "1912 used." Upon investigation, I found enclosed in each envelope a dried turtledove tongue. I placed them aside.

After finding their copy of Magnus's *Egyptian Secrets* only a day or two later, in reading I discovered a love potion that called for the user to kiss his intended with a turtledove tongue in his mouth. When I questioned my ailing uncle about the dried tongues, he meekly shrugged the incident off with his usual stubbornness as best he could. After pondering this find most of the rest of the day, the following morning I confronted him outright and asked to see their copy of the *Sixth and Seventh Books of Moses*. He laughed and told me to go upstairs to his bedroom. There, in a small, "special chest," he kept his most treasured possessions and the dreaded book, as well as the one by Albertus Magnus. Later that night, he passed away.

I was saddened (though probably in the minority) and, admittedly, disappointed, for the red cloth-bound books I found did not appear to be older than about eighty years and were in English. Knowing that my great uncle read English very poorly and that most Pennsylvania Dutch read German, I did not believe that the books were used much at all.

With my great aunt and uncle's sudden passing, I further prepared for a potential sale or demolishment, and, in doing so, I discovered bags of "Deivel's Dreck" nailed over the cow stable lintels. This substance, known as asafetida, was used in local folklore to ward off evil spirits (see chapter 24). Quite often bags of mercury were used for the same purpose, and not knowing what all this stuff was for at the time (and possibly handling mercury), I gathered everything and placed it in a box nonchalantly and headed back into the house to wash up.

Most mysterious of all among the day's finds was a homemade muslin bra concealed in a wooden box in the hayloft. My great aunt, typical of her generation, always kept money in her bosom. When I tossed the garment toward the garbage bags already filled with disposed clothes, the bra flipped upside down, revealing a paper sewn inside. When I cut it open, inside was a lengthy German verse from the Bible that was probably used to protect my aunt when she traveled on foot, and on the front of the garment were three

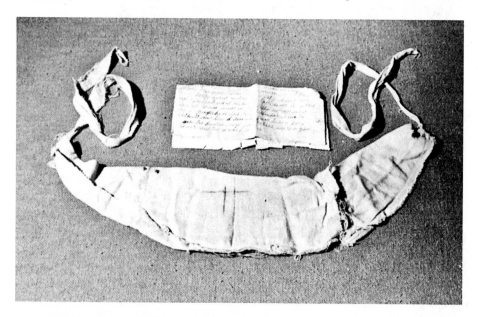

This muslin bra was discovered in the hayloft with a parched paper bearing a biblical verse meant to protect the traveler.

crosses. I then recalled from family that my aunt was always careful to protect herself while on a journey on foot, even to the local general store.

The deaths of my great aunt and uncle were surrounded by mystery, as they fell ill quite suddenly and passed shortly thereafter, within days of one another. Some family members thought Naomi might have got "ferhext" herself "as payback," or possibly consumed something toxic, subsequently passing an illness (or something else) to my great uncle, unintentionally or intentionally, depending on the family member. My observation was that my great uncle literally drank himself to death, not knowing how to survive on his own.

My aunt Naomi's health did begin to fail quickly, and "a distant relative," unbeknownst to me, had offered to take Naomi in to care for her while she was ailing. It soon became evident that Naomi was dying, and on the night of her death, she beckoned for anyone to come by her side, as she "had something important to say." Fearing that she wished to pass on her "powers" to a youthful relative (such as myself), the nurse's aide closed Naomi's bedroom door and she died in solitude.

Having been given access to some papers from my great uncle's favorite chest, by himself and other family members, I stumbled across a rare old copy of Hohman's *Long Lost Friend* that I had not seen the first time around; I was sure that was the same book my aunt Naomi had on her deathbed, because the book she had clutched so tightly to her chest was too small to be the Bible. This copy, though, was in German, much older, and (according to papers tucked inside) had been used. My family being completely uninterested, I also did not let them know that it was original from the early 19th century.

While attempting to clean the cluttered kitchen, one of my friends, who had offered to assist me, discovered a star, of the Jewish type, chalked on the underside of my uncle's favorite kitchen chair. This symbol matched others found in the *Sixth and Seventh Books of Moses*. My great uncle had a reputation for being a crackpot, and he did a great deal of hunting when he was younger. This fact became most interesting when I discovered a brass bullet shell with his hunting equipment. In this shell was a rolled piece of paper that contained a talisman charm that would cause the bullet to hit any target it was aimed to strike. In defense of my apparently eccentric uncle's ways, he was not the only person in the eastern end of Berks County who followed this folk practice. Old Earl told me a story from years earlier, when he was a much younger man, in which some of the area boys had decided to cast a bullet to kill anyone, anywhere, at any time (a practice discussed further near the end of chapter 12).

The ancient hex formula used by these boys called for the casting of a bullet at an intersection where a corpse had been driven in both directions. The place that was chosen was a local intersection at the appointed time of midnight during a full moon. The bullet was to be cast from a silver dollar. At the intersection, the boys were to make a large ring out of green Hollerhecka (elder twigs) that was to be set on fire, and inside the ring, the silver bullet was to be shot through a human skull. Once all preparations had been attended to, onlookers on the porch of the village store watched while two of the boys set out to kill the kaiser of Germany—this being the period of World War I. One of the boys became scared and ran out of the circle, but the other fired the silver bullet, and a clap of thunder was heard from the direction of town as though a landslide had occurred.

In the following moments, to the great dismay of the sole boy in the circle, a dark figure began walking toward the circle with its hand outstretched as though for a handshake. The boy quickly escaped the circle, and the image disappeared. I was assured that the boys never again engaged in any similar activity! (I also suspect that Earl may well have been one of these boys.)

My relatives on the paternal side of my family had long stayed mum on this topic. But after numerous inquiries, as I became educated (or, more accurately, "enlightened") on the subject, they finally confided their Hexerei encounters. Mostly, they were sundry in nature, but nevertheless most typical of the region, as they were the victims. It seems that my paternal grandmother was "ferhext" as a young woman by a neighbor while living in Ephrata when my dad and his siblings were very young. After consulting a Powwow doctor in the area, she was told to take nine new needles and place them in a pot of her urine, which was to be boiled on top of the stove. She did this very religiously, and the following morning, when she passed through the alleyway that connected the front of the row house to the backyard, she found a black snake. She killed the snake, and on the morning of the third day the suspected neighbor woman was dead.

My grandmother went on to live to a ripe old age, somewhat affliction free after that experience, and she shared much of her other knowledge of the rich Pennsylvania Dutch culture—most favorably, her cooking! But in one humorous episode, my grandmother informed me of her close cousin being "ferhext" while she lived a county over in the Dutch Country. As with my grandmother, a Powwow doctor instructed that needles and urine be boiled; however, in this case, the cousin attempted to keep the process a secret and placed a corked bottle of urine in the oven. After several hours, the bottle blew up and the stove fell apart. The cousin, slightly younger than my grandmother (and obviously not as wise), had to buy a new stove with help from the family. However, they all had a good laugh, and everything turned out well. On hearing these details, I was finally able to piece together this story, which I had heard several times in my youth. (I had always wondered why she put a glass bottle in the oven in the first place!)

Throughout the Dutch Country, the people who have specialized knowledge of Hexerei are generally wise grandmothers. In a case that occurred in the Kutztown area several years ago, a husband with a young daughter lost his wife, and he made an arrangement with another woman who had a child but no husband. Living together, the circumstances seemed ideal, until one day the woman and her child left. The man then asked his daughter's grandmother to take care of her while he worked. The wise grandmother asked the daughter if she wanted the woman and her child to come back. The girl lamented, "Yes." So, the grandmother instructed the girl to set plates on the dinner table for the missing parties. Then, as the grandmother and girl sat down to eat lunch, the girl was told to converse with the missing people just as though they were there.

The following day, the woman and her child returned, to the delight of the young girl. But later, the woman again left the man, and again the grandmother was called. This time the grandmother said to the girl, "We will get them back for good!" The daughter again eagerly set the table for the missing parties, but this time the grandmother turned to the walk-in fireplace and called the name of the woman up the chimney three times. The next morning, the father received word that the woman had suffered a slight heart attack and wished to come back for good.

Through these early life experiences, and soon as a fledging teacher of social studies, I became very intrigued with the local practice of Hexerei in my area of Berks County. Throughout the years, I have never missed an opportunity to acquire a unique piece or rare publication; more important, I have had the good fortune of meeting and learning from the best collectors and most knowledgeable people in the fields of the Pennsylvania Dutch folk arts, furniture, folklore, and so forth.

To the average person, such accounts of witchcraft appear to be absurd and coincidental; however, after collecting these accounts for the past twenty-five years, I have found that they are not isolated ideas and happenings, but rather part of a pattern. For instance, in many cases of Hexerei or witchcraft, when the victim breaks the spell, the witch invariably calls upon the family to borrow something. In other instances, the witch may want to bestow a gift on the victim. In either case, if one accepted the gift or lent something to the witch, she would obtain a greater hold on the person.

A universal belief in the Pennsylvania Dutch Country is that witches cast spells on people by obtaining items that belong to their victims. Therefore, in the Dutch Country, there has long been the belief that one does not give anything away for free. The practice was to charge a nominal price for the article, perhaps as little as a penny; this way, the item was sold and you were no longer the owner. Another feature of spell breaking was to always avenge the witch. For example, if your butter would not churn because it was bewitched or ferhext, you plunged a red hot poker into it. Soon after doing this, you would find that the suspected hex had been badly burned. It was not uncommon for the act of breaking the spell to result in the hex or witch's death.

The most common method of testing for a witch was to observe the restlessness of the animals: "If a witch is around, the horses cannot stay tied." Cattle became very uneasy in any stable where evil spirits were present. A test for a witch under these circumstances was to place a broom in one's oven; when a suspected witch came to call, the broom would become hot, and the witch would be very restless and wish to leave. One of my father's aunts was given a black belt to wear by a Powwow doctor, and when she was in the presence of the hex, the belt would tighten. Also, at one time in the Dutch Country (pre–1950s), it was a common practice for young children, especially those attending one-room schoolhouses, to wear bags of "Deivel's Dreck" around their necks to protect them from all manner of evil sickness. This practice was no different from that of using this substance in stables to protect the cattle (covered extensively in chapter 24).

2

Braucherei

Its Counter (Powwow and Hex Doctors)

The Witch and the Bewitched

In the realm of witchcraft, nothing is safe from being bewitched—not people, not animals, not even matter. Ferhext (bewitched) persons were numerous in the past and still presented a problem in contemporary 1950s and 1960s Dutchland. Every year there was a percentage of people who believed themselves to be ferhext and sought the help of Powwow and hex doctors. While the nature of their bewitchment varied, it generally fell into one or more of the following categories:

1. "The witch keeps their sleep from them so they will be many days without rest."
2. "The witch will prevent them from having an appetite or receiving nutrition, and thus they will waste away."
3. "The witch will invoke a physical sensation such as choking response, or the sticking of a pin, etc."
4. "The witch will 'bless' them with bad luck, and they will fail in any endeavor they may pursue."

Of these four classes, the first two made up the largest percentage of all known Hexerei cases. If the victims of these two types of bewitchment could not break the spell(s), death was certain. In the notorious witch murder case of York County in 1929, it was the thought of eventual death that prompted the ferhext person to make sure that the witch was dead by burning the body in kerosene. Usually the bewitched persons are successful in breaking the spell(s) with the help of the highly gifted doctors of black and white magic.

A Dutch farmer's most valuable possessions have traditionally been his animals; therefore, they were a prime target for witches. Of all the animals on the farm, the cow was the most frequent victim. To tell if his animals were ferhext, the farmer looked for several symptoms, such as the following:

1. Animals losing hair.
2. Animals' hair becoming bristly.
3. Animals losing their appetite.
4. Animals becoming very restless.

Once a farmer suspected that one of his animals was ferhext, he would consult a nearby Powwow or hex doctor. If he followed their directions, the animals could usually be saved. In one ferhext-cow case in eastern Berks County, the wisdom of the Powwow doctor was not heeded and the cow died. The case was recorded as follows:

> One of the best milking cows of a farmer became ill, and if it continued not to eat, it was certain to die. The wise grandmother of this family told the farmer that the cow was not sick of natural causes but "ferhext" and that the farmer should ride to Reading to see the Powwow doctor. He was reluctant but went into Reading anyway. The Powwow doctor told the farmer that when he went back to the farm he would receive a visitor: the witch. This visitor would bring him a present, but he was by no means to accept the gift and bring it in the house. If this warning was heeded, the cow would once again be a good milker and eat regularly.
>
> That day, while the farmer ate supper a visitor came knocking at the door. The family could see that it was old Bess, who was long suspected of being a witch in the community. Without any warning to the farmer, the hired hand quickly jumped up from the supper table, ran out on the porch, grabbed the basket of apples that Bess had with her, and dumped them all over the front lawn. The hired hand, knowing what the Powwow doctor had said, did not wait for any orders from the farmer and, of course, surprised not only old Bess but also the farmer. Because the hired hand did not act tactfully, the farmer and his family took pity on old Bess and went outside, gathered the apples, and brought them in the house. The following morning the cow was dead, and the grandmother of the father said to her dying day that the family should have followed the Powwow doctor's advice.

The Hex Doctor of the Dutch Country

Located in various parts of the Pennsylvania Dutch Country were Powwow and hex doctors whom the local folk sought out and relied upon for help in dealing with white and black magic. In general, the Powwow doctors specialized in curing physical sickness and injuries through the use of secret incantations and ceremonies. (This form of Pennsylvania Dutch faith healing would only work if the patient believed in God.) On some occasions, those who were bewitched enlisted the help of these wizards to break the spells. Although the Powwowers would never cast a "black" spell, the less popular hex doctors not only broke black spells but also cast them. A hex doctor's area of specialization was Hexerei itself, and there were very few deeds he could not perform. People who sought revenge could (for a modest fee) have a hex doctor cast a spell on another person. (The number of hex doctors in the Dutch Country most likely never included the number of Powwow doctors in any area.)

The power of the hex doctor was derived from the Devil via the several hex books available to him. Since the nature of the hex doctor's occupation was so notorious, he would often have to travel about the countryside to recruit clients. Many cases are recorded of a cow or other farm animal stubbornly refusing to be herded into a barn until the "noble" hex doctor (who just happened to be in the neighborhood) was asked to induce it. Of course, out of gratitude, the "Doc" would be rewarded for his successful effort in restoring the animal to a good disposition.

In Dutch occult folk medicine, there is the belief that if a person should come into contact with an object used in either black or white magic curing, that person might catch the disease. For instance, there was the case of a hex doctor in Berks County who was accused of drawing off a sickness or spell from one person and transferring it to another person close by. In this way

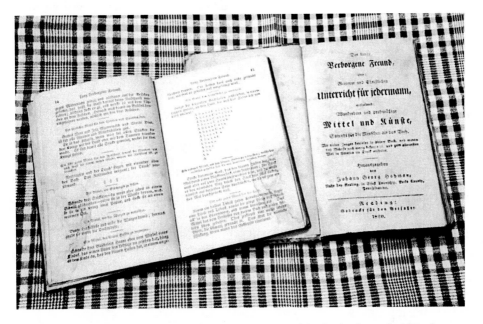

German-language occult books of this type were used in the backwoods of Berks County by many hill folk and practitioners in the 19th century and up to the mid–1900s. These books were not refuted until the establishment of Commonwealth English rural public schools in 1834.

the doctor guaranteed himself an abundant supply of patients with ailments to be cured.

In some instances, the hex doctor was not always clearly free from guilt in cases of witchcraft, and he was often considered no better than the actual witch. Certainly, these doctors had as much power as any witch, since they also had the occult books of knowledge in their field. Some of these hex doctors became so influential in their communities that the proper use of their power and talent was never doubted. These doctors had a great reputation, and their fame spread over many miles.

Unlike with the Powwow doctors, the bewitched people who came to the hex doctors did not have to believe in God or in the power of the Devil. (However, the very fact that they were bewitched, and being tormented, was proof enough for them to believe in the existence in a God and Devil.) Once cured of the bewitchment, the patient did not owe his soul to the Devil, but he was expected to reward the hex doctor with some sort of compensation. If the amount was not to the liking of the doctor, there was always the fear that he might use his power in black magic to make his former patient aware of that fact.

The success of both the hex doctor and the Powwow doctor is attributed to the religious nature of the Dutch folk who believe in the personal existence of God (through Jesus Christ) and the Devil. For centuries in Germany, and for a few hundred years now in Pennsylvania, the existence of these two supernatural beings has been made very real and vivid in this culture in a number of ways. The most popular instrument that has kept alive the personal nearness of God has been the "Himmelsbriefs" (letters from Heaven). These letters are believed to have fallen from Heaven, at various places in Europe and at different times, written by God.

Himmelsbriefs typically contained certain religious ideas or commandments pointing out that the children of God must walk the straight and narrow path, or they cannot expect to enter into the Kingdom of Heaven. Of these letters, the most well-known example is the Magdeburg Brief, which was believed to have been written in gold and to have descended in that community in 1783. It is a popular belief that if anyone carries a brief with him, or keeps one in his home, that person cannot be harmed and that home cannot be struck by lightning, fire, or other disasters. Many soldiers in the Dutch Country have carried them in war and have returned unharmed.

Next to the existence of the widely circulated Himmelsbriefs in the Pennsylvania Dutch Country is a spiritual book called *The Heart of Man: A Temple of God or the Habitation of Satan*. In this book, through a series of pictures, is depicted the human soul as it starts out in life and subsequently progresses.

A LETTER

WRITTEN BY

God Himself, and Left Down at Magdeburg.

It was written in golden letters, and sent by God through an Angel; to him, who will copy it, it shall be given; who despiseth it, from him will part

The Lord

Whoever works on Sunday is cursed. Therefore I command you that you do not work on Sunday, but devotedly go to church but do not adorn your face, you shall not wear strange hair, and not carry on arrogance; you shall give to the poor of your riches, give plenty and believe, that this letter is written by my own hand and sent out by Christ himself, and that you will not act like the dumb beast; you have six days in the week; during which you shall carry on your labors; but the seventh day (namely, Sunday,) you shall keep holy; if you do not do that, I will send war, famine, pests and death among and punish you with many troubles. Also, I command you, everyone, whoever he may be, young or old, small and great, that you do not work late on Saturday, but you shall regret your sins, that they may be forgiven you. Do not desire silver and gold; do not carry on sensualities and desires; do think that I have made you and can destroy you.

Do not rejoice when your neighbor is poor, feel moreover sorry with him, then you will fare well.

You children, honor father and mother then you will fare well on earth. Who that doth not believe these and holds it, shall be damned and lost. I Jesus, have written this myself with my own hand; he that opposes it and scandalizes, that man shall have to expect no help from me; whoever hath the letter and does not make it known, he is cursed by the christian church, and if your sins are as large as they may be, they shall, if you have heartily regretted and repented of them, be forgiven you.

Who does not believe this, he shall die and be punished in hell, and I myself will on the last day inquire after your sins, when you will have to answer me.

And that man who carries this letter with him, and keeps it in his house, no thunder will do him any harm, and he will be safe from fire and water; and he that publishes it to mankind, will receive his reward and a joyful departure from this world.

Do keep my command which I have sent through my Angel. I, the true God from the heavenly throne, the Son of God and Mary. Amen.

THIS HAS OCCURRED AT MAGDEBURG IN 1783

This English version of a Himmelsbrief (letter from *Heaven*) was concealed in an Amish black felt hat used in Lancaster County. Note that the first statement is "Whoever works on Sunday is cursed." None of the Plain People work on Sundays, which has been a longstanding religious tenet.

Either the soul can be inhabited by God and be an agent for good or it can be the workshop of the Devil and be an agent of evil. These vivid illustrations, needless to say, have certainly left their mark on the minds of the Pennsylvania Dutch, as many folk have been exposed to them from early childhood. The *Heart of Man* has been printed many times in the Pennsylvania Dutch Country and was actually quite common.

Hex Books of the Dutch

In the 18th century a substantial attempt was made by the Pennsylvania Dutch folk to record known formulae of both white and black magic. These early manuscript collections were the forerunners of the published books of white and black magic printed in the early 19th century. Undoubtedly, the person responsible for the great awakening of Braucherei and Hexerei in the early 1800s was John George Hohman of Berks County.[1] His widely popular occult book, *The Long Lost Friend*, has never been out of print since it was first printed in 1820.[2]

Das

Herz des Menschen,

ein

Tempel Gottes,

oder

eine Werkstätte des Satans.

In

zehn Figuren sinnbildlich dargestellt.

Zur

Erweckung und Beförderung des christlichen Sinnes.

Nach der fünften verbesserten Augsburger Auflage, 1815.

Reading,
gedruckt und verlegt bey Heinrich B. Sage,
1822.

Das Herz des Menschen (The Heart of Man) is a spiritual book that depicts the human soul as it starts out and progresses in life.

This book, although dealing mostly with Powwowing formulae, gave particular attention to witchcraft. The 1820 hex book was a favorite tool of all Powwow doctors and always a good seller for any printer in the Dutch Country. Listed in Hohman's works are more than 180 different formulae, which were good for treating typical sickness and disease (occult and non-

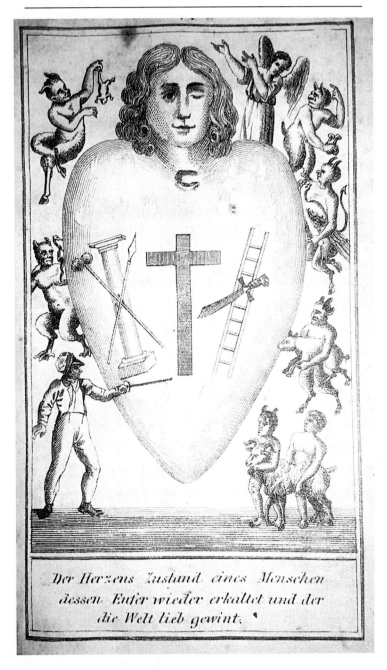

Der Herzens Zustand eines Menschen
dessen Eifer wieder erkaltet und der
die Welt lieb gewint.

A vivid illustration from *Das Herz des Menschen* (The Heart of Man). These images surely left a mark on all those who paged through this book, enlightening readers regarding the many temptations to be encountered in their earthly lives.

occult) of man and beast. However, many more Hexerei practices could be found in two other books—Albertus Magnus's *Egyptian Secrets* and, to a lesser extent, the infamous *Sixth and Seventh Books of Moses*.

In the three-volume work *Egyptian Secrets*, there are more than 590 different entries on black and white magic. It cannot be ascertained whether the 13th-century German scholar Albert the Great investigated any of these formulae or was the author of this book that bears his name. During his life, Albertus Magnus did investigate and experiment with formulae similar to those found in the book, but it is not believed that *Egyptian Secrets* is a report of his findings. The more probable conclusion is that his name was associated with this book of formulae so that the book would be accepted by readers. False imprints were a trick of many printers at an early age. For example, Hohman's *Long Lost Friend* (which can also be translated as *Long Forbidden Friend*) was reprinted around 1839 in Montgomery County. However, in this printing, Hohman's name was deleted and Albertus Magnus was given as the author. The book was known as Albertus Magnus's *House Friend* (Haus Freund), even though it was an exact copy of Hohman's 1820 edition.

The only definite observation that can be made about the book *Egyptian Secrets* is that it was originally from Europe (Germany) and was not written by a Pennsylvania Dutchman. The influ-

The most circulated book related to the practice of the occult in the Pennsylvania Dutch Country was John George Hohman's *Der lange Verborgene Freund* (*The Long Lost Friend*), printed in Reading as early as 1820. As we will see, there were numerous reprints of this compilation of sympathetic medicine.

ence of this book was first apparent in the Dutch Country after the Civil War, and an edition was printed in Allentown, Lehigh County, in 1869.

The term "Sixth and Seventh Books of Moses" is an ambiguous one, and according to Pennsylvania Dutch folk tradition, any hex book known to have great power was awarded this nickname. Ironically, though, there does exist such a book printed several times in the German language. However, it is doubtful that its use in the Pennsylvania Dutch Country was ever as deep rooted and widely practiced as the other two books (*Long Lost Friend* and *Egyptian Secrets*). For the most part, this book (containing three volumes) consists of many unintelligible seals, designs, and hieroglyphics. Listed in the back of the book is a key designed to use the Psalms of David in curing various ills.

There is little evidence to support this book's existence in the Dutch Country earlier than possibly 1871. In one particular example of the *Sixth and Seventh Books of Moses* (printed in Philadelphia in German), there are a few of Hohman's 1820 formulae incorporated in the contents. This multiple Hexerei edition may also have had a false imprint and could have been published in Europe. Considering the Hexerei formulae found in use in the Penn-

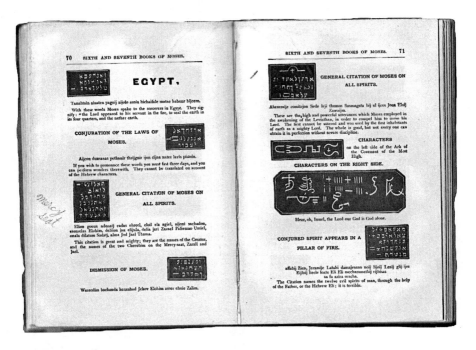

Almost 600 entries on black and white magic can be found inside the three volumes of the *Sixth and Seventh Books of Moses*.

sylvania Dutch Country that are traceable to the known *Sixth and Seventh Books of Moses*, it is definitely 20th century in origin. Therefore, it would appear that the current book known by this name was relatively late in appearing on the Hexerei scene in Pennsylvania.

Among the Dutch folk, there was the general belief that all Hexerei formulae were written by the Devil, and if anyone conspired to use the material in the hex books, they would automatically bind their souls to the Devil and be eternally damned. According to folk belief, a person who reads from a hex book must reread backward all he has read forward, or that person will be under the power of the Devil. Thus, if a person wanted to cast a spell, he could read that particular part of the book and cast it, provided that he could reread backward to keep from becoming damned. Reading oneself "fast" (reading too much in the book and not being able to read oneself out) was a very serious matter. In order to break the Devil's hold, the victim had to seek the assistance of a Powwow or hex doctor.

However, it was also widely believed that a possessor of a hex book would gain fortune and be very lucky. In the later issues of Hohman's hex book, the following memo provided some reassurance to readers: "Whoever carries this book with him, is safe from all his enemies, visible or invisible; and whoever has this book with him, cannot die without the Holy Corpse of Jesus Christ, nor be drowned in any water, burn up in any fire, nor can any unjust sentence be passed upon him. So Help Me."

3

Pennsylvania Dutch Powwow Carvings and the Occult

Among the rare objects collected in the Pennsylvania Dutch Country of the southeastern region of the state, none are as provocative or crude as the wooden, carved effigies of actual people. These were used by natives in a secretive Powwow cure meant to save a mortal from harm or death. The Pennsylvania Dutch sometimes relied on ancient, bizarre Braucherei or Powwow methods to survive in this rough hinterland, living an agrarian lifestyle removed from urban medicine and veterinary assistance for their animals. These early rural farm families continued primitive sympathetic folk medicine, which had been brought from Germany by their immigrant ancestors and practiced up to the late 20th century.

In the secluded area of Pennsylvania's Appalachian Mountains at Fredericksville, Berks County, where some say the moon rarely shines through the dense woods, I came to meet a hard-working District Township farmer who knew I was recording local hex stories. A few days later, he confided in me his true account of the hex (evildoer) who lived down the road from his parents. His mother had told him that when he was an infant, he was very sick and no one knew what to do, and there was great fear that he would die. His astute Pennsylvania Dutch grandmother warned his parents that this illness was not natural but an evil spell. She explained that his father must go to the nearby Moravian town of Emmaus, Lehigh County, to consult a wise "Braucher" (faith healer). The father reluctantly drove there to see this Good Samaritan, whom he had never met before.

Upon arriving, the father was astonished to find that the gifted Braucher knew his name before he actually spoke it, and the Braucher had also foreseen the vexing problem worrying the farmer before he was able to tell him. The wise Powwow doctor, in consoling him, went on to explain how to save his child by avenging the mysterious hex: in order to break the spell, the father was to go home and carve a wooden figure of the hex and pierce this dummy with a pin or nail—but not in the heart, or this person would die. Confident in the wisdom of the Braucher, the humble farmer did as instructed and buried the wooden figure to rot under the eaves of his house.

To the astonishment of the family, a woman down the road suffered a broken leg that week, the same leg that the farmer had pierced on the wooden dummy. However, it was no surprise to the grandmother, since this woman was a somewhat peculiar person. She never set foot on their property again, and the child (my informant) became well and grew stronger, going on to live a full life. This account was now told without any fear of reprisal, since the hex had died a few years earlier, "knock on wood."

In colonial times, when deists were few and the masses believed in a personal God and the existence of the lost books of Moses from the Bible, ancient mysticism was viewed as very plausible. Without listing the large number of Braucherei healings attributed to Hohman and the art of Pow-

Discovered in the Emmaus area of Lehigh County, this 11½-inch hand-carved figure (circa 1900) was used in a Powwow cure to break a Hexerei spell prescribed by the Braucher of Emmaus, who was also consulted by the Fredericksville family in District Township.

wowing, these testimonies by surviving victims everywhere in this part of Pennsylvania have convinced the public that this Germanic form of healing worked. The 20th-century term, "Powwowing," used by non–Germans for the proper healing term "das Brauchen," is a slang designation for John George Hohman's Christian art of calling on the Lord to "Bless Away Illness or Affliction."

Braucherei faith healing is based on Jesus Christ's words in Matthew

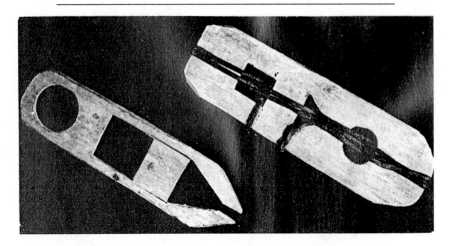

These 19th-century boards, about four inches long, were used in a Berks County occult ritual. The circle, square, and triangle cut into the wood are symbols of alchemy, standing for earth, fire, and water. The board on the right (with a shoestring woven into it) was found in Kutztown, whereas the board on the left (with a chip out of the triangle) was discovered on a Rockland Township farm.

18:20: "For when two or three are gathered together in my name, there am I in the midst of them." The operative word "three" indicated the patient, the Braucher, and a third party who introduced them. This secret Christian Divinity Covenant appears to have cured ailments historically, but, again, no one was cured without divine intervention. Because deists in the early 1800s no longer believed in a deity who answered personal prayers, Hohman included in his 1820 edition historic formulae and charms used in Germany when the medieval church dealt with forces of good and evil (besides sorcery) to convince his readers of mortal dangers and the Lord's power to heal.

Unfortunately, these ancient medieval charms became the book's most interesting feature, causing it to be reprinted more than any other book published in the 19th century. Thus, some Braucherei incantations became suspect by modern people reading them in connection with other occult material. Denied access to expensive books in Europe, German immigrant commoners were taken advantage of by the early 19th-century German press in Pennsylvania, which sought to make a large profit by publishing all sorts of books and broadsides, religious or otherwise, to sell to gullible countrymen.

In 1943, Dr. Earl F. Robacker, in his study of Pennsylvania Dutch literature, called John George Hohman's *Der lange Verborgene Freund* "no more and no less than a book on practical witchcraft for the needs of 1819 Pennsylvania German citizenry." In regard to the portion of Hohman's *Long Lost Friend* dealing with religious healing incantations, Robacker states that certain "successful" Brauchers were the reason that Powwowing existed surreptitiously through the ages. We can only guess that Hohman's dynamic charisma in the early 1800s allowed him to heal his afflicted countrymen miraculously, where all others had failed. His incantations to stop a person from bleeding to death were most popular.

Mysterious Powwow episodes were common in this part of rural Pennsylvania up to the early 1900s; however, the Emmaus area is where the original wooden dummy artifact was discovered. Crudely carved, not as a doll, this wooden figure was intended for avenging a hex or evil-doer through paranormal "voodoo," but it showed up at auction to an astounding price, as most artifacts of this type were buried or placed somewhere to rot, as instructed. This dummy had a hole drilled into its posterior, still plugged with dried material. In some occult formulae, in order to avenge the hex, a lock of the victim's hair must be plugged in a hole to break the evil spell. Perhaps representing an ancient use of mod-

Crudely carved with applied arms, this figure's meticulously carved head completes the six senses. Note the mysterious hole drilled in its posterior, possibly serving as a place in which to plug a lock of hair.

ern DNA, this identified the hex by reversing the spell back to that individual! This effigy figure was carved out of native American wood and appeared to have an old bloodstain on its chest, but it survived because it was not buried in the ground.

Old Frank Miller from Crow Hill, Washington Township, whose family were members of the Roman Catholic Church at Bally,[1] was recorded as being ferhext as an infant in the early 1900s. His father was told by a Braucher to drill a hole in the threshold beam of their doorway, where people entered the home, and plug it with a lock of hair from the infant without telling anyone. Thereafter the culprit, revealed by the ominous Braucher, would become deathly sick and the spell would be broken.

Pleased to see the infant get well and grow again, the family almost forgot their occult cure, except that one day they wondered why that "certain neighbor" no longer came around. But that was the age-old trick of the Powwower to reverse the curse! Old Frank went on to live a long life in his parents' home, but no one ever dared to remove the plug of hair from the threshold beam. A psychosomatic effect may have happened when the family sought the help of a powerful third person, thereby becoming more cautious in their daily routines and omitting their careless habits, which had allowed for a natural cause to afflict their loved one, but no one doubted the wisdom of this wise Braucher.

4

Abracadabra
An (Antediluvian) Amulet of Protection

The most famous Pennsylvania Dutch sympathetic cure that was handed down through the ages to local Brauchers in America was the cure for ague, known as *ABRACADABRA*, which was written as a cryptogram amulet of protection. It became a household word used among native children for fun, but *ABAXACATABAXA*, another popular Hohman cryptogram, is rarely heard in public anymore, if ever. Most of the surviving Powwow doctors in the 20th century were located in the backwoods of Pennsylvania, where modern medicine was slow to reach Rhineland natives.

One brazen Powwow practitioner who had set up just east of Kutztown, a stone's throw away from busy Route 222, had interactions with my family. On clear summer nights in the 1900s, farmers residing in Maxatawny Township, Berks County, could hear him bellowing German Powwow prayers, echoing over the fields and meadows. One of our most eccentric faith healers, "Doc Moyer" (as his believers called him) used two carved wooden figures of a snake devouring the image of a person in his rituals, purchased by the late Hamburg antique collector, Richard Machmer. Each carving had a secret chamber in the rear where hair, from either the victim or the hex, could be placed while the ritual was performed to cure or break the evil spell. A definite follower of John George Hohman's German sympathetic arts, Doc Moyer was well known among the local rural folk.

Another Braucher living in the wilderness of Rockland Township, Berks County, "Doc Sterner," followed the ancient Powwow practice of "drawing off the evil spell" cast on a person by using a lock of the victim's hair. He did this by plugging the hair into a pre-drilled hole in one of his property's growing trees to contain the evil, so no one else would become a victim. There was also a clump of three trees in his backyard where he carved three crosses in the bark, symbolic of the Holy Trinity.

Allie Day, a neighbor of Doc Sterner at Fredericksville, Berks County, in the 1960s, often remarked on how Doc Sterner, in curing his victims, did not destroy the disease but carelessly discarded his diseased objects. Day's point was that some local person might contract the evil disease and need to pay Doc Sterner to break the spell again! It was customary not to pay the Braucher in cash, instead giving him some market goods to eat or bartering for his service. Despite Doc Sterner's antics and some locals wondering whether he even performed the white magic part at all, several informants agreed that Doc Sterner was so revered that people came from miles around to seek his blessing, and that he always wore a silver dollar necklace that could repulse the evil that had consumed some of the victims who sought his help. Although impressed by old Doc Sterner's success in curing his

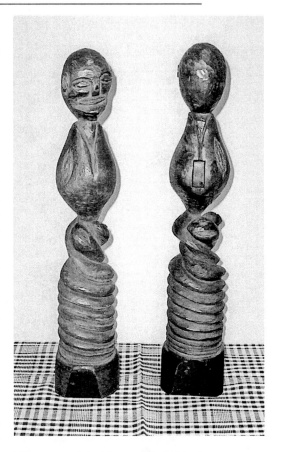

These turned bedposts carved into Powwow figures were used by Doc Moyer from the Maxatawny area of Berks County. They have small removable chambers in the rear where the "doctor" placed hair or cloth taken from the person to be cured in the ritual.

many patients, Allie Day and other mountain folk would not cross his property, where people had lined up in the woods on a Saturday night to wait their turn for exorcism. This caution demonstrated the locals' concern about contacting an occult disease and becoming ferhext.

In many cases, the Powwow doctor could determine from a brief examination whether his patient had a natural affliction or was actually bewitched; if the latter, the Braucher could tell who the person was who had caused the bewitchment. Amazingly, most often the wise Braucher did not know who the people in the patient's home territory were, but he could mysteriously

Three trees representing the Holy Trinity in Doc Sterner's backyard, where he transferred evil sickness to end an evildoer's hex-spell (photograph early 1970s).

name a certain person who more than likely was the hex. Usually coming as a surprise, this eagerly sought information gained the confidence of the victim, and they would try whatever solution the Braucher recommended out of desperation.

Coming across as religious and a person who knew his Bible, the Braucher's demeanor as a man of the cloth disturbed the church hierarchy, forcing local clergy to oppose these laymen faith healers. Ultimately, the practice of Powwowing went underground for most of the 20th century as modern medicine advanced. Like New Englanders, Rhinelanders who settled above Philadelphia were religiously oriented, having immigrated from Europe during the Reformation Period, and one's salvation was really a matter of his faith.

Reverend Thomas Brendle of Egypt, Pennsylvania, who was an authority on sympathetic medicine among the Pennsylvania Dutch, wrote or lectured that in order for "sympathetic folk medicine" to work, the victim had to be a "thinking person" who believed in Christianity. He often laughed at local, "fake" Powwow doctors who made a living off illiterate farmers in the area. According to Brendle, "when a farmer had a stubborn cow that would not come in from the fields for milking, this perturbed a farmer greatly." "And often, some fake Powwow doctor would offer to solve his dilemma for a prize or favor."

Even though there were a number of genuine Powwow healers in the region, there were also impostors who preyed upon the unfortunate. As told by Brendle, one such fake Powwow doctor was called in when a cow was giving bloody milk. The pompous quack properly asked the farmer if his family believed in Christ. Brendle stated, "The farmer replied indeed they did." Con-

A typical ritual layout of a Braucher, whose powers of healing in the art of "white magic" are derived from God (the Holy Trinity). The Pennsylvania Dutch have not hesitated to use Braucherei in the healing of their sick and afflicted.

A Traditional Pennsylvania Dutch Verse to Stop Bleeding

And when I passed by thee, and saw thee polluted in thine own blood, I said unto
thee, when thou wast in thy blood, Live; yea, I said unto thee, when thou wast in thy blood,
Live.   Ezekiel 16, 6.

° Where words are underlined insert name of subject.

This imprint gives a traditional Pennsylvania Dutch verse to stop bleeding; numerous hill folk could effectively cure specific afflictions such as blood stopping or pink eye, but they were not considered Brauchers.

fident, the doctor entered the stable where the cow lay and prepared to heal her. Speaking in German and bad Latin, the fraud pronounced over the cow's head a marvelous incantation, but not before asking the cow if she, too, believed in the Holy Trinity. Almost laughing out loud, Brendle, a German dialect linguist, realized that the gentleman did not know for sure what he was doing, but God cured the cow's milk anyway by the end of the week![1]

My maternal grandfather, from north of Kutztown, Berks County, could Powwow for blood stopping, having learned the incantation and acquired the power from an old Rhineland woman. Like so many other freelance people who knew only one incantation, he was good at curing that specific affliction but knew no other cures. Only the most gifted Brauchers earned the right to be called "Doctor" by the country folk.

5

Rural Superstitions of the Pennsylvania Dutch Country

While interviewing Berks County families on the subject of Hexerei for the past twenty-five years, I learned of the ancient German occult power held by individuals who possessed the *Sixth and Seventh Books of Moses*, among many other folk beliefs. But this particular fabled work, according to the Pennsylvania Dutch hill folk of the region, allowed those who renounced Christ to turn themselves into mysterious creatures to do the Devil's work! Published secretly in German, and sought after by devious people, the Lost Books of Moses were confused with Hohman's 1820 *Long Lost Friend*. Thus, many hill folk possessing any of Hohman's early German editions either tore out the title pages or pasted them shut so others would not accuse them of having evil intentions.

My grandmother heard of individuals who supposedly owned the lost books of Moses and had the ability to turn themselves into cats (or other creatures) at night to roam around doing mysterious things. Once, when I showed an elderly Berks County Pennsylvania Dutchman a copy of Hohman's German Powwow book, he became startled and rebuked me for handing it to him. Mistaking it for the fabled *Sixth and Seventh Books of Moses*, he immediately turned to the last page and read in German the last seven words backward, which, according to tradition, would protect him from merely holding Satan's powerful works! There was actually a local radio program in the 1940s that older folk remembered that covered the topic of Pennsylvania Dutch hysteria and individuals whose mental health was damaged from the fear that was invoked by this book.

But the 18th-century German immigrant's belief in the possible existence of additional books of Moses, beyond the first five printed in the German Bible (which was secretly denied to commoners by the church hierarchy because it dealt with the paranormal), gave credence to the idea that occult powers existed. Through the ages, starting in Europe, there have always been enterprising printers who would publish unintelligible occult books to sell to the credulous public to make a quick dollar. Local German printers in the Pennsylvania Dutch Country would include on the imprint page of such devious occult books "Gedruct fur den Kaufer" (printed for the buyer), which, in itself, should have been a warning.

According to legend, if a person wished to use one of the Devil's devious formulae, one could read and find in the hex book the spell they wanted to cast. But then, as explained earlier, one must reread backward all that he has read to get out of Satan's contract, or he will be eternally damned. Therefore, if a person innocently picks up the lost books of Moses, he should immediately read backward the last seven words to be saved (as did the gentleman I spoke to).

The hysteria of the 1940s came when curious people opened the *Sixth and Seventh Books of Moses* and read too much of the German text, becoming unable to remember which passages to read backward. The popular term used to refer to such a victim who thus became trapped by the Devil through reading the Devil's book, was "read himself fast," meaning one who was too curious to know what favors Lucifer could grant. The news media of the time attempted to make the older public aware of this fraudulent ancient medieval travesty, which had nothing to do with the recipes in Hohman's *Long Lost Friend*!

Old Abe Carl from near Sally Ann Furnace, Berks County, informed folklorist Dr. Alfred Shoemaker that the most traditional way to sign a contract with the Devil was

> to summon Lucifer, all one needs to do is climb to the top of a tall manure heap in the barnyard with his manure hook. Standing atop this heap at twelve midnight, one shall swing the hook around his head three times, and say: "Here I Stand on a Pile of Manure and do Jesus Christ Abjure." Legend has it, Satan will then appear and have one sign his book, and if Lucifer does not materialize, Great grandma and the rest of your German church congregation will appear soon afterwards to give you a Pennsylvania German dialect tongue lashing for your stupidity!

6

Secrets of a Pennsylvania Dutch Witch in the Oley Hills

The Pennsylvania Dutch Witch

Witches in the Dutch Country do not wear black capes, keep black cats, ride on brooms all night, or toil over caldrons. These people are ordinary country folk, but, for some reason, they have chosen to enter a contract with the Devil for supernatural powers. Of course, by becoming a member of the Devil's league, they are eternally damned and will never enter the kingdom of God. In return for their souls, the powers that are given to these persons can be used to their advantage on earth. The mysterious powers of these witches are sometimes beyond the wildest flights of imagination.

One of the most common witch practices is stealing the milk from a farmer's cow; so common is this occurrence, in fact, that many people in the Dutch Country have reportedly observed the witches doing it. Without being anywhere near the cow or the farm, the witch is able to milk the cow (remotely) in her own kitchen. To do this, the witch drapes a towel over the back of a kitchen chair and places a container on the floor beneath it. She then milks the towel by pulling on the ends of it and directing the milk into the container. Meanwhile, at a nearby farm, when it is time to milk the cows that day, the farmer will find that one or more of his cows has been milked dry. If a witch would like to cause further trouble for the farmer, she can make the cow give bloody milk. To combat this witchcraft, the farmwife must take the bloody milk and heat it on the kitchen stove in a pan. As it heats, she will stir the milk in the motion of a letter X, and very soon the cow will give pure milk again.

According to folk tradition, there are several ways for a person to become a hex (witch). Nearly all of the methods require the prospective witch to renounce God and, furthermore, accept the leadership of the Devil. The methods may change, depending on where one is in the Dutch Country, but all methods follow similar patterns and are seemingly medieval in origin. Two of these methods are as follows:

1. To become a hex, take a black cat and boil it alive in a kettle of hot water. When the bones and flesh have boiled apart, take a skimming ladle and collect all the bones with it. Take these bones to a nearby stream and place them in the water; all will sink but one. The bone that does not sink will come to the top of the water and float upstream against the current. When this has been done, that person will be able to hex.

2. If you are really sincere and wish to be a witch, go to the kitchen and draw a large circle on the floor with a piece of coal. Then step inside this circle and hold your hand out; the Devil will come and make his mark in the palm of your hand. After this acceptance, you will be a hex.

Unsurprisingly, persons in the Dutch Country suspected of being witches became social pariahs in their respective communities. The folk believed that if anyone passed the house of a witch or crossed a witch's property, that person might become ferhext (bewitched). Likewise, if one met a person believed to be a witch during hunting season, she had to be kept from touching the hunter's gun or making any sign with her hands. Should the witch cross her apron strings, for example, she would be able to affect the hunter's aim, and he would not be able to hit any game. As mentioned in the previous chapter, it was also a popular belief that with the *Sixth and Seventh Books of Moses*, witches could turn themselves into almost any type of animal. Particularly widespread was the belief that witches turned themselves into cats and roamed the countryside.

Among the Pennsylvania Dutch dialect–speaking farm folk of Berks County and beyond, anyone who practiced evil witchcraft on their neighbors was referred to as a person who could do more than *Brod essa* (do more than eat bread)—a euphemism that would not cause the witch to retaliate against the person who exposed them. Powwow faith healers, or "Brauchers," should not be associated with this term, since they cured individuals by calling on the Holy Trinity (Father, Son, and Holy Spirit) to bless their sickness away. But there were always evil souls that sought out the powers of Satan among earthly mortals, using ancient German texts like the ominous *Sixth and Seventh Books of Moses*.

Below are a collection of interviews conducted over a number of years with Richard Shaner about his notorious aunt and their interactions with some of the unique Irish hill folk who also settled among the native Pennsylvania Dutch in the backwoods of southeastern Berks County:

Annie Buchert-Bieber was often accused of witchcraft bedevilment by her rural neighbors, who relied on the wisdom of Doc Sterner for breaking her Hexerei spells (photograph 1955–60).

So when I met my uncle's neighbors in the Oley Hills at a hinterland place called Ruppert's "Eck" (Corner), I was not surprised to hear that his wife, Annie Buchert-Bieber (1874–1960), could do more than *Brod essa*. Living secluded on an eighty-acre mountaintop farm in Rockland Township, he was a basket maker and she assisted him in weaving their melon-shaped oak potato baskets. On my frequent trips to visit them, I would stop in at the Fredericksville Hotel run by Russell and Alma Stahl, two Pennsylvania Dutch people. When the hill folk at Fredericksville learned that I was a blood relative of Freddie Bieber (1885–1978), they looked at me with suspicion. Allie Day in particular was uneasy if by chance I sat down alongside him at the bar.

One day as I sat down at the bar in the Fredericksville Hotel, just a mile or so away from Ruppert's Eck, the oldtimer who knew I also collected hex books quickly moved away. Deciding to have fun with him, I got up and again moved alongside of him. Quite uneasy, the old gent mumbled under his breath "Leek mich im orsch" three times. As I was bewildered, the bartender explained in private that if you fear a person is a hex, to protect yourself you say "Kiss my ..." three times.

Near the end of her life, I soon became aware of the fact that my recluse aunt Annie (who only spoke the Dutch dialect) was feared by a number of hill folk for being able to do more than *Brod essa*. She was an elderly woman who walked with a cane because of a back injury she once suffered at an apple butter boiling fire when she fell into the

The abandoned home of Doc Sterner in the secluded Rockland Township forest. A wise Powwow practitioner, he could draw off sickness or break evil spells, and he wore a unique silver dollar amulet around his neck for protection (photograph early 1970s).

fire (1957 or 1958). She was nice to me but admired my twenty-three jewel Buliva wristwatch I wore from high school graduation, because she did not own a watch.

One true story told to me by Jonas Day (Allie Day's brother), also of Ruppert's Corner, was that his son as a child was cranky and could not sleep! Therefore, he sought advice from Doc Sterner, a local Powwow doctor from the village. The "Braucher" said someone has robbed your son of his sleep; we must do something to break the spell. Sterner instructed Jonas (similarly to Doc Moyer in Chapter 1) to take the next diaper the child messes in and wrap it up, but Doc S. had Jonas put it high in his attic under the rafters. Doc Sterner assured Jonas the witch would come the next day bearing a gift, but by no means accept!

Sometimes I wondered if Doc Sterner was getting a kickback from Annie Buchert, since whenever she was accused of witchcraft bedevilment, the hill folk relied on the wisdom of Doc Sterner by rewarding him for breaking her bad spell incidents. Another story Jonas told was when a neighbor volunteered to give Annie a buggy ride home from the Lobachsville store. She accepted, crawled up on the seat and pulled out a revolver, exclaiming that she wanted a ride only. The hex doctor along the ridge specialized in breaking spells, and Jonas and others doubted if he engaged in Powwowing.

In fact, one oldtimer told me he did not trust seeing the "Doc." The old gent believed that the doc did not destroy the spells but passed them on to innocent people he came in contact with, thus creating more patients for himself. Lewy Angstadt told me of a story how one time a neighbor farmer had a cow which would not go to her newly

Annie and Freddie Bieber's home, high in the Oley Hills, far away from the nearest highway or the nearby villages of Lobachsville and New Jerusalem, was not electrified in the 1950s. Freddie Bieber became known for crafting his white oak trees into split oak hand-woven baskets. He and his wife, Annie Buchert, lived deep in the forests of Rockland Township; he resorted to this ancient craft to sustain a self-sufficient living pattern for himself and Annie (photograph circa 1962–1963).

born calf. Doc Sterner, who happened on the scene, offered his services and in a short while charmed the cow to walk by his side as he led her, without any grip, over to her calf.

Mysteriously Freddie Bieber, the split oak basket maker, and his wife, Annie, were robbed by two thieves in 1960 who believed these two recluses had cash buried in their remote home. Annie was beaten severely and needed medical help from the medical doctor in the village of Oley. She had a friend in the Eston Herner family and stayed there to be nursed. But she got worse, and fearing that she would die, she motioned to Mrs. Herner to utter her "last words," and the two men who beat her and Freddie up were never found.

What I eventually found out was Annie may not have been the evil one at all; as I learned when I bought this enchanting farm from my uncle, it seemed Annie and Freddie lived in a crude frontier lifestyle was because an urban real estate mogul had owned the land leading up to their house, and the real reason they lived so primitively was because Gladys Paddock would not allow them to obtain a right of way; therefore the Metropolitan Edison Electric Company could not install electricity to their farm to live normally.

Years later, in sitting with the Met Ed executives, I finally got Paddock to agree to allow Met Ed a right of way over their land to electrify the Bieber home, but not until I promised to give Gladys Paddock the cast iron kitchen range of Annie Bieber in return for this electric pole right of way. It seemed to be a bizarre condition for electrifying the Bieber farm, but when my neighbor and I took down the cast iron stove pipe to this early cast iron stove, we discovered that the pipe fitting was molded with unusual cast iron dragons on either side. Perhaps Paddock was fearful that Annie had cast one last spell meant for her uncooperative neighbor.[1]

7

Hexerei
Application and Folk Tales

Witchcraft Formulae

Hexerei formulae in the Dutch Country can be divided into four general areas: (A) protective and preventive; (B) spell casting; (C) spell breaking; and (D) supernatural power. Simply, protective and preventive witchcraft is any method used to prohibit witches and evil spirits from bothering both man and beast. Spell casting encompasses any magic formula used to cause a reaction in either man or beast. Spell breaking, by contrast, refers to any method used to terminate or break a spell that has already been cast. The fourth category, supernatural power, is any type of formula that enables a person to do more than what is considered normal. In the following Hexerei material, several samples of each category are given. These formulae have been passed down from generation to generation.

Protective And Preventive

1. Against Evil Spirits and All Manner of Witchcraft

I.

N. I. R.

I.

SANCTUS SPIRITUS

I.

N. I. R.

All this be guarded here in time, and there in eternity.

Amen.

A page of sympathetic formulas from *Haus Freund*, a reprint of Hohman's 1820 book from a dialect press in Skippackville, Montgomery County, Pennsylvania.

2. If a Man or Beast is attacked by Wicked People, [this is] how to banish them forever from the House so that they may never be able to do any Harm.

Bedgoblin and all ye evil spirits, I forbid you my bedstead, my couch; I forbid you, in the name of God, my house and home; I forbid you, in the name of the Holy Trinity, my blood and flesh, my body and soul; I forbid you all the nail holes in my house, and home, till you have traveled over every hillock, waded through every water, have counted all the leaflets of the trees, and counted all the starlets in the sky, until that beloved day arrives when the mother of God will bring forth her second Son.

This formula three times spoken in the house of the person whom we seek to aid, always adding, in the right place, both his baptismal and other names, has been found excellent in many hundred cases.

3. To Prevent Witches from Entering a Stable

Take white elfencoop wood, make plugs there from, and drive them into all the doors and thresholds of the stable, and no witch can enter. If a witch is already in the house, it cannot leave.

4. To Protect Cattle from Witchcraft

The following must be written on paper and the cattle made to swallow it in their feed.

SAVOR AMC TENET OPERA ROTAS

5. To Secure One's Self Against Wicked People whilst Traveling and Being in Danger of Being Attacked

Speak three times: Two wicked eyes haves overshadowed me, but three other eyes are overshadowing me too, the one of God, the Father, the other of God the Son, the third of God the Holy Spirit, they watch my blood and flesh, my marrow and bone, and all other large and small limbs, they shall be protected in the name of God.

6.

A Preventive, which must be carried upon the Body, for the Arts and Wiles of Gypsies Just the same as the prophet Jonah, the prototype of Christ had been provided for during three days and three nights in a body of the Whale, so may the Almighty God protect me against all danger with his fatherly kindness. J. J. J.

SPELL CASTING

1. To Prevent a Person to Escape

Take a needle wherewith the gown of a corpse was sewed, and draw this needle through the hat or shoe of him whom you seek to fasten, and he cannot escape.

2. A Charm to Gain Advantage of a Man of Superior Strength

I [name] breathe upon thee. Three drops of blood I take from thee: the first out of thy heart, the other out of thy liver, and the third out of thy vital powers; and in this I deprive thee of thy strength and manliness.

Hbbi Massa danti Lantien. I. I. I.

3. To Compel a Thief to Return Stolen Goods

Early in the morning before sunrise you must go to a pear tree, and take with you three nails out of a coffin, or three horseshoe nails that were never used, and holding these toward the rising sun, you must say:

> Oh, thief, I bind you by the first nail, which I drive into thy skull and thy brain, to return the goods thou hast stolen to their former place; thou shalt feel as sick and as anxious to see men, and to see the place you stole from, as felt the disciple Judas after betraying Jesus. I bind thee by the other nail, which I drive into your lungs and liver, to return the stolen goods to their former place; thou shall feel as sick and as anxious to see men, and to see the place you have stolen from, as did Pilate in the fires of hell. The third nail I shall drive into thy foot, oh thief, in order that thou shalt return the stolen goods to the very same place from which thou hast stolen them. Oh, thief, I bind thee and compel thee, by the three holy nails which were driven through the hands and feet of Jesus Christ, to return the stolen goods to the very same place from which thou hast stolen them.

The three nails, however, must be greased with the grease from an executed criminal or other sinful person.

4. That No Wolf or Dog May Bite or Bark at You

Speak the following: Thus did it happen, on a Friday it was, when our Lord God rode over a field of grass, he carried neither money nor purse with him; for he owned naught but his five holy wounds. May God protect us against wolves, dogs and hounds, he gave to St. Peter the keys for the locks, wherewith to close the jaws of wolves and of dogs. In the name of JJJ.

5. To Prevent Anyone from Killing Game

Pronounce the name, as, for instance, Jacob Wohlgemuth, shoot whatever you please; shoot but hair and feathers with and what you give to poor people. Amen.

SPELL BREAKING

1. When a Man or Cattle is Plagued by Goblins, or Ill-Disposed People

Go on Good Friday, or Golden Sunday, ere the sun rise in the East, to a hazelnut bush, cut a stick there from with a sympathetic weapon, by making three cuts above the hand toward the rise of the sun, in the name of the Holy Trinity. Carry the stick noiselessly into the house; conceal it so that no one can get hold of it. When a man or beast is plagued by evil disposed people, walk three times around such a haunted person while pronouncing the three holiest names; after this proceeding, take off thy hat and hit it with the stick and thus you smite the wicked being.

2. When the Milk Leaves a Cow

Take a new earthen vessel, for which you must pay without bartering. In this dish place the water of such an afflicted cow, whilst calling the three highest names; also put a knife, with three cents, in the dish. Thereupon put the dish in a locked chest, and the chest again in another larger chest, and the latter in a trough, so that the earthen vessel is closed up by three locks. If, after this, somebody calls to obtain something from you, do not give it to him.

3. How to Relieve Persons or Animals After Being Bewitched

Three false tongues have bound thee; three holy tongues have spoken for thee. The first is God the Father, the second is God the Son, and the third is God the Holy Ghost. They will give you blood and flesh, peace and comfort. Flesh and blood are grown upon thee, born on thee, and lost on thee. If any man trample on thee with his horse, God will bless thee, and the holy Cyprian; has any woman trampled on thee, God and the body of Mary shall bless thee; if any servant has given you trouble, I bless thee through God and the laws of Heaven; if any servant-maid or woman has led you astray, God and the heavenly constellations shall bless thee.

Heaven is above thee, the earth is beneath thee, and thou art between. I bless thee against all tramplings by horses. Our dear Lord Jesus Christ walked about in his bitter afflictions and death; and all the Jews that had spoken and promised, trembled in their falsehoods and mockery. Look now trembleth the Son of God, as if he had the itch, said the Jews; and then spoke Jesus: have not the itch and no one shall have it. Whoever will assist me to carry the cross, him will I free from the itch, in the name of God the Father, the Son, and the Holy Ghost. Amen.

4. A Remedy to Cure Sickness

Let the person in perfect soberness and without having conversed with anyone, make water in a pot before sunrise; boil an egg in this urine, bore three small holes in this egg with a needle, and carry it to an anthill made by big ants; and the person will feel relieved as soon as the egg is devoured.

SUPERNATURAL POWER

1. To Cause a Witch to Die within One Minute

First, try to obtain a piece of the heart of the cattle which had been attacked, then take a little butter and fry the piece therein, as if prepared for eating, then take three nails from the coffin of a corpse, and pierce with them the heart through and through. Piercing the heart and killing the witch, are facts of the same moment. All will be correct at once. Good and approved.

2. To Make Oneself Invisible

You must obtain the ear of a black cat, boil it in the milk of a black cow, then make a thumb cover of it and wear it on the thumb, and no one will be able to see you.

3. How to Be Able to See in the Darkest Night

Grease the eyes with the blood of a bat.

4. For Gaining a Lawful Suit

If anyone has to settle any just claim by way of a law suit let him take some of the largest kind of sage and write the name of the twelve apostles on the leaves, and put them in his shoes before entering the courthouse, and he shall certainly gain the suit.

5. To Win Every Game One Engages In

Tie the heart of a bat with a red silken string to the right arm, and you will win every game at cards.

6. To Obtain Money

Take the eggs of a swallow, boil them, return them to the nest, and if the old swallow brings a root to the nest, take it; put it into your purse, carry it in your pocket, and be happy.

Popular Witchcraft Folk Tales

Since true believers recognize the existence of a personal God and his evil counterpart, the Devil, many folk tales in the Pennsylvania Dutch Country focused on the struggles between these infinite beings. There was hardly a community in the entire countryside that did not have its favorite storyteller and witchcraft tales. As the powers of both God and the Devil were without limits, so were these tales that spoke of the supernatural and how humanity was caught between two opposing forces. Each example was so real to life that storytellers usually inserted the names of people within the community, and listeners did not doubt for a minute that the story was true, attesting to the prevalence of the folk belief systems in this region.

The most famous tall tales from the Dutch Country are those of Eileschpiggel, a wise young Dutchman who seemingly delights in outsmarting the Devil. He is the Paul Bunyan of the Pennsylvania Dutch. There are endless tales of his adventures, but the following two are among the most popular:

> One day Eileschpiggel and the Devil were talking, and the Devil boasted of how hot it was in Hell. Eileschpiggel retorted to the Devil that the hotter it was, the better he liked it. The Devil then made a challenge with Eileschpiggel to see which one of them could stand heat the best. The challenge was accepted, and the two of them went off to a nearby bakeoven. They fired the bakeoven, and then both of them crawled inside. After a very short while, Eileschpiggel feared that he would soon burn up, and he started to crawl out the door. The Devil yelled at him, "Where are you going?" Eileschpiggel replied, "It's too cold in here, I am going to put more wood on the fire!" At that instant, the Devil quickly followed him out and said, "You win, you can stand the heat better than I can."
>
> In another wager, the Devil challenged Eileschpiggel to a swimming match to see who could swim the farthest. They decided to meet at the Schuylkill River; the Devil showed up on time, but young Eileschpiggel was late. When the Devil was just about to go to look for him, he saw Eileschpiggel coming down the dirt road dragging a calf. As he got closer he said to the Devil, "Go get some wood for a fire." The Devil, puzzled, asked, "Why?" Smart Eileschpiggel then replied, "You don't expect me to swim for forty days and nights without first having a good meal!" With that reply, the Devil considered Eileschpiggel the better swimmer without even getting in the water.

Many other tales were told of how certain people had particular powers to provide for themselves without appearing to have the necessary resources. Such is the case in the following tale, in which a Dutchwoman was observed to have more than normal luck with her butter:

> A farmer, who suspected his neighbor woman of having supernatural powers, knew that she made an enormous amount of butter but only had two cows from which to get the cream. One day, he crept to her springhouse and hid under the roof to watch her make butter. As he watched through the crack in the floor of the loft, he saw her place a red rag in the churn before she closed the lid. In just a few minutes, the butter was churned. She then took pound after pound from the little churn, much more than the churn was capable of producing.
>
> When the old woman left the springhouse, the farmer secretly made his exit and went home. The following day, when it was time to churn butter, he told his wife that he would like to take care of the chore. However, this time he put a red rag into the churn with the cream and began to churn. When the butter had just about come, the lid of the churn slowly started to open, and out came the hand of the Devil. To the very frightened Dutchman, the Devil held out a book and said, "It won't do you any good, my friend; your name *ain't* in my book yet!"

Part II

The Mysterious and Unexplained

8

John Ross
and the Supernatural

When John Lesher, of later Revolutionary War fame, established the Oley Forge in 1744, he took in two other partners: his father-in-law John Yoder and a "gentleman" from Philadelphia named John Ross. The forge business was operated under the name John Lesher & Company, so no one ever thought too much about the involvement of the other two partners. However, John Ross was more than just a "gentleman," as Morton Montgomery puts it in his elaborate 1886 *History of Berks County*. John Ross was one of the most prominent lawyers of colonial Philadelphia and would have been considered the equivalent of the president of the bar association. Born in 1714, Ross was a very influential citizen, but he died on the eve of the Revolution in 1776.

The ties were also strong between the Lesher family and colonial Philadelphia, for John Lesher had a few townhouses there. The Rosses and the Lesher family were very friendly. It may also be significant that John Lesher had a daughter named Elizabeth while one of the most famous members of the Ross family was often referred to as Betsy; indeed, our nation's flag designer, Betsy Ross, was a cousin to John Ross.

In the letter reproduced below, John Ross tells of an experience he heard of in the port city that had supernatural overtones. This letter is arguably the most interesting document Ross ever penned, as it provides insight into life in colonial Philadelphia. Written in 1748, when Ross was 34 years of age, the letter was addressed to a gentleman friend, Doctor Cadwalader Evans, who was residing in Jamaica, of the West Indies, at the time. The boy whose death is related here is John Kinsey, Jr., son of John Kinsey, the chief justice of the Supreme Court of colonial Pennsylvania. Note the casual reference to "B. Franklin" (Benjamin Franklin).

Dear Dr. Evans-

I am going for New Castle early in the morning—I just heard of a vessel going to Jamaica before my return, so in haste determined to give you one scrawl, least you should think the neighbourhood forgot you—but you may depend that will never happen—we gratefully and cordially remember you often; even at the widow Jones's—I would tell you all the news in a word if possible with all haste—to begin—Our neighbourhood [is] just as you left us, only B. Franklin lives in your house. The Col. Hollier not yet gone to sea.—I think all your acquaintance continue well, save poor John Kinsey junior on tuesday the 8th inst. by accident shot himself dead coming over Gray's ferry by Schuylkill falls while in the boat.—He had loaded his gun, and as is supposed, let the butt drop on the bottom of the flat, the gun erect, in a line with his body by his side went off, when half cock'd—The whole load of shot struck his left cheek, and went up directly into his brain—he dropt and was dead in an instant—never groaned—Great sorrow attended his father and all his friends for the accident.—He had strange apparitions of his death the night before, which he informed his aunt Bowene of at breakfast that morning of the accident, which I must relate you, as it is as true as surprising—He talking with his aunt at breakfast concerning his being admitted as an attorney and going into business, for his time he thought was not long in this world—He said that last night he was strangely disturbed in his sleep with dreams and apparitions—that his cousin Charles Pemberton who died last Spring appeared to him wrapped in a sheet and said to him, "Kinsey your hour has come you must go with me" and he disappeared.—Soon after appeared a person before him in the form of an angel (according to the idea he had of an angel) and said to him, "Kinsey your hour has come you must go with me" and instantly he thought a flash of lightning struck him on the cheek and he instantly died: this was followed with a severe clap of thunder and lightning that awaked him from his sleep, and all these particulars came fresh to his memory, and gave him great uneasiness—(Note, no thunder or lightning that night)—Upon this he endeavoured to get to sleep again and after dosing a short time he was awaked again by the noise of a person walking across the room, giving one heavy groan—he heard or saw no more, but got out of bed, went into the other room called the Scotch boy to bring in his bed and lay by him the remainder of the night—In the morning at breakfast, tuesday last, he communicated all the before related to his aunt Bowene and Hannah Kearney—He seemed much dejected upon it.—was confident he was near his end: but to divert himself for that day he determined to take his gun and go fowling with young J. Desborow young Oxley and two or three more—They walked to Coulter's ferry and crossed Schuylkill, and up to the falls ferry—he told the company several times as they walked, he wished no accident might befall him before he got home.—On their return, crossing the ferry, in the boat, the unhappy accident happened him—Thus you have the particulars of this melancholy affair as fully as I could relate it, if with you—And I chose to be particular in it, because I have met with no story in history so well attested as this concerning the premonitions from Heaven of our dissolution.—The flash that struck his cheek when asleep clearly answered the flash of the gun, and the shot thereof first striking—His aunt laboured to persuade him not to go a gunning that day, and he agreed; but afterwards meeting his company they prevailed with him as they had all agreed to go the night before. Our President Palmer is married to the young widow that lived at Harriet Clay.—Old Doctor Kearsley is to be married this week to Mrs. Bland Mrs. Usher's niece that lives near the burying grounds—Doctor Bond is gone to spend the winter at Barbadoes in a low state of health; it is thought he will continue there if the climate agrees with him—Last week Judah Foulke had a son born—no small joy—About 20 of us baptized it last monday at John Biddle's in hot arrack punch—and his name is called Cadwalader—John Smith has passed one meeting with Miss Hannah Logan—I would give you more, now my hand is in, if I could recollect; but I have wrote by this conveyance to my relation Doctor Ross, as duplicate of my letter by you, I pray you will say from me to him—And let me hear from you as often as possible and how you are like to succeed.—I shall write per next to Dr. Curnesby concerning Noxon's estate—Your father and all friends are well.—I sincerely wish you all imaginable felicity and with all the haste I began I cannot help now concluding that I am

your very affectionate Friend
and Humble Servant

John Ross[1]

9

ESP + 1750 Mansion = Historical Insight

Today interest in the occult is a multi-million-dollar business in the United States, ranging from zodiac monograms to the more mysterious tarot fortune cards, mediums who communicate with deceased loved ones, and psychics predicting one's destiny. Excepting the academic investigations led by Dr. J.B. Rhine and Dr. J. Gaither Pratt some decades ago, there are only a minority who are interested in the scientific aspects of the occult, as opposed to the vast majority who are amused and intrigued by the mere thought of its existence. As an occult collector of the Pennsylvania Dutch culture, I came to respect the science that attempts to study the occult, known as parapsychology.

The author of the letter from the previous chapter, John Ross, was partners with eventual Revolutionary War hero John Lesher, who supplied General George Washington's troops with ammunition from the forge he co-owned with Ross. Lesher's mansion was finished in 1750, and that is the location where our next ESP encounter takes place.

Note: The following event, although true, has been reconstructed from an old tape cassette recordings, vintage notes, and recollections of five willing interviewees present that evening. I have used fictitious names and dates to protect the identity of those participants who chose to remain anonymous; however, the location and interactions that follow did happen, and they are presented as such.

It was not surprising that in the fall of the new school year, some of my elective psychology and sociology students challenged me to hold a séance at my home, as I had told previous classes of past paranormal accounts from former residents. The students, who were all upperclassmen, were curious and looking for amusement; as for myself, restoration was just finished on the 1750 colonial mansion, which was quite the locale for a séance. At the time this idea was conceived, neither this teacher nor the young scholars ever

The mansion of Colonel John Lesher (built circa 1750), overlooking the Manatawny Creek, site of the Oley Forge and location of séances.

dreamed that the mansion would be so fantastic that they would continue to have sessions all year. Since the students thought of the idea, they were given the task of finding a reputable medium to hold what was to be the first séance. Having searched the Berks County area to no avail, yet meeting some very interesting bohemian fortune tellers, the students enlisted my help.

Knowing the curiosity of the nearest city's newspaper, a call was made to its offices and employees were asked if they could give us the name of a suitable medium. Within a few days, we had not only a medium but also a newspaper reporter to follow the events. The medium, Helen Terrel, was the daughter of a famous local medium. She was a woman in her 40s, from a distance of about forty miles away, and one who was unfamiliar to the students, me, and the *Valley*. In fact, Ann Kovalenko, a reporter with the newspaper, became our only source of contact with the medium prior to the séance. The date of the séance was set for 8:00 p.m., Halloween eve night.

Two students were to rendezvous with both the reporter and the medium at the former Moselem Springs Inn on Route 222 and lead them south into the historic Oley Valley. The night was clear, and the moonlight was reflected on the narrow macadam roads as the two cars traveled along the foothills of the mountains. Finally the cars arrived at Lesher's mansion, a large pre–Georgian dwelling that was built on the side of a limestone cliff, overlooking the Manatawny Creek. The home was originally part of the Oley Forge (established in 1744), which encompassed hundreds of acres of land. With the passing of time, the forge and other buildings fell into ruin, and only the mansion was left amid walnut trees that provided seclusion.

Our medium was greeted as she got out of the car and walked down to the house with the rest of her party. Although it was damp, Helen insisted on taking off her shoes and walking barefooted down the slope of the cliff to the mansion door. As we approached the house from the front, she could see that the home was illuminated by candlelight, and that there was a large group of students, about thirty, waiting inside. As the home had been built

After massive interior restoration, the Lesher mansion was discovered to have seven fireplaces, a large vaulted root or wine cellar, and a medieval "kick" at the eaves of the roof.

by an ironmaster, it was quite fashionable for its day, and it had seven elegant fireplaces. In the dining room, a large table was set up, covered with a red velour cloth, upon which rested a large black candle and a skull.

After a very brief tour of the house, the time had come for the séance. As the entire decor of the home consisted of authentic antiques, the atmosphere was right for contacting spirits of an earlier day. Candles, one by one, were snuffed out until everyone seated in the dining room was in total darkness. Helen was seated at the end of the velour-covered table, and her hands rested on an open 19th-century German Bible. Seated at the table were about eight of my students, and Helen asked everyone in the group to sing "Rock of Ages" to welcome the spirits. After singing several verses, everything became quite still and quite dark. For the first time, some of my scholars realized that this was the real thing. Our medium friend, who was a non-trance medium, announced that there were many spirits present and that the Lesher mansion was "indeed haunted by spirits."

Although in the dark, Helen was facing the drawing room, which was directly across the hall from the dining room. She perceived there a tall man with a tall hat, shirt ruffles and white hair. This man and later spirits were only seen by the medium, but at times a few students witnessed what they thought were spirits. Helen then went on to talk about healing lights and other personal problems of several of the students. *(In order to follow a certain historical pattern, I will delete references by the medium to material that is non-historical.)* After a short while, Helen reported that the spirit of a very large dog roamed throughout the house, and she believed that this dog belonged to the original owner. During a high period of excitement, Helen saw a woman standing in the hallway in a long-flowing white gown. This woman was carrying a candle and crying; Helen said she was weeping because she was happy and that she, too, was a dominant spirit of the house.

In subsequent communications, Helen asked if there was a small room upstairs, to which I answered in the affirmative. She then said that in this room would be two chairs, and that the woman who wept would always move the chairs no matter where we placed them. (The room to which Helen referred was to be a small den with "two chairs," which was only an idea at that stage of our remodeling, not known to anyone.) During the evening, Helen stated that I would come across two fancy chairs for the mansion and that I was by no means to discard them. Papers were also yet to be discovered, as well as an antique or two, still hidden from view in the mansion. Among the last of the spirits to be seen by Helen was a lackey who went through the hallway—"a very short male servant."

The séance lasted about two and a half hours, but it did not reveal any more clues about the mansion or its owner, John Lesher. However, the non-historical highlight of the evening was a possessed rocking chair owned by my late great aunt, who was reputed to be a witch (see the discussion of Naomi in chapter 1). No matter who the occupant of the chair might be, great aunt Naomi would cause the chair to rock wildly without any human propulsion being necessary.

At this point, it is necessary to point out that John Lesher, the owner of the Oley Forge, was a waggoner in the French and Indian War (1754–1763) and later became a colonel in the American Revolution (1775–1783); after independence, he was elected to the General Assembly of Pennsylvania for five terms. Though he was evidently very wealthy and politically important, there is no description of Lesher's physical appearance or any portraits of himself or of his five daughters and two sons. Likewise, there have been curious statements in legal documents that have teased historians and genealogists as to the character and nature of the family of John Lesher. All of these mysteries were to be solved through ESP in later sessions.

In the days following the séance, my students graduated from being curious to becoming scholars in parapsychology. It was amazing to them personally that most of the individual precognitions of the séance did come true, and they conceived that it was highly likely that Helen possessed genuine powers. Needless to say, plans were made for the next séance, and Helen this time decided to bring along her personal hypnotist.

So on February 20, several of my students and a few friends reconvened at the candlelit Oley Forge mansion for another séance. Helen had brought with her Mr. Barry Schlenker, her hypnotist. Mr. Schlenker and Helen went to one of the upstairs bedrooms to place a post-hypnotic suggestion in her subconscious so that she could enter a trance state when the séance began. Again seated at the end of the long velour-covered table, Helen began the singing of "In the Garden" as the candles throughout the house were extinguished. Unfortunately, she became too self-conscious to allow herself to be hypnotized into a trance state. At this point, the hypnotist asked if anyone in the room wanted to be hypnotized to contact spirits, and most agreed. A candle was lit on the center of the table, and those who wished concentrated on the candle as the hypnotist guided their thoughts.

About half the guests went under the trance (I was among those who did not). Mr. Schlenker said if there was any spirit that wanted to make itself known, it should do so through the trance state of these individuals. My brother-in-law, Bruce, who was just home on leave from military service, was in a trance, standing at the window. His face began to show anguish, and it was evident that something was wrong. The hypnotist went over to Bruce and said, "What do you feel?" to which he replied, "Pain ... all over my body ... a burning pain." In order to save Bruce from discomfort, Mr. Schlenker brought him out of the trance. At the table, a colleague of mine also showed signs of disgust and later revealed that he had found himself in the cold, empty house of his deceased aunt.

Everyone who was still under was brought out of the trance, and Helen had a session in psychometry, while the hypnotist and myself conversed in the drawing room. Having been familiar with retrocognition, I asked the hypnotist if he would like to turn one of my guests into a time machine and take them back to the 1700s. He agreed, and I asked my brother-in-law if he would be the subject for this experiment, as he was familiar with the idea. Having consented, our group now concentrated on Bruce, who was put into a trance at the opposite end of the table from the medium.

The following comes from the accounts of an old cassette recording:

> The hypnotist said to Bruce that he was going to make him into a time machine and he was turning the dials on his shoulder blades back to 1920. "All right, it is 1920, Bruce," said Mr. Schlenker. "What do you see?" Bruce said replied that he could see a chandelier and a sofa across the room, and that was all. Mr. Schlenker announced that the owner was entering the room: "Whom do you see?" Bruce said, "No one."

Mr. Schlenker said he was turning the dials back to 1870: "What do you see?" Bruce answered, "A large carpet, a chair in the corner and that is all." The hypnotist said, "The owner is coming into the room; whom do you see?" Bruce replied, "A man and a lady; the man is wearing a gray suit and the woman a fluffy pale dress." "What are they doing?" asked Mr. Schlenker. "They are not doing anything," stated Bruce. "They are considering buying the home."

Next Mr. Schlenker said, "I am turning the dials back one hundred more years to 1770 from today; what do you see?" Bruce replied, "It is dark; there is a fancy type of a sofa across from me, an iron candle chandelier." "What are the colors of the room?" asked the hypnotist. "The walls are dark blue and the woodwork is brown or wood," remarked Bruce. Mr. Schlenker said, "The owner is coming into the room; whom do you see?" Bruce said, "A tall man with a very large dog. I never saw a dog like that; it has short hair and has several markings."

Mr. Schlenker then asked him to describe the man. Bruce began, "He has curly hair, he is not as old as he looks, he is wearing a wig, he has a long coat that goes down to his knees." At this point Bruce began to laugh wildly, and the hypnotist asked him to share his humor with the guests, but Bruce just laughed for a good minute. Mr. Schlenker asked Bruce, "Who is this man; is he well liked?" Still very jovial, Bruce said, "It is Colonel Lesher," and, breaking into laughter, said he was very well liked. Finally, the hypnotist begged Bruce to tell the group what was so funny. Bruce exclaimed, "He's wearing white socks that go up to his knees!" Bruce, like most American teenagers, had an aversion to anyone wearing white socks, let alone white socks clear up to their knees!

Bruce was in a trance for an hour, and without leading him or his imagination, we asked him questions that led him to see in retrocognition the following events. The lead question was "What does the colonel do for a living?" Bruce at this point went outside (in his mind) and talked to the group as he mentally saw, smelled, and experienced part of a day in 1770. Bruce continued, "The colonel is in a stone building; there are other men; it is hot, very hot. They seemed to be heating something; there is a man on horseback down at the stone bridge. To the distance, you can see wagons coming" (he pointed toward Philadelphia); "they are big white wagons—no, they are Conestoga wagons. There's a wine cellar under the house; it is slimy and stinks. The wagons arrived at the forge; they are unloading them, black slaves are unloading them. They are taking boxes out of the three wagons; the boxes are wood and are empty. Now, a big very hairy man, with a leather apron, is putting something heavy into the boxes, bars of metal."

Occasionally, as Bruce saw the colonel during his discourse, he would break out laughing at his flashy white socks. When the hypnotist brought Bruce out of the trance, he instructed Bruce to remember everything that he had seen; on coming back to the present, Bruce remembered the tall colonel and his clothing, and he could not get over the fact that our ancestors really wore "extraordinary long white socks."

Two interesting facts were substantiated through hypnosis—that is, according to Bruce (who was not at the first séance, nor was he told about it), Colonel Lesher was a tall man and he did own a very large dog. Since he had slaves at the forge operation, it is likely that he may have had a lackey as well. It also occurred to me that through hypnotic retrocognition, we might be able to check for certain leads as to how the forge and mansion were originally designed and what happened to some of Lesher's descendants. Thus, another hypnotic session was set up for the following month, on Friday, March 13. Since we were dealing with the unknown, I requested that my students have permission from their parents if they wished to engage in the experiment. At least eight students were ready to set out on a journey to the colonial period at the third session. The session began at 8:00 p.m., and four of the eight students were given chairs at the head of the table in the dining room to be put under hypnosis.

Mr. Schlenker had little difficulty in placing all four students (two females and two males) into a trance. The boys were tested first; one was unable to make the transition back (in time), and the other, while able to go back, was limited in perception. The boy who made it back to the 1770 period saw unrelated (though real) images. One such image, which he at first thought was a spear, turned out to be the iron handle of a colonial octagon pump. The same boy also located a fireplace in one of the bedrooms that had long since been walled up. The two girls were taken back in time simultaneously, with the hypnotist snapping his fingers to represent the clicking of dials on a time machine. This time, we were careful to choose a date when the American Revolution would be going on, taking the girls back to 1777.

The following accounts come from an old cassette recording:

> Jen said she could see a fancy sofa in the dining room covered with burgundy material. The girls were asked to look for a large kas (wardrobe); both agreed that there was such a piece of furniture on the left side of the doorway to the dining room. (The colonial kas was against the largest wall of the dining room, covering the hole in the wall for the German five-plate stove, which the girls knew nothing about.) The girls not only located the only probable place for the kas but also saw the five-plate stove where in reality the wardrobe was standing. Knowing that early furniture was often monogrammed and dated, I asked the hypnotist to have the girls check the kas for an inscription. Both girls saw a date and words above the doors but could not read them because they were in a different language, "possibly German," according to Pat.

Although I am an expert on antiques, my students were not trained in the least to recognize such artifacts, so I instructed them to read the date on the kas. Pat and Jen both saw "1, 7" in front of the German word "Ein," but they could not see any other part of the date. Realizing that dates were often split in half by the inscription, I instructed the girls to look at the end of the inscription for the other two digits. The girls acknowledged "4, 8"; both verified each other's findings, and the date was 1748. The kas was tall, about eight feet high; it had two doors and drawers at the bottom. I instructed Pat to open the kas so we could see the clothing inside; Pat was very reluctant and said "no." I asked why; she said he (Lesher) would not like that. After I explained that it would be all right to take a peek, she was ready to open it, but then a servant came into the room.

Pat described the servant as a black woman, coming from the kitchen, wearing a white scarf over her hair and an apron. We asked what she was doing; Pat said, "She is looking out of the dining room window at a tall man wearing a powder blue silk coat with tight-fitting gray trousers down to his knees." She guessed the man's age to be about forty. At this point, we asked if Colonel Lesher had any secret hiding places. Pat said, "Yes, a trap door in the corner, a window nearby." Mr. Schlenker said, "Let's open the door and go down into the hiding place; I'll go with you" (mentally). Pat said, "There is a ladder; the hole smells musty like ground; the ladder leads to a narrow room. The room [corridor] is long and turns to the left into another room." "What is in the room?" Mr. Schlenker queried. Pat said, "It is dark; I cannot see." Mr. Schlenker said, "I will light a candle; now what do you see?" Pat said, "Guns, all around the room, and boxes." "What kind of guns?" asked Mr. Schlenker. "They are long rifles," answered Pat. "What are they doing here?" asked Mr. Schlenker. Pat said, "There is a war; the owner is involved; he is on the side of the 'colonies,' they are against Britain."

At this point, Pat and Jen were both asked if Colonel Lesher knew any important people connected with the war, and if any of them came to the forge. Pat answered, "Lesher knew Franklin but did not like him; Washington sent messengers here for supplies, and Lesher gave guns and metal for the war. A Polish general came here, Pulaski, and a German who had a title, Baron von Steuben." Speaking of the war activity at the forge, the girls remarked on the ten buckskinned soldiers who had now assembled on the front lawn. The hypnotist asked what happened to the secret passageway. Pat said he (Lesher) filled it in with mud and dirt; he was angry. Here, Jen came into the discussion: "Yes, he was angry, mud and dirt." We asked why he was angry; Pat said it was because his son John was always playing there. Recalling the Pennsylvania Dutch stories about hidden treasure, I asked if Colonel Lesher had concealed any treasure. She said he had, at the base of an old tree. What kind of treasure? "Gold and silver coins and paper money." I asked what happened to the treasure, and Pat said he (John Lesher Junior) stole it and ran off to France. Pat and Jen, showing disgust on their faces, said he spent the money; he liked to live high, drinking and carousing.

Remembering a part of Colonel Lesher's will, I asked what Lesher meant when he stated that "son John is unable to keep himself." Pat said he was a ladies' man; he was always running around and never took anything seriously. Distracted by the riflemen outside on the lawn, Pat and Jen said that now there were more of them wearing uniforms, and they were admiring the cannon that had just been made at the forge. Jen said to me of the men, "They are cute looking."

Concerned with the domestic side of the Leshers' lives, I instructed the hypnotist to ask the girls about their social life and entertaining. Mr. Schlenker said to the girls, "I hear music; where is it coming from?" Pat said, "In the house—they are having a party. There is harpsichord music in the drawing room; the colonel and his wife are dancing with other friends." What was the occasion? According to Pat, "It is son John's birthday that they are celebrating. He is not favored because he is always in trouble; they are just celebrating his birthday."

Hoping to discover which bedrooms belonged to the various members of the family, we had the girls go upstairs. According to them, the largest bedroom belonged to George; as it turned out, Lesher's daughter Hannah had married a George Focht. John Junior's room turned out to be the most elegant paneled fireplace bedroom, across from the one belonging to George. Colonel Lesher's bedroom was the one at the head of the stairs. However, most interesting of all was the small bedroom where, according to the medium, two chairs would move continually. This was Lesher's mother-in-law's room, and she shared it with Elizabeth, the Leshers' youngest child. Elizabeth (or Betsy, as she was often called) was not married at the time that the will was framed. Could this be the female spirit that wept in the house, because she was happy and about to married?

In Betsy's room, the girls discovered a lovely dower chest, but they could not read its inscription, because this was written in French (the chest had been given to her by a Frenchman). The date of the dower chest was 1772, and, according to the girls, it was decorated with flowers and birds. The girls were asked when the mansion was built, and Jen said the site was picked in 1745, and Pat stated that it was built in 1749 and 1750, which was historically accurate.

Both girls at this time had visions of the building of the house and reported that the "Indians" were attacking the workmen. One particular workman was seen being shot from a position on the building by both girls, without their conversing, though they simultaneously made a disgusted facial expression. Jen said Lesher did not pay for the land and that was why the Indians attacked and why it took so long to build the house. The two partners in the forge with Lesher, as mentioned in the previous chapter, were his father-in-law, John Yoder, and John Ross of Philadelphia. Pat said, "John Ross came to the forge because Philadelphia 'smelled,' but John did not like the Indians any better." She also remarked, "John Ross was a cousin to Betsy Ross."

Having spent a great deal of time with Pat and Jen, we decided to end the hypnosis session and brought the two girls up to the present date and released them from the trance. As in the previous session, both girls were instructed to remember everything that they had seen under hypnosis. The reactions of the girls were quite unexplainable, for they could not believe that they had traveled to a different time and were equally amazed that they could compare notes about what they had seen and verify each other's experiences.

Most of the students were intrigued by the secret passageway, wondering whether Lesher had filled the entire corridor in with dirt. It was quite exciting to realize that somewhere there was a hidden passage that might not be entirely filled. Pat said she believed that she could recognize the corner where the trap door was if she was in the basement on the ground floor where she had visualized it. The next day, several of the boys arrived at the mansion with shovels, hoping that Pat could locate the area of the trap door. Much to their dismay, in almost every corner limestone outcroppings were discovered that proved the trap door was not in the basement.

After several weeks had passed, I attended a séance that Helen Terrel held at a home in Macungie, Lehigh County. At this time, I told her of the secret passageway (she had not attended the hypnosis session) and of our dead end in the basement. Helen said that she felt we would not find the passageway from the inside of the house; rather, we would find it on the outside. She also said that she felt strongly that the passageway went straight into the cliff and not down. Most surprising of all, Helen told me that I would have a visitor and he would locate the secret room.

Giving Helen's advice some consideration, I recalled a curious foundation that stood about forty feet away from the house at the side of the cliff. The foundation was covered with garbage and refuse thrown there over many years by previous owners. The stone foundation was about fifteen by twenty feet rectangular, and the southernmost end protruded above ground about nine feet. The northernmost end was buried in the cliffside under several feet of ground and rubble. However, parallel to the wall, running the length of the building, was an inner stone wall that formed a space three feet wide between the two walls. It seemed just possible that if the rubble was dug out of the foundation of this building, it might prove to be not a foundation alone but about 75 percent of the building.

My students, who were ever willing and able, were more than eager for a chance to investigate the old ruin. In several evenings we had dug the rubbish out from between the two parallel stone walls and were at a depth of eight feet inside. Most of the rubbish was from the last couple of decades, but the last three feet proved to be dirt, bones, and occasionally broken colonial tile. Having reached a certain depth, we continued to dig toward the cliffside in what evidently was a corridor about fifteen feet long and eight feet deep. A door was discovered on the other side of the parallel walls to the rest of the building, but no access was discovered to the corridor from inside or outside the building.

After reaching a depth of about twelve feet at the cliffside, which was a solid limestone outcropping, we discovered that the floor at this end of the corridor was protected by a small wall, and under the wall was a fill of charcoal and lime mortar, heavily binding rocks. For safety's sake, and because we needed a backhoe to make room for the entire fill we were digging out by hand, I decided to call a halt to the project. In the interim, we agreed to have a fourth session including the hypnotist to see if we were digging at the right place. Pat and Jen, who had previously made the journey into the past, again offered to be of service. On May 8, in the bright sunshine on the front lawn of the mansion, the girls were placed under a trance and followed the life-history of the mysterious foundation.

The following accounts come from notes and an old cassette recording:

> Thus, in hypnotic discovery, we found that during the pre–Revolutionary War period, the building was a storage unit for the wooden boxes used to pack the bar iron, which was sent to the wharves of Philadelphia. Later, after the war broke out, in 1777, Lesher made a secret hiding place to store Washington's provisions. Hidden behind the boxes, in the corner of the storehouse, was a trap door leading into the secret passageway and room. After 1779, the passageway was discontinued and filled in with dirt; a wall was then built to conceal the passageway's location.

After the girls were given time periods progressing into the future, allowing them to watch the building deteriorate to its present condition, they were brought out of the trance. Jen was quite confident that the trap door was located at the cliffside of the corridor and that the secret room was approximately under the lawn; Pat agreed with Jen's judgment but could not be more precise as to the exact location under the lawn. Jen stated that she did not believe that anyone could dig out the original passageway because of the efficiency used to seal it off. Having satisfied our curiosity about the secret room, we reconvened in the house to learn more about the colonel's life.

Pat was the most receptive that evening and talked about Lesher's friends. As mentioned, the colonel did not like Benjamin Franklin and thought *Poor Richard's Almanac* was "a lot of poppycock" (rubbish). General Edward Braddock of the French and Indian War period was a "stuffed shirt and did what he should not do." The man Lesher most favored was Baron Von Stiegel, the glass maker (prized Stiegel glass). Both Stiegel and Lesher sat in on committee meetings together; Lesher bought much glass for his house from Stiegel. Lesher did not have any portrait of himself because he was not vain; he was a Virgo, as explained, French Huguenots as a lot were not vain. When asked what the colonel did with the notes from Washington, Pat said he burned them because they were important.

A few days after the last hypnosis session, early on a Sunday morning, when only Berks County farmers and their cows were stirring, I received a visitor. It was Eli, an old farmer and family friend from Rockland Township, whom I had not seen in well over a year. He began, "I came to see this secret passageway you think you found." In my stocking feet, I climbed down the cliff with Eli to show him the corridor and where our digging had been done. After some study, Eli remarked, "I have never seen a building with such a design. This is certainly no farm dwelling and, by my experience, it does not make sense to have an inner stone wall where this is placed" (pointing at parallel wall). "Where do you believe the passageway goes from here?" he asked. I then told him what the girls had told us during the session.

Not quite satisfied, Eli asked for a pair of pliers and said that he would try to dowse for the passageway and room, considering that a great deal of moisture and water would have collected if they were still hollow. Beginning at the house, Eli walked straight along the lawn; sure enough, the pliers dipped right before the rose garden, and about ten feet after that point, they dipped again. This would be the supposed dimension of the room; additionally, when Eli pinpointed the room's location, he was right in front of the corridor by the necessary twenty-five feet the girls had predicted. Now Eli walked along the cliffside near the corridor, and as he came across the end of the stone

The stonewalled pigpen alongside Colonel Lesher's home had a secluded double wall at the back in which supplies for General Washington's troops could be hidden, which could only be reached through a trap door in its attic room, at a time when British soldiers were an eminent danger to American patriots living in the Oley Valley.

walls, the pliers dipped again. But this time they dipped so hard that Eli could hardly fight against the pull. "Well," said Eli, "I believe this is it; I sure would like to see this opened."

As I looked over my nice lawn and rose garden, I admitted to Eli that I did not know whether I would go so far with the digging as to undermine the front lawn. After Eli left, my wife called to my attention the fact that Helen had said someone was going to show me where the secret room was. Although I was now not too keen on allowing my students to continue their excavation of my lawn, I did allow them to dig deeper into the heavily mortared charcoal and rock, and one evening one of the boys discovered a coin near the passageway entrance. The coin was a half penny, not too tarnished to be dated in a coin book, and it was listed as a British coin minted between 1740 and 1750. Perhaps Colonel Lesher had dropped it, or more likely his son John had done so in pursuit of a girlfriend.

Overall, it had been a very interesting school term for everyone involved, including the curious farmer who helped much with his backhoe. However, the most bizarre occurrence did not happen under hypnosis or with a medium, but rather in the solitude of the house; this incident was one I kept from the others. One night, as I lay half asleep sometime after the second séance, I heard a little girl recite, "Twinkle twinkle little star, I wonder how you shine [sic]."

Was this the weeping woman? Was it Betsy? Was this a clue to the passageway or perhaps an undiscovered treasure? Perhaps it was just the lament of a happy spirit that had not seen so much company since the old days of the elegant colonial mansion. My wife and I did hear the whimpering of Colonel Lesher's great dog, but we hadn't used Betsy's room. Whatever became of son John and his lavish lifestyle? There are no records tracing him in America. Did he ever come back from France? Perhaps he never went? These are questions to be answered in time, living in a most remarkable house in the secluded countryside of the Oley Valley.

10

A Colonial Lobachsville Homestead in America and Ties to the Occult

The Keim Homestead of the Oley Valley of Pennsylvania stands just a few miles away from the forge, having been built at roughly the same time. This homestead is important for several reasons, but for the purposes of this book, I will concisely say that it represents the regional colonial architecture of a homestead in this historic valley, remains in excellent condition, and is a classic example of an ideal Pennsylvania Dutch homestead, possessing architecturally unique Germanic qualities. There is no precise evidence for construction dates of either the manor house or the colonial stone cabin, alongside where the Keims first would have resided while constructing the manor house (or else used as a bachelor pad while Jacob Keim courting). However, both buildings are attributed to 1753 and 1746, respectively, and both, in retaining their original condition, can be architecturally placed in the realm of the first half of the 18th century for certain.

The popular oral tradition throughout the area attempts to place greater emphasis on this homestead at Lobachsville, since a local belief is that Johannes Keim first settled there in 1705, making it the first homestead in the territory.[1] There is, however, no documented proof that Johannes Keim ever purchased land on this 320-acre track or subsequently built a home here. There is, however, documentation that Johannes's youngest son, Jacob (by his first wife), developed this tract in the mid–18th century when he bought one of two tracts of land from his future father-in-law, John Hoch (a purchase recorded in 1753). The purchase price was 150 pounds for 50 acres. In 1761, after marrying Magdalena, John Hoch's daughter, the second 50-acre tract was sold to Jacob for only 50 pounds, "out of love and affection for our son-in-law and for his advancement into the world."

Even President Abraham Lincoln's ancestry can be traced to this nearby

Located on a back road away from the village, Jacob Keim erected a large, medieval-type manor house in 1753 with quaint, brick-arched Dutch doors and narrow windows. A huge walk-in fireplace made of stone was used to heat this home and cook the family's meals (even after cast iron cook stoves became commonplace) (photograph early 1970s).

paranormal hotbed at Exeter Township in the Oley Valley. In the modest amount of work I have done in checking up on President Lincoln's ancestry through the years, I've uncovered documented evidence that the former president, for a long period of time, had been searching for his own forebears. He believed himself descended from the Lincolns of Berks County, Pennsylvania, and thought that they had been Quakers. Clues were never uncovered suggesting that he might have actually settled the matter within his own mind, establishing his line back so far as Exeter Township, until I came across a newspaper story that appeared to verify that President Lincoln did establish his missing links before his death. The *Pottstown Weekly Advocate*, on May 4, 1895, printed a brief story stating that John Lincoln, a distant cousin of the martyred president, had journeyed to the capital during the years of the Civil War, "and the cousins had quite a chat during which the relationship was fully established." The *Advocate* went on to describe John as "a tall, muscular

During restoration, celebrated architect John K. Heyl discovered, among other things, that the current raised-panel Dutch doors on the main floor of the stone cabin had originally hung on the back doorway to the 1785 addition to the Keim manor house.

man, clean shaven, and his features much resemble those of President Lincoln."

Mordecai Lincoln, great-great-grandfather of Abraham Lincoln, came from England and settled in Massachusetts, where his wife died; around the year 1735, he left Massachusetts and settled in what is now Exeter Township, taking up 1,000 acres of land. He brought with him one son, whose name was John; this son was the great-grandfather of the future president. Mordecai Lincoln married again in Berks County, allying himself with the Lincolns in Massachusetts by his first marriage and those in Pennsylvania by his second, including (eventually) the sixteenth president of the United States.

Another interesting footnote is that Mordecai Lincoln had seven sons by his second marriage, and one of them, whose name was Abraham, married Anna Boone, a first cousin of Daniel Boone of Kentucky fame, who was born in Exeter Township, Berks County, in 1733, and not in Bucks County, as often stated in certain historical accounts (and backed by more than just my research). Daniel Boone frequently returned home to Berks County from Kentucky and always spent some time with his cousin, Anna; his glowing accounts of the south and west might have been an inducement for President Lincoln's ancestor, John Lincoln, to move to Virginia around 1750, but that is a subject for another book. Nonetheless, this area has historical significance, as well as much paranormal activity.

The Mysterious Occult Link to This 18th-Century Family

When the last of the Keim sisters, "bearded" Betsy (perhaps the biggest perpetrator of haunts on the 320-acre colonial plantation), died on October

Betsy Keim (d. 1911) was one of five spinster sisters who lived on the 1753 Jacob Keim plantation near Lobachsville (photograph circa 1908).

5, 1911, at 82 years of age, one of America's last living ties to the ancient occult folk practices was gone. A strange farmwoman with eccentric medieval German folkways, Betsy's folk customs were traced to primogenitor Johannes Keim, who settled in the Oley Valley at Pikeville in 1707. Betsy was one of five spinster sisters who had lived on the 1753 Jacob Keim plantation; after her death, villagers often talked of ghosts and paranormal experiences attributed to her family.

Since stone houses of the time took a year or more to build, the Keim family most likely stayed in this earlier stone cabin until the 1753 manor house was finished. The early stone cabin became an ancillary building later, used as a workhouse.

The American Folklife Society operated the historic Jacob Keim farmstead in Pike Township as a Pennsylvania Dutch Museum in the 1970s.

As Rhineland immigrants were often predisposed to follow ancient practices popular in their homeland, when the Jacob Keim (1724–1799) branch of this family settled near Lobachsville in the backwoods of America, they lived much the same way as they would have in the picturesque territory of the Black Forest in faraway Germany. In colonial times, surrounded by many other Rhineland immigrants, the family's peculiar folkways were not noticed until the following century. Located on a back road away from the village, Jacob Keim had erected a large, stone medieval-type manor house with quaint, brick-arched Dutch doors and narrow windows.

A prodigious Germanic central walk-in fireplace made of stone was used to heat this early home and cook meals, and the farm family continued the ancient practice of open-hearth cooking long after their neighbors had adopted cast iron cook stoves, making open-hearth cooking an outdated method in the 19th century. A brilliant, native orange clay-tiled steep roof covered the 18th-century manor house and the quaint woodworking building alongside it.

The workhouse had an additional two colonial walk-in fireplaces: one in the cellar for butchering and the main floor fireplace for washing clothes. Unique to this structure was a cold storage basement that was cooled by a spring, where milk and cream were refrigerated and butter freshly churned, partitioned off from its cooking room. A bell tower at the peak of the roof was built in the early 1800s and called local farmhands in from the distant fields for noonday meals when they were out cutting grain and storing hay in the steep-roofed bank barn, opposite the main house.

This root cellar, with an arched doorway, was once part of the foundation to Magdalena Keim's colonial bakehouse (photograph early 1970s).

The prominent Hansel and Gretel–style bakehouse, once located at the east end of the Keim manor house, has long since crumbled—the victim of too many firings in baking the Keim generations' bread. Only its ancient, vaulted root cellar survives, as well as part of its structural base. This cave-like, arched-stone dungeon, with a wooden batten door, would certainly have been able to hold the fabled Hansel and Gretel until the fire was ready to bake them up above! As time moved on and the rest of the world progressed, Jacob Keim's descendants continued tilling the soil and harvesting their crops in awkward colonial fashion. Self-sufficient in farming, they were hardly dependent on the outside world, nor were they exposed to change and new inventions.[2]

Old John Keim (1822–1897), Betsy's bachelor brother, was the last family head to operate the prodigious farm with hired hands, following an industrious German work ethic and aided by his five loyal sisters. Enforcing a family creed begun by the Keim ancestors in 1753, he did not allow the family to cut timber from a 100-acre tract of virgin woodland that dates from pioneer days, and his ghost is still occasionally seen riding on horseback, "protecting" the property. This enchanted forest with native birds and animals formed the tree line of the Oley Mountains as they met the tilled farm fields of the plantation stretching to the north—one last vestige of Penn's woods not cut down by ambitious frontiersmen!

Since the old farm road, which cut through their plantation, did not lead to active commerce, there was little traffic except for farmhands and an occasional visiting huckster or peddler who knew the household would welcome him. This pastoral farming scene was rarely upset, except for occasional lightning striking tall trees in the virgin forest on the mountainside, and the undisturbed woods were a formidable deterrent for people who might steal from the Keims living in this isolated corner of Pike Township. As recluses, no one had reason to visit them, and conversation with one another was conducted in their habitual age-old German dialect proverbs.

Any peculiar cause and effect or accidental occurrences were often attributed to the realm of the paranormal, as they would have been in medieval times. The early craftsmen who had built the Keim manor house were also Rhineland immigrants; thus, the features of their mysterious houses were neither American nor British. These Palatinate pioneers facing the wilds of a mysterious New World incorporated safeguards in protecting the occupants of the colonial Keim manor by calling upon occult folk practices of the Old World. Subsequently, there were forces of evil in this wilderness, not experienced by humans beforehand, which needed to be counteracted.

Related by marriage to Peter Lobach, founder of the village of Lobachsville, the Keims depended on this small hamlet for milling their grain at Wilhelm Pott's gristmill; they also made use of Peter Lobach's fulling mill for their textiles. Although the Industrial Revolution rendered some of their colonial trades obsolete following the Civil War, the Keim women continued to grow flax, spin and weave linen throughout the Victorian period until their deaths. Amazingly, the estate sale following Betsy Keim's death featured 97 handmade linen tablecloths and 40 homespun cases for rope-bed featherbeds. Thus, the romance and adventure of this unusual early American lifestyle had been kept alive in the historic Oley Valley by the industrious Keim family, who sustained their German antediluvian living and beliefs for generation after generation.

In wintertime, the Keims' 18th-century lifestyle was particularly noticed by the public, as woodsmen chopped firewood by the cord to feed the five fireplace hearths to heat both buildings in which the family cooked, washed their clothes, and plied early American trades. Three of these hearths fed hot coals into German Continental five-plate cast iron stoves, which were used until later six-plate iron stoves replaced them in the post–Revolutionary War period. By 1894, John M. Keim, concerned with wood as a fuel source, put a codicil in his will demanding conservation by his sisters and forbidding the felling of trees in the ancient forest on the hillside unless it was absolutely necessary.

The homestead was bordered on the south side by a vast swamp, which separated the Keims from the colonial Johan Hoch plantation, where Jacob Keim's wife, Magdalena (a twin), originally lived (as mentioned earlier, it was her father who had gifted Jacob Keim the land upon which the homestead was built). The only time anyone ventured through this dense tree-grown swamp was when gypsies who camped along the Manatawny Creek lost their way and showed up at Betsy's doorstep—"or so they said!" There were real dangers in the early Oley Mountains, where wild boars attacked woodsmen, and nearby Sheep Hill was so named because of wolves that still lingered in this part of Pennsylvania and attacked the unsuspecting.

As time moved on, and the original pioneer generation around Lobachsville passed out of existence, German descendants who had learned to respect their elders were unusually aware of this eccentric, aristocratic Keim family. These land barons not only had the "first Continental dollar ever made" but all the additional wealth accumulated by past generations, adding to the mystique surrounding this old pioneer family that spread near and far and, oddly enough, was not exaggerated.

At the time old Betsy Keim died, her family's fortune equaled a king's ransom, and the executors were astonished at how much money was concealed all over the manor house. Much of the money, which the five sisters had hidden, was in pure gold and silver coins in a lard can in the attic that held as much as $8,000. Back at the turn of the 1900s, this would have been considered over 200,000 stashed in today's market, according to numerous inflation calculators. Together with the real estate and virgin woodland, as well as the revenue from the 3-day auction in 1911, attended by antique collectors from numerous states, the total funds amounted to a considerable sum. Today, author Charles J. Adams III, who has written about the famous Keim ghosts observed after the death of Betsy Keim, has called attention to this mysterious manor house, in which the former occupants continue to live on "in spirit" long after their mortal demise. Thereby, the Keim legend, reevaluated in the last decade or so, continues to bring about new inquiries.

When John K. Heyl, the noted restoration architect from Allentown, did blueprint measurements on the Keim houses for the American Folklife Society in the 1970s, he noticed the exceptional hand-forged iron hardware.[3] Made by a local German-schooled blacksmith, they were artistically fashioned in the early 1700s period style with rat-tailed pintles, upon which iron strap hinges held the raised-panel doors. However, some of the forged iron hinges of these buildings had an unusual feature distinct from all others used on the property (and, for the purposes here, most relevant to this book). Concealed from view when the doors were closed were mysterious Xs painstakingly

The Huguenots of Lobachsville followed in William Penn's teachings and did not use noble titles from the Old World. They painted flat "Huguenot hearts" on their children's dower chests to express their love of mankind. On the door to the Keim woodshop is an early drawing of four flat hearts that created a tulip outline design, the folk symbol of fertility. That is today the logo of the American Folklife Institute of Kutztown (photograph 1972).

embossed on the strap hinge roll as it was fitted to the pintle on the doorjamb. The manor house, divided into a typical Continental German floor plan—a kitchen, *Stube room* (stove or "great room"), and *Kammer* (back or downstairs bedroom)—was outfitted with exceptional iron strap hinges on all the doors.

However, the most unique feature was the first-floor Kammer, adjacent to the Stube room, which had three mysterious Xs forged into the iron hinges. This area of the downstairs Kammer, or small bedroom, was known as the dying room in colonial times, as it was where ill members of the family slept and drew their last breath before departing this life. In local folklore, brought from Europe, a *Seelen Fenster* ("soul window") was often located in this room on the outer wall; it was only opened via wood plug to allow the deceased's soul to leave his or her body, exit the home, and depart to Heaven. Cracking or opening the window of a deceased person's bedroom is still done in Berks County today, so that the spirit may enter Heaven.

Although the Keim workhouse did not have a Kammer on the first floor, it did have a board partition dividing the kitchen from the Stube room. Upon further investigation, the iron hinges on this earlier batten-board door revealed the largest Xs secretly punched on its underside to protect the pioneer occupants who slept behind the door. As was customary in pioneer days, the great room of the manor may have been used to worship with other Pennsylvania Dutch French Huguenot neighbors, as today's Plain Dutch cousins, the House-Amish, continue to practice. A molded cornice along the open beam ceiling in this room still has its Bible and songbook bookshelf in place to hold religious texts.

The meeting room, heated by an iron German jamb stove like the room above, was supplied with hot coals through an opening in the back wall of the central fireplace. Of all the ornate ironwork in the manor house, the escutcheons on the forged iron locks seen on entering the Stube room were especially elaborate. The blacksmith had incorporated into these Moravian-style locks an elegant (good luck) swan with a curved neck on top and a reverse motif at the bottom. The X marks on the backs of iron interior strap hinges were the result of the folk belief in ancient German sympathetic magic used to protect the family's inner sanctum.

Unlike "hex signs," which were not used at the early Keim farmstead, true occult magic is hidden from view. An X is the symbol for Christ (in the Greek alphabet), and three in a row represent the Holy Trinity, often used in popular secret Powwowing rituals. Another ancient Pennsylvania Dutch folk belief (as mentioned) was that if a witch crossed her apron strings while looking at a hunter carrying his gun, she could steal the fire from his gun; thus, when he attempted to shoot at game, the gun would not ignite and the hunter would

The door handle and attractive escutcheon of the second-floor great room door. An elegant (good luck) swan motif incorporated into these Moravian-style locks was a very elaborate touch by the blacksmith.

miss his intended target, as initiated by bearded Betsy. According to Dr. Edwin M. Fogel, who collected Pennsylvania Dutch folklore in the early 1900s, "If a gun is 'ferhext' (bewitched), stick two pins on the gun in the shape of a cross to break the spell. And if you really want to avenge the witch, lay the bewitched gun in a creek and the 'hex' will not be able to urinate until she personally comes to the owner of the gun to ask for forgiveness."

Old Rhineland folklore was also known for the use of talisman charms, which were carried by flint gun huntsmen in case they came upon such a sorceress while hunting game, so that the amulet would ensure their accuracy. Old John Keim, Betsy's brother, never allowed people to trespass in the 100-acre forest on their property, so hunting was definitely forbidden! There were confirmed accounts of the Keim sisters stealing fire from the guns of would-be hunters seen trespassing near the homestead. It was also common knowledge among people living near Lobachsville that the Keim women had other supernatural powers, and, as the German dialect phrase goes, *Brod essa* ("they could do more than eat bread!").

11

Cross My Heart
and Hope to Die!

Johann George Hohman, famous for his occult Powwow book, *The Long Lost Friend*, published in Reading by Carl Bruckman in 1820, was no stranger to the Keims and their neighbors in Lobachsville. In an earlier German 1818 household arts book, his list of local Lobachsville patrons included William Lobach, Salomon Peter, Jacob Bieber, and Samuel Hoch, as well as Johannes Keim.

As an antiquarian of Pennsylvania Dutchland for many years, I once purchased an 1811 Pennsylvania long rifle (popularly called "Kentucky rifles" for their prevalence and use on the frontier) at a farm sale. At the urging of my mentor, Richard Shaner, I continued to bid and eventually won the rifle, but at a pretty hefty price tag for a college kid. Richard had feared the price would go sky high if he bid on it, with many eager participants in the crowd recognizing him and looking on as we went over the finer primitives at the sale. We noticed the rifle had not three but nine primitive crosses inscribed on the underside of its gun stock, most likely to ensure a good game season for the owner. (Unfortunately, after the auction, I foolishly bartered away the gun to Richard.)

Later on, in keeping my eyes out for such objects, I discovered an 18th-century whetstone holder made out of a bull's horn with three Xs carved on it, representing the Holy Trinity. The only conclusion I could draw as a young folklorist was that the farmer who had carried the whetstone holder to sharpen his grain cradle or scythe believed the Powwow charm would protect him from snakes during the summer harvest. Local farmers often came across deadly copperhead snakes in this part of the Appalachian Mountains, with the grain fields of rye standing waist high.

Even in the enchanted Keim woods, with virgin walnut and spreading oak trees near the farm fire pond and swamp area, there were vast sunning places for copperheads along the upper ridge. After the Keim woods were purchased in the 1900s and timbered by Mahlon H. Boyer of Pine Grove, Pennsylvania, adventuresome farm boys trapped the copperheads, but only after Betsy's estate was settled. It is also likely that whichever Keim sister was in charge of butchering the chickens drew an X on the chopping block where she held the neck of the fowl between nail posts before chopping off its head. A common Pennsylvania Dutch folk practice, chickens were beheaded in this manner so they would not flop around and make a bloody mess afterward.

Some of the more ancient habits of the spinster Keim sisters carried on from the 19th century into the beginning of the 20th century were these, making them stand apart from most of the outside world.[1] Rarely did these recluse sisters leave the farm to be seen in public, even when motorized buggies became popular and drove by their home; instead, they would hide and call them "lightning wagons" in German. Relying on two to three cows for milk and cream for butter, each sister had her own chores, and they ran the household and farm cooperatively. If by chance a cow gave bloody milk, they might follow the sympathetic formula of boiling the tainted milk on the stove, stirring it in the design of a cross or letter X to break the evil spell and exorcise the hex from the bewitched cow.

Old local occult folk beliefs, though not practiced by everyone, are a significant tie in Pennsylvania Dutch culture to the religious world civilization from whence it has evolved. On occasion, hard-working farmhands were allowed to enter the large Keim manor kitchen for noontime meals and were summoned to the main house by the dinner bell still used atop the workhouse belfry. Of course, no one was ever permitted to go upstairs to the family's inner sanctum. To do this, the guest would have had to climb the spiral staircase alongside the *Feier Eck* (fire corner) of the large, medieval Central German fireplace. Here, there was a wide door; unsurprisingly, an X was carved into the wooden lintel board above the threshold, serving as an amulet, carved to repulse any evil (or curious farmhand) from passing through. Is it a coincidence that the Huguenot carpenter carved a three-foot X above the threshold of this spiral staircase leading to the inner sanctum, or was he following the blacksmith's occult artwork? Regardless, this mystical, sanctimonious passageway taunted many of the Keim neighbors, who wondered what secrets were hidden beyond these closed doors guarded with incantations.

In a 1974 interview undertaken by our institute, an elderly neighbor of Betsy Keim stated that as a young boy, he was sent to the Keim house by his mother to fetch an unremembered item. Betsy, speaking in her authoritative German tongue, sat him down on the spiral staircase alongside a gallon crock filled with coins while she looked for the item. "Shaking in his boots," as he

The brick-floor kitchen and hearth fireplace of the 1753 Jacob Keim manor house as it appeared in 1974 at an open house. The iron kettle hangs from a crane in the corner. Note the large mysterious 3' X above the doorway leading to the second floor.

recalled, he dared not move or make her *cross* (upset) until she came back to "release" him.

Not far away, on the hillside beneath what used to be the Keims' enchanted forest, the first generation of Keims rest in a stonewalled family cemetery, keeping a watchful eye over the manor house and estate. Before Jacob and Magdalena died, they built an addition on the east end of the manor, circa 1785, in which the extended family lived and prepared meals on a second hearth fireplace. The younger Keims were not buried with the older generation; instead, they lay in a second cemetery in an orchard area where an age-old, underground pipeline passed by and brought water from an unfailing spring in the mountainside that once trickled down to their animals and household. It filled a large, long iron water trough in the backyard, flowing day and night like eternity itself.

The Keim houses are no longer occupied by mortals, but the historic presence of the former occupants abides within every corner of this hand-fashioned and reverently utilized interior, which seems to let one know that the colonial past is only an echo away. On occasion, the ghost of Betsy Keim has been reported peering out the windows at passersby, and John Keim's ghost is still heard roaming on horseback where the enchanted forest once stood along (old) Boyer's Road in Pike Township, looking to avenge those who destroyed his virgin forest!

The Early Keim Workhouse or Ancillary Stone Cabin

Although the brick-arched doors and windows of the Keim cabin match the manor house architecture, this in itself does not mean the two buildings were built at the same time. Architect John K. Heyl discovered that the current raised-panel Dutch doors on the main floor of the stone cabin were not the originals but in fact once hung on the back doorway to the 1785 addition to the Keim manor house. The crude wooden batten-board doors, which still hang on the rat-tail hinges of the early cabin's gable end cellar doorway, are

A 1973 sketch done by Gerald O'Brien of the earlier Keim stone cabin, notably with a bell tower at the peak of the roof (added in the early 1800s). The bell called in local farmhands from the distant fields for noonday meals when they were out cutting grain and storing hay in the steep-roofed bank barn, opposite the main house.

more than likely original. When the 1785 addition was renovated during the Victorian period, its Dutch doors, being in good condition, were used by frugal carpenters to replace the worn-out frontier batten doors from the main-floor doorway of the old stone cabin.

The later displaced raised-panel Dutch doors fitted on the early stone cabin gave it a later appearance than its real pre–1753 origin. Given the early crude iron hardware and even cruder interior carpentry, this cabin, built over an unfailing spring with the German Continental Stube room fed from its central fireplace hearth, was likely the first home built for Jacob Keim, making it far more than just an ancillary building. The early Keim stone cabin, which later became a domestic workhouse to support the extended family living in the large manor house, is very unique, as it has two original walk-in fireplaces incorporated into its layout. Therefore, it is evident that Jacob Keim and his wife practiced a trade from the very early years when they built this first home, as he was listed as a weaver. And the Stube or stove room on the main floor, with its fenestration of large windows for light, was ideal for weaving (or possibly wood turning), as reported by historian Philip E. Pendleton.

12

X Does More Than
Mark the Spot

For centuries, native hunters in Pennsylvania's Dutch Country have stalked the region's forests carrying amulets and talisman charms to invoke God's blessing on their kills. Among these ancient rites, many of which are now forgotten or lost in antiquity, none was perhaps more obscure than the sign of the X carved on numerous rifle butts. Today, many authorities agree that the X mark used for supernatural protection and good fortune was a corruption of the Greek symbol of a fancier-looking X, which was the initial stand-in for "Christ." Used commonly by early Christians, the X was placed on chests and doors as a blessing of protection. Over time, the meaning of this Greek figure was lost, to the extent that some people in the Pennsylvania Dutch culture mistake it for the evil of hexing.

The practice of marking Xs on a gun stock for good luck was commonplace and at one time integrated into the overall concept of folk art gun embellishment. We can now look in a museum at an elaborately designed and decorated Kentucky rifle of the period; yet we cannot fully grasp the significance of its historic evolutionary motif(s). Silver inlays on a valuable early Kentucky rifle undoubtedly originated in the marksman's desire to protect his gun; a universal formula to break a spell over a bewitched gun called for the discharge of a silver bullet therein. The need for protection while hunting was real to the Pennsylvania Dutchman, who believed that if a witch crossed her apron strings in the presence of a hunter, she would steal his aim or "fire" and the gun would not discharge. Given such a widespread belief in the paranormal during America's early years, it is understandable that a Christian huntsman would use amulets and incantations to seek divine protection.

Another of Edwin M. Fogel's recorded Pennsylvania Dutch folk beliefs, besides using pins in the shape of an X to exorcise evil from a ferhext gun, tells of how to discover a witch: "One should draw an image of her, load his gun with a silver dime, and shoot at the sketch." "The portion of the body that is stuck on the image will correspond to a 'mark' that will appear on the suspected person."

Since the number 3 is a number of great power, representing the Holy Trinity in the Pennsylvania Dutch culture, it is not uncommon to find this crucifix letter or symbol in a series of three. In the previous chapter, I mentioned how once, on an 1811 Pennsylvania long rifle, my mentor and I discovered a series of nine X markings secretly carved on the bottom side of the curly maple stock; there was no other decoration on the gun except for two silver inlays. Since the number 3 stands for the Holy Trinity, nine X marks, being divisible by three, was a show of extraordinary faith or caution.[1]

Old Rhineland folklore promoted the use of talisman charms, which were carried by huntsmen to guard against any sorceress they might encounter while hunting game. One of the most common methods was to carve Xs in a series of three, representing the Holy Trinity, on the rifle butt and/or powder horns to prevent witches from "stealing" one's fire.

The most famous or utilized of all the huntsman charms were gathered by John George Hohman in his 1820 *Long Lost Friend*. On this topic, no mention of incantations or charms would be complete without listing the most widely used talisman for outdoorsmen included by Hohman for publication, which features two Latin phrases with the sign of the Holy Trinity between them; on top of the three crosses are three stars. This talisman is so powerful that the huntsman is warned mysteriously not to shoot more game in the forest than meets his needs! Hohman, the most published of all sympathetic folk practitioners, sought out and established the validity of these charms in his books and thus popularized them in the early 19th century. In my family artifacts, there is an empty brass shell containing this talisman inscription for bagging impressive game (it was to be hidden in one's game bag).

Pennsylvania Dutch housewives have traditionally used the mark of the

X in slaughtering their fowl. In this practice, the woman cuts an X between nail posts on her chopping block, which will "still" the bird upon death; thus, she avoids the bloody mess the headless fowl could cause through flopping around. A primitive whetstone holder seen by the author featured another series of Xs carved on one side; it was made from a cow's horn and discovered in Lynn Township, Lehigh County. Dating from the late 1700s (or even earlier), the shield was likely used at harvest time as the farmer cut grain and periodically sharpened his German cradle scythe. One can only theorize about the occult implications, but folklorists have recorded patterns of witchery involving pens and knives. Since the whetstone shield was clipped to the harvester's belt, it may have been a personal gesture of protection to ward off copperhead snakes sunning in the grain fields, as mentioned previously.

But if one were going to ask for protection, it most certainly would be for one's home and family. There is no better example of this concept than the Keim manor house, which features Xs on the backside of several door hinges. Inscribed in a series, and hidden from view, these Xs do not seem to be an integral part of the forged art work. Even in the kitchen of the Keim manor house, the door leading to the upstairs bedrooms displays a prominent mold-carved X across the entire panel atop the entrance. Although this bead-grooved X at first appears to be aesthetic, there's no matching bead-molded artwork anywhere else.

The Keims resided at this site from colonial days until 1911, and they maintained a "virgin stand on the woodland" covering nearly a hundred acres. The family rule was that there would be no hunting in this refuge. Most famous among the bizarre criminal happenings in this area is the episode of the Herbein gentleman whose gun was bewitched by one of the older Keim sisters who last lived there. Sneaking into the woodland to hunt partridge, the intruder found that his gun would positively not fire. As Fogel would say, "the witches had stolen his fire."

Although not a charm, there was also the prevalent remedy to stop a bewitched cow from giving bloody milk. In this counteraction, the milkmaid would take a portion of the bewitched milk into the kitchen and bring it to a boil on her stove. While the milk boiled, the maid would stir it in the figure of an X, which broke the spell. A second countermeasure for bloody milk recorded by Fogel called for the use of an X stake from a zigzag or worm fence. One was to locate an X stake along the fence line that contained a hollowed base, and a portion of the tainted milk was to be poured into the hollow end of the stake, which would then be returned to its original position.

However, the largest X that can be made is that which is formed when two roads form an intersection. This is considered the most powerful of all

Pennsylvania Dutch farmwives would solve the problem of a cow giving bloody milk by heating the milk on their kitchen stoves, thus breaking the witch's spell.

supernatural locations, and one should never pick up money found at a crossroad, for it will bring bad luck. The crossroad was long considered the gateway to the *World of the Supernatural*, and the square formed in the center of the intersection was considered a "no-man's land," not belonging to anyone. In the Oley Valley, there was a famous oak tree that stood in the "middle of the road." Known as Huguenot Oak, it was located on (then unpaved) Oak Lane, Oley Township, and had long been an obstacle to traffic but was not removed out of "fear" for a number of years. This landmark oak, which also marked the intersection of four land grants, resided safely in the "no-man's land" up until the late 20th century. Although the state now has the power to eliminate such an obstacle on a public road, in years gone by what landowner would dare wield such power over the no-man's land?

In addition, according to Pennsylvania Dutch occultists, it is at the "apex" of the crossroads that a silver bullet can be cast to shoot anyone, anywhere, at any time. Tradition states that first two corpses must pass over the intersection, crisscrossing diametrically. Then, at midnight, a bullet can be cast in the "no-man's land" surrounded by a burning circle of brush, discharged through the eye of a skull as the marksman named his prey. There are also numerous stories of pioneer settlers who cheated their neighbors by moving boundary markers and thus, if found out, were condemned to walk the earth after death, never to have eternal rest.

As we look back upon the past, I am intrigued by the ingenuity of our ancestors and their belief in the wonderful and adventuresome mysticism of the New World. Whether or not folk practices are accepted literally from the past, or mutely found integrated in American folk art, they are part of the romance of American civilization. Representing an innocence of our heritage as told in human values that touch the soul and renew our curiosity in the still unknown universe, folk beliefs are milestones in humanity.

13

18th-Century Yoder
Ghost of Oley Valley

Note: The following account of the Oley Preacher's Ghost of 1748 (ironically, or perhaps coincidentally, the same year that John Ross wrote of a supernatural event, as detailed in chapter 8) is translated from a mysterious event taken from Christopher Saur's works, Erscheinungen der Geister, *printed, of course, in German at Colonial Germantown, Pennsylvania. The preacher was Johannes Yoder (German: Joder), who lived in the Oley Valley during colonial times. The appearance of the Yoder ghost caused a great deal of interest in religious circles, and a number of people from far and wide came to Oley to interview the people involved.*

After Joder left this world for two years and several months, he was granted permission to revisit his favorite daughter, Elizabeth, for whom he had a particular message. It has been the premise of clairvoyants that those unfortunate departed souls who have been unable to complete their earthly mission, or who have a special bit of intelligence, may find no peace in the far beyond and, upon rare occasion, may be granted permission to return, thus freeing themselves of the weight of their unrest.

"On August 14, the before-mentioned Elizabeth Joder was overcome by great sadness, fear, and anxiety. She said to her mother, 'I think father is coming to me.' She was so anxious that she continually looked about her and imagined that her father stood behind her or near her. Because of her anxiety she could not eat or sleep.

"Now, as she went about her work on the 15th of August, she was again overcome with anxiety and felt such a strong urge to go into the house that it became impossible for her to wait until the work was finished. As she entered the house and went to fetch something from her room, she looked around and saw her father sitting on the bed. He said to her very kindly,

Views from inside the intimidating 1741 Yoder homestead looking eastward at the 19th-century toll house used for collection to cross the 126-foot Pleasantville covered bridge, built in 1852 (photograph December 2016).

'What are you doing, my child?' Whereupon she was so frightened and horrified that she could not answer but dropped everything and, trembling and shaking, ran out of the house and fell down.

"Her mother was perplexed by this, fearing that there might be unfortunate aftereffects. She said to her daughter, 'You must go live on another farm for a while. It will be a change and do you good.' This the daughter did, but she continued to be restless and felt a continuous urge to return home.

"So, on the 16th of August, under a strong impulse, she returned to her home and went immediately to her room. Her mother and another woman talked to her and told her that if she should again see her father, she should not run away again. They would remain outside the door. She again entered and, after she had sat for a while on the chest, everything became quite dark to her eyes as though it were night. When this had passed everything became bright again and her father was standing by the bed. Then, in terror, she screamed, 'Oh Jesus! He is here.'

"Then her mother and the other woman came in wishing to see him, but he had again disappeared. Then the daughter signaled them to leave the room, which they did, and the father reappeared immediately. He sat with her on the chest, talking to her with gentle kindness. 'What are you doing, my child? Where are your brothers?' The daughter said, 'They are not here.' He said, 'I have just taken leave of this world and have said nothing to you. I think this is as good a time as any. So now, obey your mother and do not mock her. She is on the right path and when she departs she will come to a good place.' She answered several times, weeping constantly, 'Dear father, I will do everything you tell me.'

"She asked him, 'Why do you come now for the first time?' He said, 'There was no time. I could not come sooner.' She asked why he did not appear to others. He said, 'I have a special relation with thee.' She said to him, 'Where are you now and how are you?' He answered, 'I am in a good place and I am well.' She asked him, 'Where is your dear brother?' He answered, 'He is with me and we are well.'

"Then he said to her, 'Why did you run away from me yesterday? It was not necessary. I am indeed your loving father. You have no need to be afraid. Because you were afraid of me and ran away from me you must undergo a severe illness. The third night will be worst. Death will approach you three times and you will just escape. But you will recover! Completely and your life will not be shortened thereby.' Then he said more things that concerned the daughter alone.

"When he had said all these things it seemed that he was pulled away from her with these last words, 'Now I go forth and come not again.' Once again she looked back under the door and could still see the glow of his presence. She said that he had become so beautiful and shone so brightly that the light in the room caused an afterglow. Moreover, he was in the clothes and condition in which he had been laid in his grave."

Part III

Faith Healing
of the Dutch Country

14

Frontier Faith Healing in the Pennsylvania Dutch Country

Of all the folk characters who have inhabited the "Dutch Country" from colonial days to the present, none can compare to the mystique of John George Hohman of Alsace Township, Berks County. An indentured servant who came to Pennsylvania in 1802, Hohman was destined to become the father of black and white magic in the United States. The occult powers of John George Hohman are amazing to 20th- and 21st-century Americans, but his wizardry was very real in the 19th century, and his powers were sometimes feared.

Was Hohman a witch or a wizard? There is a good comparison drawn between him and the benevolent Mountain Mary of the Oley Valley, whose talent for curing the ill and afflicted bordered on the supernatural. The supernatural, in this case, is the occult power possessed by only a few people in the Pennsylvania Dutch culture, which is known as Braucherei or, to use the slang term for it, Powwowing. Braucherei is nothing less than a Pennsylvania Dutch form of faith healing, and the agent who performs this sympathetic magic freely admits that he is not doing the healing; rather, it is God. No individual can be cured with Powwowing if they do not believe in God, and incantations uttered by the Braucher always end with or include the Holy Trinity.

People who could Brauch (bless) were always respected in their community and would usually cure about half a dozen types of sicknesses. Two very popular ailments cured by this method were *Wildfeier* (erysipelas) and blood stopping. To appreciate the full power of the Braucher, one must realize that certain illnesses and afflictions were believed by the Pennsylvania Dutch to be evil in origin, from either a witch or the Devil himself, and a person so afflicted could not very well be cured by home remedies or medicine.

Hohman explained the ground rules for Braucherei, which was based on the existence of God and Satan, thus in 1819: "There are many in America who believe neither in a Hell nor any Heaven; but in Germany there are not so many of these persons found. I, Hohman, ask: Who can immediately banish the wheel of mortification? I reply, and I, Hohman, say: All this is done by the Lord. Therefore a hell and a heaven must exist; and I think very little of anyone who dares deny it."

Hohman was indeed a master Braucher, according to people who possess the power to Brauch, and if such individuals do not practice their gift, the force builds up within them until they are compelled to show their compassion for their fellow men. Such must have been the case with Hohman, and his ability to heal people of literally scores of elements and afflictions surely compelled him to publish his occult incantations in 1820. Hohman's 100-page work, printed in German, was called *The Long Lost Friend*. In his own words, "I did not wish to publish it; my wife, also, was opposed to its publication; but my compassion for my suffering fellow-men was too strong, for I seen many a one lose his entire sight by a weal, and his life or limb by mortification.... Besides that, I am a poor man in needy circumstances, and it is help to me if I can make a little money with the sale of my books."

In the introduction of his home and occult book, he gives a number of testimonies from people he healed along the Pricetown ridge of the Oley Hills and states that he will not "secrete or hide himself from any preacher." Hohman responds to the most famous argument among some Pennsylvania Dutch that the use of the Lord's name in Brauching is blasphemous by using the following logic: "If men were not allowed to use sympathetic words, nor the name of the most high, it certainly would not have been revealed to them; and what is more, the Lord would not help where they are made use of. God can in no manner be forced to intercede where it is not his divine pleasure."

Hohman justifies the practice of Braucherei by arguing that the "Lord says in the fiftieth Psalm, 'Call upon me in the day of trouble: I will deliver thee, and thou shalt glorify me.' Woe onto those who, in obeying the direction of a preacher, neglect using any means offered by this book against mortification, or inflammation, or the weal." Whether one believes in Braucherei or not, the simple truth for Hohman was that it does work, and he personally healed many in the Oley Hills and beyond. It is apparent from Hohman's writings that there were people and preachers who opposed this folk practice in his day, as there are at the present time. Despite the advantages of modern medicine, there are still certain afflictions such as "wildfire" that are probably more likely to be cured by a contemporary Braucher than by a score of physicians.

The Origins of Black and White Magic

In the preface to Hohman's *Long Lost Friend*, he states that some of his formulae and sympathetic words were taken from a gypsy book, others from secret writings, and still others from all parts of the world. The late Reverend Thomas Brendle, a foremost authority on folk medicine among the Pennsylvania Dutch, once stated that Hohman's SATOR formula was traced to 200

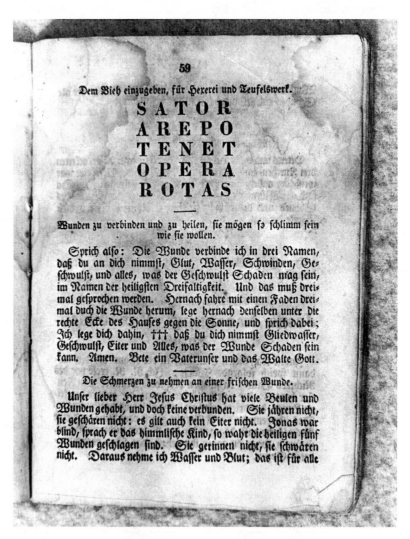

The SATOR formula, including the mystic words SATOR AREPO TENET OPERA ROTAS, is the most common charm for protection against the occult.

B.C. in India. Since Hohman was obviously a very religious man, it is difficult to understand why he included some black magic witchcraft formulae in his 1820 work. However, since he did include excerpts from various European sources, he no doubt included several devious recipes from early alchemist studies attributed to Albertus Magnus of the 13th century.

In spite of the fact that Hohman had knowledge of witchcraft, there is no evidence that he ever practiced it. However, his popular 1820 occult book eventually became the handbook for practitioners of white and black magic alike. But because of the inclusion of black magic formulae in Hohman's book, no self-respecting Dutchman would ever admit publicly that he owned one. Sometimes the title page was pasted shut, as mentioned, so that the identity of the book would not be readily noticed.

The Enterprising Hohman

It is not known if John George Hohman had a trade or occupation other than being one of the many individuals who were part of the broad agrarian economy of the early 1800s. However, it seems that from the time that he was an indentured servant until possibly his death, he was an itinerant peddler of broadsides (single printed sheets of paper, such as ballads and so on). At one time he purchased for resale a number of birth certificates, which he possibly might have illuminated in the Pennsylvania Dutch fraktur style.

Obviously an educated man, Hohman might also have been a school-teacher in one of the many one-room schools in the Pricetown area. To the countless people whom Hohman aided in his lifetime, he must have been a savior. Certainly he was well respected early in life, as attested to by the huge number of Oley Valley citizens who subscribed to his first book, *Die Land- und Haus-Apotheke*, (a medical text) printed in Reading in 1818. Hohman also published a Himmelsbrief (letter from Heaven), which, according to German tradition, was a letter written by God and dropped to Earth for mortals to read (see chapter 26). The Pennsylvania Dutch tradition is that if you possess a Himmelsbrief in your house, it will be safe from floods, fire, and lightning.

A first edition of Hohman's *Long Lost Friend* is a rare find among book collectors and very much sought after. This book has been reprinted many times, by a number of dialect presses, in all parts of the Pennsylvania Dutch territory. Late English translations were poorly done, and in some alchemy formulae that call for the use of human urine, publishers just stated "catch rainwater in a pot."

An Incantation to stop bleeding

I walk through a green forest;
There I find three wells, cool, and cold; the first is called courage,
The second is called good,
And the third is called stop the blood.

An Exceptional Biography of Hohman

In a 1949 issue of the *Pennsylvania Dutchman* published at Lancaster, Pennsylvania, Dr. Wilbur H. Oda wrote an excellent biography of John George Hohman. Oda was an avid book collector of Pennsylvania German imprints, and he lived near Bally, Berks County. The following is an excerpt and only account ever published at the time in such detail:

> John George Hohman and his wife arrived in Philadelphia, on the ship *Tom*, from Hamburg (Germany), on October 12th, 1802. His wife, Anna Catharine, was indentured to Samuel Newbold, a farmer who lived in Springfield Township, Burlington County, New Jersey. A week later, October 19, 1802, Hohman found himself as a servant to Adam Frankenfiehl (Frankenfield) of Spring field [*sic*] Township, Bucks County. He was to serve for three years and six months and was to receive customary freedom, suits and twenty dollars in exchange for payment of his passage which amounted to eighty-four dollars.

"Hohman's name is first found in print in a broadside called the 'Grodoria Himmelsbrief.' This broadside was brought to America in 1802 and later published by Hohman, probably in Easton. At this time Hohman was living near Hellertown, Northampton County." Hohman's name next appears in the *Adler* account books on May 29, 1805. He is charged with the printing of 800 sheets of songs. It is impossible to ascertain at the present time the name or nature of these songs. They cost nine dollars and fifty cents, but it was not until September 29, that Hohman made a "partial payment of one dollar and a half."

HOHMAN PUBLISHES BROADSIDE

We next hear of Hohman in a broadside titled "*Trauergeschichte*," which is the story of the famous Mayerhof murder. According to a note at the bottom of the sheet, it was published as a warning to those who were not inclined to follow the straight and narrow path. Hohman admitted to having changed certain words so that the ballad would be better adapted to singing. He also added three stanzas of his own, which had never before appeared in print, and signed it as "Johann George Homan, District Township, Berks County, January 8, 1811." This was the only time Hohman ever mentioned District Township, and it may have been about the time that he attended the Church of the Holy Sacrament at Bally (Catholic). On December 23, 1812, Hohman bought for the first time *Taufschiens* (birth certificates), but as far as historians and folklorists know not a single *Taufschien* signed by Hohman has been found.

Mr. Stapleton, in one of his articles on German imprints, mentions the fact that Hohman published a book about "the wandering Jew": *Das Buch von dem Ewigen Juden*. It was published in 1813, according to an advertisement in the Reading *Adler* of April 27, 1813. However, no copy of this book is known to historians. Around May 10, 1815, Hohman published a broadside containing three hymns, one a confirmation hymn for the historic Mertz Church near Dryville, Berks County.

EARLY MEDICAL BOOK

In 1818, Hohman published his first American book, *Die Land- und Haus-Apotheke*, which was a general medical book for both man and beast. There was also an appendix that discussed dyeing (with, strangely enough, a special section devoted to the dyeing of hats). In the year 1819, Hohman published two editions of the *Evangelium Nicodemi*. It must be mentioned that this book had been printed as early as 1748 in Ephrata (Pennsylvania). Hohman's editions were, however, more complete and contained additional material, including the *Testament und Abschrift der Zwolf Patriarchen*. These aforementioned two books belong to the "Lost Books of the Bible."

The year 1819 also saw the appearance of Hohman's Catholic catechism; according to the best information that can be found, this book (like many of Hohman's other publications) was copied from other sources. Oral tradition claims that it was printed for the Church of the Holy Sacrament at Bally.

THE LONG LOST FRIEND

Obviously, the most popular of Hohman's publications, repeatedly mentioned and referenced in this book, is *The Long Lost Friend*. The first edition actually appeared in 1819, coincidentally (or not) the same year that local saint and fellow faith healer Mount Mary died; the book became readily available by 1820. This book has been republished frequently, even up to present day, but with very generic covers.

Hohman published little of importance after 1820, but in 1842 there appeared *Aufblick der Seele in den Himmel oder neue schoene geistliche Buss- und Bekehrungs-Leider ... Zum Druck befoerdert von Johann Georg Hohman, Berks County, 1842*. As the title implies, these songs (or rather hymns) were of a religious or spiritual nature—a call to repentance or conversion. The first one began as follows: "Ach arme grosse Sunder, Helf uns Herr in uns'rer Noth" (translated: Ah, poor Sinners that we are, help us, Lord, in our distress). All the hymns contain the same religious fervor and are signed by Hohman. The hymns are followed by several ballads, among them "Die arme Witwe" (The Poor Widow) and "Die Sultans-Tochter" (The Sultan's Daughter).

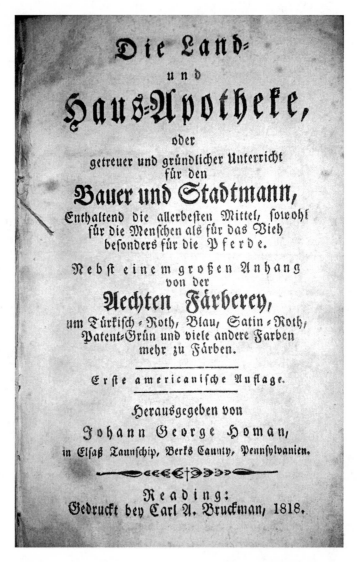

Hohman's first American book, *Die Land- und Haus-Apotheke*, was printed in Reading, Pennsylvania, in 1818; according to the title page, Hohman was a resident of Alsace Township, Berks County, at the time.

HIS LAST BOOK

Hohman published his last book, as far as is known, in the year 1846. It was titled *Der Fromme zu Gott in der Andacht* and printed in Reading. The first part consisted of Hohman's version of another pseudepigraphical book of the Bible called "The Childhood of Jesus." This book was supposedly written around 200 A.D. and was recognized by some early sects, including the Gnostics, as a genuine book of the Bible. In it, among other things, we find the story of the child Jesus molding little birds of clay, putting them on a fence, and making them fly away. The latter part of Hohman's book consists of many of the songs that he had already published in broadside form. Among these folk poems are "Die Kinder im Wald," "Concordia," "Susanna Cox," and "Adam und Eva im Paradies." Although many of the songs are in the form of hymns, in only one case does Hohman sign himself as the author. The first stanza of the hymn is as follows:

> *Folg Jesu in Kreuz und Leiden,*
> *In der groessten Angst und Noth,*
> *Denn er kann da Schicksal leiten,*
> *Und befreien von dem Tod.*

FINANCIAL STATUS

Hohman's name does not appear in the Reading tax list until the year 1815, when he paid the sum of $0.15. In this year, there were forty-four H names on the Alsace Township list, and of this number, 33 paid more than Hohman; one paid as much as he did, and only nine paid less. Hohman continued to pay approximately the same amount until the year 1825, when he paid only $0.12. In order to explain this drop in taxes, one has to go back to 1819, when the deed books of the Reading courthouse show that Jacob K. Boyer, a Reading merchant, had sold Hohman on May 1, 1819, a plot of ground (three acres and fifty-four perches) in Alsace Township.

Thus, everything seems to have gone well with Hohman during this time until August 13, 1825, when the sheriff, Danial Kerber, was commanded by writ of *fieri facias* to seize "the goods and chattels, lands and tenements" of "J.G. Homan" in order to raise money in the sum of $52.50, owed to Jacob K. Boyer. The sale was held December 24, 1825, where the record states, "Did on the twenty-fourth day of December last expose the premises aforesaid to sale by public venue or outcry and sold the same to Joseph Smith of the County of Berks aforesaid for the sum of ninety dollars he being the highest bidder." What a bleak and cheerless Christmas this God-fearing man and his wife must have had that year.

As far as can be learned, Hohman continued to live on the property after he was sold out, and it is probable that Smith soon sold the property back to Jacob K. Boyer. Strange as it may seem, Hohman paid the highest county tax he ever paid, $0.33, in 1826, the year after the sale. (In comparing his tax with that of others in his township, it is of interest to note that in 1826 William High paid $23.44.) Mr. Buck writes, "Homan attained to a good old age through the comfortable provisions he had made by his industry," which seems a gross exaggeration when the records indicate that Hohman was apparently in financial straits for the greater part of his life.

No Longer on the Tax List

Hohman's name is not found in the tax lists for years of 1827 and 1828, but appears again for the years 1829–1833. In 1834, instead of John George Hohman, we find the name of "Caspar Homan," who paid $0.26 county tax and $0.21 state tax. In 1835 and 1836, Hohman's taxes amounted to $0.08 per year, and in both years he was allowed a deficiency in the full amount of his tax by the collector, John W. Burkhart. This seems to indicate that Hohman was, at this time, poverty-stricken. His name does not appear after 1836 in the Alsace Township tax list, but in that same year, Hohman published a broadside in which he stated that he was living two miles north of Pricetown (near Fleetwood). From that time on, the historic record loses track of Hohman; nothing is known about him, not even when he died or where he was buried.

In 1975, a Pennsylvania folklorist offered a $100 reward to the person who could find the grave of John George Hohman. To date, no one has ever collected this reward. Perhaps his grave was unmarked since he was poor, or perhaps Hohman moved in his old age from the Oley Hills to live with his son. Nevertheless, the reward still stands, if anyone can locate the gravesite of John George Hohman, who died sometime after 1846; the American Folklife Institute now has on deposit $500 for this purpose.

Of the many books and pamphlets that came off German presses in early 19th-century Pennsylvania, the great majority were religiously inspired. Of the remainder, a surprisingly large number dealt with home cures, remedies, and arts. Some dealt specifically with horse diseases, and several others were advertised as "new recipes" and "approved cure[s] for man and beast." These ranged from the "Ephrata-style" midwives' manuals of the late 1790s to the well-known *Land- und Haus-Apotheke*, written by famous Hohman and printed at Reading in 1818 by Carl Bruckman. *Die Land- und Haus-Apotheke* really had something for everyone and involved both the farmer and the town dweller. As mentioned previously, this book included a marvelous section on dyes and inks.

Die Land- und Haus-Apotheke is of special interest to me, as my great-great-great-great-great-grandfather was one of the numerous subscribers to this work. Of similar design is the 450-page *Haus und Kunst-Buch*, printed in 1819 at Allentown by Heniuh Ebner. Additionally, the rather well-known *Ballmer cures* (only 40 pages long), printed in 1827 by F. Goeb in Schellsburg, brags of fifty-six cures for snake bite, dog bite, ringworm, and similar afflictions. Most of the cures are supposed to work as well on animals as on people!

Popular Books on Home Cures

A closely related genus of cure books is made up of those that involve the Holy Trinity and use sympathetic formulae. Hohman's *Long Lost Friend* is obviously the most well known in this category, but there are others that would greatly interest any folklorist. Some use charms that are said to be derived from gypsy kings or, like Himmelsbriefs, arrived on Earth via angels (or dropped from Heaven). Because these books are on the mystical side of things, the printers often omitted their bylines and the title pages, merely stating, "Printed in Pennsylvania AD 1847" (if they even gave that much information).

The most exciting of these books is the *Soli Deo Gloria*, or Helfenstein book. According to his autobiography, George Friedrich Helfenstein was born in Holland in 1730 to poor parents and was soon orphaned. He was aided by a cousin and through hard work became a respected and successful physician. On his way to inspect a new patient, Helfenstein met an old gray man who told him to return home, as the patient was cured. The old man then told him that he (Helfenstein) was lucky, as he had been selected to be taught a more powerful method of medicine. After Helfenstein, with the aid of the Holy Spirit, learned these cures (all of which are said to be presented in this book), the old gray man disappeared before Helfenstein's very eyes.

Using the Bible to prove that such actions are sanctioned, Helfenstein quotes Matthew 7:20 and Mark 11:22–23. He states:

> I was not prompted by financial gain to print his book but rather by compassion for my fellow humans. And were it not for the great expense involved in its printing I would like to be able to sell it for less. One will find it of great value, however, and not mind at all the investment. If one follows my instruction and believes in the power of the Spirit one will be amazed at strength of the cure. To be sure, however, to only use these for a real and sincere cause.

Haus-Freund edition—this rare 1847 occult book is a copy of Hohman's *The Long Lost Friend* that belonged to my grandmother. Hohman's hex book was a favorite tool of all Powwow doctors and was always a good seller for any printer in the Dutch Country.

HELFENSTEIN OCCULT BOOK PRINTED IN AMERICA

After Helfenstein's death, his book continued in print, and an edition consisting of seventy pages was attributed to a southeastern Pennsylvania press; however, there was no imprint line. This edition was never bound; instead, it

Der

Lang Verborgene Freund,

enthaltend

Wunderbare und Probmäßige

Mittel und Künste

für

Menschen und Vieh.

Herausgegeben von

Johann Georg Hohmann.

Demselben ist beigefügt

Dr. G. F. Helfenstein's

vielfältig erprobter

Hausschatz der Sympathie.

Evangelium Marci, Cap. 11, v. 22, 23.

Harrisburg, Pa.

Gedruckt bei Scheffer und Beck,

1853.

1853 Helfenstein edition with the German spelling of the author's last name. Listed in Hohman's works are more than 180 different formulae, which were good for treating the typical sicknesses and diseases (both occult and non-occult) that afflicted man and beast.

consisted of loose pages in a cardboard box, 1.5" × 7" × 9", and was covered with wallpaper. Usually there were two wax seals on the lid to give it proper authority. While these books are relatively scarce, they have turned up at public auctions as part of estates of long-established Berks County families. One such account, although somewhat humorous, involved the late collector and redware potter Lester P. Breininger, when several years ago a Helfenstein edition was to be sold in his part of western Berks County, Pennsylvania. Here is a brief account (minus the expletives): "While the uninformed public 'pawed' through seven cartons of nondescript books and papers, the unbound pages were scattered throughout most of the cartons!" After much anguish, Lester believed most of the pages were returned to the box, and the "set" was purchased.

Secret Powers of SATOR

Many of these cure books contain formulae consisting of names, letters, numbers and signs; some are Latin phrases mixed in with fragments of other languages. The frequent recopying by uncomprehending hands has resulted in some rather undecipherable words, unintelligible meanings, and untraceable origins. The most frequently occurring formula, though, is the SATOR one, which consists of five lines of five letters each. Carrying a copy of this formula protected the bearer and his house, and copies were fed to men and beasts to cure a variety of ailments.

A small, rather uncommon, twelve-page tract was attributed to a Pennsylvania press of the 1820s that reproduced this same formula. The title page merely stated that it was translated from the gypsy tongue and printed at the expense of a gypsy ("Gedruckt auf Koster eines Zipeuners"). Concerning the SATOR formula, it says, "This is the song (first letter of each word used) sung by those three men, Shadrack, Mesack and Abednego, those that were allowed to be placed in the fiery furnace by King Nebuchadnezzar; then did God send [his] holy angel." This is the only version that gives a specific biblical source for the origin of the formula. The formula can also be found in Amos Husy's 1846 arithmetic book—a more unusual place is hard to find, but its intended use is of great interest.

There are certainly additional pamphlets and Pennsylvania German imprints on this general subject of cures that are little known and deserve study, and interested readers are urged to contact our institute so that a comprehensive bibliography can be compiled. Interestingly enough, the following is a partial listing of people who bought Johann Georg Hohman's *Land- und Haus-Apotheke* (1818). Did these people also subscribe to his notorious *Long Lost Friend* two years later? For local historians, note the prominent Oley Valley citizens who are given in this partial patron list, with the township given first:

Alsace: George Heyer, Jakob Schmehl, John Wummer, Henry Haberacker, Major H. Leiss, Isaac Jung, George Schadel, John Kissinger, jun., Johannes

Klein, Peter Leiss, Johannes Pfaff, Jakob Becker, Johannes Wehn, Henrich Kapp, Bernard Zweizig, Wilhelm Adam, Johannes Klee, Johannes Muller, Jacob Brautigan, Johannes Fiess, Enoch Koller, William Mack, Joseph Stocker.

Pike: William Lobach, William Steplethon, Daniel Dotterer, George Eister, William Lee, Andreas Weiand, Joseph Angstadt, Mathias Kruck, Jakob Herzog, Heinrich Meyer, Johann Fronheiser, Daniel Drumheller, Jokob Aulenbach

Rockland: Jacob Bertow, Melchior Heist, Johannes D. Roth, Peter Gerhart, Salamon Seiert, Abraham Joder, Catharina Angstadt, Ludwig Scheure, Samuel Joder, Jakob Joder, Jakob Reider, Heinrich Staudt, Johannes Roth, William Roth, Heinrich Hehnig, Georg Devies, Paul Frey, Johanna Sparrow, Jonathan Friedrich, Johannes Barral, Daniel Keller, Johannes Bick, Johannes Ritz, Jakob Rohrbach, Johannes Keim, Johannes Hofner, Adam Emrich

District: Joseph Zweyer, Abraham Bohm, Joseph Kemp, David Johnson, Adam Bartman, Johannes Facher, Abraham Weler

Amity: Jokob Schroder, Michael Reider, Jacob Strunk, Jokob K. Christ, Johannes Koch, Abraham Griesemer, Joseph Griesemer, Johann Ross, Jokob Kreider, Georg Lorah, Johanna Ludwig, Peter Nagel, Johann Lorah

Exeter: Christian Spatz, Paul Bar, Benjamin Kustard, Philip Meyer, Peter Hill, Daniel Guldin, Peter Hausum, Daniel Guldin, Daniel Oesterly, Jocob Levan, William Braun, Heinrich Beyer, Johannes Leber, Johannes Strunk, Johannes Faber, Adam Jung, Samuel Kissling, Johann Neukirch, Daniel Joder, Jacob Joder, Johann Ludwig, Heinrich Bechtel, Georg Deterk, Abraham Deterk, Jokob Bechtel, Jokob Heyer, Abraham Levan, Jakob Kuhn, Daniel Ritter, Isaac Levan, Johann Geiger, Daniel Knab, Jakob Ritter, Jakob Sauder, Isaak Kloss, Jokob Steinmetz, Johann Hiester, Georg Hitter, Benjamin Hitter, Johann Kloss, Caterina Schneider, George Armand, Johann Guldin, Conrad Dieter, Samuel Dieter, Jocob Christian, Heinrich Hein, John Miller, (2)

Oley: Jakob Schroder, jun., Daniel Leinbach, Catharina Mull, Jokob Bieber, Johann Bertow, Salomon Peter, Johann Weiser, Daniel Levan, Peter Miller, Samuel Sewitsch, Daniel Herbein, jun., Johannes Wust, Johannes Focht, jun., Peter Knab, Daniel Herbein, Johann Berdole, Jakob Schafer, Samuel Filbert, (12), Daniel Joder, Martin Joder, Jakob Reiter, Henrich Fischer, Johann Guthmann, Johann Griesemer, Samuel Hoch, jun., Daniel Griesemer, Johann Dirolf, Jakob Griesemer, (Miller), Henrich Spang, (Stohrk), Johann Hufmann

Ruscombmanor: Jakob B. Griesemer, Paul Barral, Abraham Thransu, William Dalton, Isaak Thransu, Johannes Lesch, Jakob Reich, Jakob Miller, Friedrich Miller, Isaak Staudt, jun., Johann Riehl, Balentin Unangst, Peter Thransu, Michael T. Wilhelm

15

Mountain Mary
Berks County's Most Beloved
Faith Healer

"Mountain Mary"/Anna Maria Jung/Die Berg Maria (1749–1819) is an enduring Pennsylvania Dutch legend, yet a somewhat elusive historical problem. As legend, the story has grown from a cryptic notice in the 1790 census of the United States to an effusive flood of words that gush forth from regional historians. This legend has had many formulations, including *Die Berg Maria*, the novelette here translated. Not all versions of the legend agree; details vary. So the historical problem of digging out the truth about Mountain Mary remains. There are some who have denied that such a person ever existed. Perhaps the best account of Berks County's most prominent faith healer can be found in Ludwig Wollenweber's 1880 romantic novelette (written in High German, parts of which have been translated throughout this chapter by the author) about Mountain Mary. He provides local details that have been lost about this American legend; however, very little (if any) mention is made of her practice in healing.

These moralistic stories of the legendary "Berg Maria" (Mountain Mary), a Pennsylvania Dutch frontier widow who lost her newlywed husband in the American Revolution, form a heartwarming tale of God and country. This German immigrant was a beloved friend of Lutheran patriot Dr. Henry Melchior Muhlenberg, and she became a hermit high up in the Oley Hills, near Hill Church in Pike Township. She healed the sick and afflicted through Christian faith and American herbs. A homegrown Protestant saint, Mountain Mary became a pioneer model for anyone who lived alone in the Oley Valley, especially hard-working immigrants who were sold into indentured servitude by greedy colonial sea captains in exchange for their passage to the New World.

Actually, there are two historical problems that are so interwoven within

Treu bis in den Tod.

—o—

Die Berg-Maria,

—oder—

Wer nur den lieben Gott läßt walten.

—Eine—

Geschichtliche Erzählung

—aus—

Pennsylvanien.

—Von—

L. A. Wollenweber,

(Der Alte vom Berge.)

Mit Illustrationen von F. Schlitte.

Philadelphia:

rlag von Z. Kohler, No. 911 Arch Straße.

1880.

Ludwig Wollenweber's 1880 German romantic novelette about faith healer Mountain Mary provided local details (many of them fictional) about this real American legend who lived high in the Oley Hills of Pike Township.

the local culture and what exists in factual documentation that a critical historian may extract the truth only with great difficulty. The question is basic: Who was the historical figure about whom these legends have grown? And what is the meaning of these legends for the field of Pennsylvania Dutch studies and for Pennsylvania history? Evidence remains sketchy, only partially deduced from objective fact. Therefore, I will present the best evidence that has been compiled.

It is said that Anna Maria Jung (Young) was born near Frankfurt-am-Main, Germany, around 1749. She is said to have migrated to Pennsylvania, arriving sometime between 1764 and 1773 (the date is uncertain). If her father's name was Jacob—a fact not yet established—there are two possibilities: a Johann Jakob Jung signed the ship list of the *Jenefer*, November 29, 1764, Captain George Kerr commanding; and a Jakob Jung made his mark on the ship list of the *Minerva*, September 17, 1771, Captain Thomas Arnot commanding. Neither list mentions dependents. However, if her father's name was not Jacob, then we have to examine the thirteen other persons with the family name Jung who arrived between 1764 and 1773.

The Jung family, having arrived in Pennsylvania, may first have settled in Germantown, but this is far from certain. The first bit of precise information about a person like Mountain Mary—and a tantalizing bit it is!—comes from the first census of the United States taken in 1790. Listing the heads of families in East District, Berks County, the census taker recorded "Mary (the Abbess)," who was then living with two other females, probably her sisters Anna Elisabeth and Maria Catherine (both of whom would later marry citizens of Oley). This cryptic statement of only three words confirms that there already was a Mountain Mary legend. But what does "Abbess" mean? Was Mary the head of a female religious establishment? Or was this a personal designation? Why was she not simply listed by her family name? Regardless, already around 1790, just a few years after her arrival in Oley, Mary was someone around whom a legend was growing.

The second bit of precise information we have is from the will of Anna Maria Jung. On March 13, 1813, a person who signed herself as "Anna Maria Jungin" (the "in" is the feminine ending) wrote a will that was recorded in Will Book D, page 343, of Berks County (see appendix at the end of this chapter). In this significant document, investigators can find evidence that both confirms and contradicts materials in the legends.

First, and perhaps most important, we know that Mary was a historical figure, confirming that the person listed in the 1790 Census was more than a creation of the imagination. Mary listed herself as a "single" person. This contradicts the study written by Wollenweber, who makes her a war widow, though she may have been betrothed to Theodore Benz. Mary bequeathed to her niece, Maria Elisabeth Schneider, a considerable sum of money, and she owned a cabin with more than forty acres of land, so she was not impoverished.

Milk, butter, and cheese were stored in Mountain Mary's house built of native fieldstone. Note the early pent roof held in place over the door of the building by "outlookers" (beams) that extended through the stone wall (photograph early 1970s).

In her will, Mary mentions books and manuscripts. Was she a scholarly recluse? Did she write? If Mountain Mary was an authoress, what treasures her works would be! She also mentions her trusty friends: Daniel Yoder (Joder) (1777–1826), a one-time county commissioner of Berks who was an affluent citizen of Oley, and Thomas Lee, of an old Quaker family in the valley. Nor was Mary solitary, as she names her two deceased sisters: Anna Elisabeth Schneider, mother of Maria Elisabeth and wife of Johann Georg Schneider, and Maria Catherine Noll, mother of John Noll, Henry Noll, Elisabeth (Noll) Helm, and Mary's namesake, Anna Maria Noll.

Mary Young was indeed a historical person. In the year 1819, just before Mary's death, Benjamin M. Hollinshead visited Oley, properly supplied with letters of introduction (from whom?) to seek information about Mountain Mary. He was accompanied by Dr. Jesse Thompson. The party set out in July. This was one of the last visits by reporting travelers. Hollinshead wrote:

> After riding a few miles along the valley, we began to ascend the mountain. On reaching the summit, and passing through woods we came to an enclosure, on the opposite side of which was situated the humble log cabin of "Mountain Mary." Fastening our horses to the fence, we lowered the bars, and walking slowly over the greensward, were met by the hermitess at the threshold of the dwelling. She received us kindly and after an interchange of inquiries on the part of her and our friends, she commenced speaking in a religious strain, informing us through a lady in our party who acted as interpreter, that on serious thought she was obliged to speak in her native language, the German.
> Her remarks breathed a strain of devotional feeling which had a solemnizing effect upon the company, and the countenance of the speaker was one of the most benign I had ever be held. After a pause which succeeded her discourse, we walked forth to make a survey of the premises. The view was bounded by the surrounding forest except in the northern direction, where a farmhouse was seen on the slope of one of the neighboring bills. Mary took us into her milk house, which was a few steps from her door, and which was beautifully supplied from the solitary cow that stood near us.
> A limpid stream from a neighboring elevation was conducted into the building and then guided peacefully away irrigating the meadow in the course down the mountain. We now walked to the margin of the woods, where we found a square enclosure of rails, which contained three graves, one of the mother, the others of the sisters of Mary, and a head and footstone for another grave. On returning to take our leave, we were surprised to find a table spread with delicious fruits; and we were invited to partake in a manner so sincere and courteous, that we did not distrust our kind hostess when she assured us we were welcome.

Mountain Mary had been ailing for several years, as can be gathered from her will. In November 1819, she was taken seriously ill and was attended by Mrs. Susanna DeBenneville Keim, wife of John Keim and daughter of the founder of American Universalism, Dr. George DeBenneville, former resident of Oley. Mary died on November 16, 1819. In spite of her fame and reputation, a search of contemporary newspapers does not yield any formal notice of her passing. However, the Mountain Mary legend continued to grow. In 1822 it

The mountain spring that once flowed beautifully above the site of Mountain Mary's log dwelling still flowed (up to the 1970s) through hewn logs to the doorstep beside her bakeoven.

The historic DeBenneville barn, belonging to neighbors of Mountain Mary, boasted three spires meant to vent the large hay mow on Dr. George DeBenneville's homestead (built in 1745). A doctor and preacher of Universalism, DeBenneville was one of the early Huguenot settlers researched by Reverend P. C. Croll in the *Annals of the Oley Valley in Berks County, PA.*

was already widely known. In that year a poem about her appeared in *The Phantom Barge and Other Poems* by the author of "The Limner" in Philadelphia. It gives the substance of the Mountain Mary legend and so is worthy of quotation:

> Whoe'er has trod by Schuylkill's shore; where Oley's hills are stretched
>   along and in romantic beauty soar,
> Has heard of Mary Young.
> They tell for many a mile around Where her lone dwelling may be found
>   And show the green hill where it stands Surrounded by its cultured
>   lands, Where yet the traveller stops to see
> The poor and humble devotee.
> Far from the world and all its strife and care, old Mary dwells alone—
>   and tho' she treads the vale of life, her mind is not o'erthrown;
> But the bright evening of her days is passed away in prayer and praise,
>   Like that fair bird, whose latest form is full of music's magic power,
> And who, in death, awakes a tone far sweeter than her life had known.
> She owns no sect—but thus has trod the path of piety from youth—and
>   she is one who worships God in spirit and in truth.
> Her praise is pure—devoid of art—the adoration of the heart;—

And that tis simple, has no less the majesty of holiness;
And shines as bright, when prayer is heard,
As oft by loftier life prepared.
As the sweet star of evening shines, when sinking nightly to repose,
Towards life's last goal she now declines,
The horizon of her close—with as much calm serenity, as tho' she waited
*   but to die:*
As tho' the toils of time were o'er, And she were lingering on the shore,
Till the light bark of death should come
To bear her to a happy home.
There is a little spot, which she
Now holds within her cottage view,—There sleeps her line of ancestry
*   and she will sleep there too.*
And tho' the name of Mary Young' Be not on earth, remembered long,
*   There is a world where virtue lives beyond the limit memory gives,*
*   And from its earthly frailties free,*
Blooms on, in one eternity.

Around the year 1825, a young friend of Hollinshead visited Oley again, curious about Mountain Mary. He found the following hearsay information: Mary was born near Frankfurt-am-Main; she came to Germantown, where she spun cotton on a wheel, living with her father, mother and two sisters; the father died; after the battle of Germantown (October 1777) she took refuge in the Oley hills with her mother and sisters; following their death, Mary lived alone. She was a recluse for thirty years. (This would mean that her sojourn in Oley lasted from 1784 to 1819.) Hollinshead's friend wrote this about Mary:

> She was said to be very intelligent and a religious woman, and was visited by her neighbors to have her advice on their difficulties, which was often so judicious and far-seeing that she was thought by some to have a way of acquiring knowledge unknown to many.
> The most interesting feature in her character ... was her great industry. She kept three or four cows, food for which she raised on a meadow near her cottage. The grass she used to cut herself, and, after drying, carry home. Her cattle were cared for in a superior manner and consequently she was enabled to make a great deal of butter, this she carried on her head to a person who took it to market for her, and who lived about three miles away. She also had bees and collected a large quantity of honey.... These appear to have been her occupations, which did not only enable her to live, but to make considerable money.

The Mountain Mary legend was growing, somewhat slowly at first, and the character of the legend was beginning to emerge. By the time that I. Daniel Rupp wrote his *History of the Counties of Berks and Lebanon* (1844), Mountain Mary had become a full-blown legend. Mrs. Charles Evans of Reading composed a longish poem of thirty-six strophes that kept this legend alive. Around the same time, Henry W. Bigony wrote some verses that were read at a Sunday school picnic on August 21, 1846. This was translated from the German by Ralph Bigony of Bally, Pennsylvania, as follows (my translation appears at the end of the novelette):

> *There, underneath this mountain stone, Lies*
> *   Mary Young, who lived alone, High on the*
> *   lofty mountainside,*
> *Beloved and honored till she died.*
> *Loved and honored by the few Who gave to*
> *virtue virtue's due, Stranger, she that's buried*
> *here Was humble, pious and sincere.*
> *The even temper of her days*
> *She passed in grateful prayer and praise—Her*
> *   heart was like a gentle dove*
> *That came from Heaven with promised love*
> *Were open to the rich and poor—*
> *Her faith confirmed her will resigned So*
> *   sweetly calmed so pure her mind The God*
> *   of mercy from His throne*
> *Looked down and claimed her as His own.*

Interestingly, as far as the Mountain Mary legend is concerned, little was said about her folk medicine, about her travels across the countryside to comfort and to heal the sick.

By 1880, the legend of Mountain Mary was given new life in the novelette *Die Berg Maria*, written in High German and translated later in this chapter. How forceful an impact this story made on a culture then already growing weary of reading German cannot be assayed. Ludwig August Wollenweber, a German political refugee during the 1830s, wrote this novelette to project the Pennsylvania Dutch mood during the colonial period, telling of the sufferings during the voyage to Pennsylvania, the sordid redemptioner system, the hard service of the earlier years, the struggle with British tyranny and all the lonely pathos of a Revolutionary War widow spending her declining years serving others. Writing during the centennial of the American Revolution, Wollenweber gave a political cast to the Mountain Mary legend.

Wollenweber was born at Ixheim near Zweibrücken in the Palatinate. He arrived in America in 1833, settling in Philadelphia, where he founded the *Philadelphische Demokrat* in 1839. He served as its editor for many years, championing liberal politics. Upon his retirement he settled at Womelsdorf, Berks County, where he wrote novelettes, dialect prose and poetry that appeared in provincial newspapers under the pen name "Der Jae vom Berge." He also became an ardent advocate of Pennsylvania Dutch matters.

Despite its lack of accuracy as far as Anna Maria Jung, the historical figure behind the legend, is concerned, Wollenweber's *Die Berg Maria* remains the classical study of Pennsylvania Dutch life during the Revolutionary period. Although this novelette takes many liberties with the facts, it stands apart from all other versions of the Mountain Mary legend due to the structure and art of its composition. However, it is myth. Its characters can do no wrong. Here all is saccharine sentiment, full of romantic idealization. Humanity's struggle, as in the old Greek myths, is against fate, against the darkness that resides in events that dominate us. *Die Berg Maria*, then, is a novelette without villain or evil in human form. Only young Peter Muhlenberg keeps his mischief (a trait he later overcomes when he becomes a famous general).

What was Wollenweber's purpose? He was building a myth, taking elements from his background, from history, and from life to fashion a tale that carries universal Pennsylvania Dutch elements. Wollenweber made Mary Young (in his version an orphan) fall in love on ship with Theodore Benz (a fictional character); this tall muscular young man was to become a *Knecht* (farmhand) in Oley for farmer Frederick Leinbach, a historical figure. Through faithful service dutifully performed, Theodore earned the farmer's gratitude. Enlisting in the Berks County Volunteers (though his name cannot be found on the muster), Theodore is said to have served in the Battle of Long Island, where he was among the missing. Thus Mary, who had married Theodore in a quick ceremony, became a war widow. This is the motivation that Wollenweber adds to the Mountain Mary legend.

Wollenweber successfully places the Mountain Mary legend into a universal mythological frame of reference. As the story of Regina Hartmann became mythological in John Birmelin's fine ballad, standing for the sufferings of frontier families during the Indian troubles, so Wollenweber's *Die Berg Maria*, by exploiting and expanding a traditional theme, has become the classical mythological projection of Pennsylvania Dutch life during the American Revolution.

Wollenweber's tremendous achievement was bought at a price that some may find too high—the distortion of the Mountain Mary history. Be that as it may, such deviations from fact are compensated for by the greater purpose that Wollenweber proposed. This, then, is a novelette not so much about Mountain Mary as about Pennsylvania Dutch life during the later years of British rule in America. In this sense, *Die Berg Maria* is a Pennsylvania Dutch classic. Thus Wollenweber's novelette stands by itself, and it ought to be seen apart from the Mountain Mary legend, for it takes sustenance from a broader theme, one that may even go far beyond the Mountain Mary story.

In all honesty, it must be said that Wollenweber's novelette did little to influence the Mountain Mary legend. On August 27, 1910, the *Reading Weekly Eagle* printed a long account of Mountain Mary by James G. Dengler of Philadelphia. Here an interesting new theme was stressed: Mary was a healer and practical nurse. Additionally, in 1934, the Mountain Mary legend was recognized by the Berks County chapter of the Daughters of the American Revolution, which erected a monument near her cabin with the following inscription:

> To the Memory of Mary Young
> "Mountain Mary"
> "Barricke Marieche"
> Who lived to the south in these hills from
> early womanhood until her death, Novem-
> ber 16, 1819, at the age of 70 years. A
> pioneer nurse, comforter of body and soul,
> benevolent, pious, brave and charitable.
> "She hath done what she could"
> *   *   *
> Erected by Berks County Chapter D. A. R. in 1934

In 1940, Luther A. Pflueger translated Wollenweber's novelette, and it was published in Dr. Preston A. Barba's "Pennsylfawnisch Deitsch Eck" in the *Allentown Call* on June 1, 8, 13, 22 and 29. This translation was somewhat pedestrian and did not put German verse into English. After 1942, periodic pilgrimages were made to Mountain Mary's grave near the Hill Church, Bechtelsville, Berks County. Notable persons attended, sharing the festivities: guests for the first pilgrimage included Dr. Barba, dean of Pennsylvania German scholars; Dr. Elmer E. S. Johnson, founder of the Schwenkfelder Library; Dr. Alfred Shoemaker; Reverend William A. Rupp; and Mrs. Mary deTurk Hottenstein, prime mover of the pilgrimage. At the second pilgrimage in 1947, John Birmelin, Pennsylvania Dutch dialect poet, read an original poem, "An de Baerrick Maria Ihrirn Graab." At the third pilgrimage in 1951, Professor Henry W. Sharadin of Kutztown explained the triptych that he had painted, expressing his views of the Mountain Mary story; yet another pilgrimage was held November 2, 1952.

In the final assessment, then, Mountain Mary is both fact and legend. There are few proven facts about Anna Maria Jung, facts that stand the tests of the laws of historical evidence. However, at the same time, legends are also historical, and the tales about this strangely attractive person of the Oley hills attest to her historical meaning. We also can see the growth of the legend itself. During the earlier period Mountain Mary was a religious recluse—in fact, an "abbess." Wollenweber made her a grieving widow of a Revolutionary hero. Now she is seen as a devoted practical nurse. While the emphases vary, all points of view may be part of the historical facts.

**Mountain Mary's original bakeoven remains in fair condition, and up to the 1970s
it was still used by the owners.**

Obviously, we cannot at this late date go back to the historical Mary, the sources being as obscure as they are. Only historical positivists insist that Mary is what Mary was. However, we must also refrain from gushing romanticism that passes itself off as history—a flood of sentiment that does credit neither to Mary nor to those who admired her. Mountain Mary is therefore both fact and fancy, both truth and interpretation, one of the more interesting Pennsylvania legends.

Die Berg Maria

THE MIGRATION TO PENNSYLVANIA

When she left Stuttgart, capital of Württemberg, by rail down the valley, in a few minutes we come to the first station, the lovely village of Feuerbach, clinging to the hillside, whose name already was mentioned in the oldest Swabian histories. Here during the second half of the 18th century our Mountain Mary was born. The names of her parents were Jacob and Maria Jung, farmers of means who gave their children, Jacob, John and Mary, a Christian education.

Poor crops, plus the high taxes that then were levied on farmers by the several extravagant dukes of Württemberg, sapped the courage of Mary's father, and he saw that each year, in spite of all industry and frugality, he was growing poorer, whereupon he decided to sell his tract of land and migrate to America, however much it pained him to leave his lovely home, where his forebears and fathers had nourished themselves and where they rested in God's acre. Still, from America there came a fine call, leading thousands to leave the German fatherland. So, too, Father Jung thought that with industry and perseverance he might establish there a new home, preparing a better future for his children than was possible in the home valley.

He quickly found a buyer for his farm and vineyard, preparing himself for the distant land and, at that time, still burdensome and dangerous voyage. Soon, with a heavy heart, he left home with wife and children. After a week's journey the family reached the port of Amsterdam in Holland, where at that time many ships were departing for the city of Philadelphia in America, and wherefrom they soon hoped to find good opportunity to sail. At that time many Europe-weary persons were to be found in Amsterdam, and every ship setting out for America was filled with emigrants who were pressed together like sheep and so poorly provided for that, after a short voyage, evil diseases arose among them and death reaped a rich harvest.

Likewise, the Jung family, after waiting several weeks for an opportunity for passage, found a ship that, in addition to discomfort, had a conscienceless captain and a rough crew. So it happened, after the emigrants had been at sea for only a few weeks, that pestilential sickness broke out aboard ship and death called for many sacrifices. Hardly had life left the bodies of the poor people than the sailors lustily cast the dead into the briny deep.

Indescribable need and fright reigned aboard ship, and, night and day, the wailing was heartrending. The parents and brothers of our Mary were taken by the pestilence, and they were sunk into the sea yet the same day. Alone, forsaken, hopeless, with tear-reddened eyes, the poor maiden sat on the bunk from where death had taken her loved ones. After the great pain had subsided somewhat, Mary gained some peace of heart again. Seeking consolation, she took up her mother's prayer book. Mightily did she pray to the omnipotent Creator of Heaven and earth! Things soon eased. Consolation and hope again came to her soul, and she grew quiet in mind.

One day she was sitting on the foredeck of the ship, gazing over the waves beneath which her loved ones were buried. Tears filled her eyes. A young man approached her, well dressed and of upright mien, wishing her a friendly how-do-you-do, trying to console her. When the maiden accepted the greeting and consoling words in a friendly manner, he also offered her his protection, which she accepted thankfully.

Theodore Benz—so this young man was named—had been born in a village near the town of Lahr in Baden, where his father had been a farmer who found it hard to support himself, as he was richly blessed with children. When Theodore, second oldest son of the family, was grown, he saw that he was of small help to his parents. So he decided to go to Amsterdam and offer himself for America, which then was looking for many strong men for farm work, promising them free passage that had to be paid for later, in order to populate America.

With parental consent and blessing he had set out on the journey to Amsterdam. He knew that his parents were poor and could not give him much money for the long voyage. Still, Theodore was satisfied. He had his parents' blessing; that was enough! He had been religiously brought up, as a good child, to honor parents and brethren. With these he felt rich.

After a two-week trek, knapsack on his back and gnarled stick in hand— but without means—he came to Amsterdam port, where he soon found an American agent who accepted him as a farm worker in America, after he had obligated himself to pay his passage and his stay in Amsterdam. In this way many persons of both sexes, even children, were hurried to America, where, alas! a sad lot was theirs, not only aboard ship but even after arrival in America, especially in Philadelphia. Hear what a certain Gottlieb Mittelberger, who also came from Württemberg, said on arrival in Philadelphia in 1756:

> The human traffic at dockside is as follows: Every day Englishmen, Hollanders, Germans from the city of Philadelphia and elsewhere, some from quite far away, come and go to the arrived ship that has brought persons from Europe, and that has them for sale, seeking among the healthy those capable of doing their work, bargaining for them for however long they have been at sea, and for how much freight still is due, and for how long they are to serve. When a bargain has been closed it happens that grown people must work it out, binding themselves for the sum, according to the competence of their strength, and age, to work for three, five or six years. But quite young persons from ten to fifteen years of age must serve until they are twenty-one. Many parents must bargain for and sell their children like cattle so that they, when the children take the [parents'] freight upon themselves, may get free and quit of the ship. As parents often do not know where their children get to, it happens that after leaving ship many parents and children do not see one another for many years, or even a lifetime. A husband, if his wife be sick, must stand for her freight and she also for a husband. And then not only for themselves but for all other sick persons, serving five or six years.

Now, turning again to our story, through their frequent meetings these two young persons, Theodore and Mary, soon found each other's hearts, and true upright love was found by these two young people. They swore never to forsake one another in joy or in sorrow, and they asked the omnipotent God by earnest prayer ever to protect them.

One day, however, when they could see the mainland, and everyone aboard ship was jolly, Benz came to Mary with sadness and said to her in a shaking voice, "My dear Mary! Just a few more days and we shall have to part! For as soon as the ship casts anchor in Philadelphia you will be able to enter the land freely, but I dare not leave ship until I find someone to pay my freight and for whom I shall have to work for several years. I am a redemptioner."

Now, Theodore thought that Mary, who was taken by true love for him, would be frightened, but she arose joyfully, giving him her hand and saying, "God—the dear God—be praised that I can help you. I shall buy your freedom. How much do you owe?" Theodore answered, "One hundred fifty Dutch guilders." "Good," the young maiden again said, "through the death of my dear parents a goodly sum has come to me as inheritance that I have carefully guarded. Come with me and you shall have the sum in a moment." With inexpressible gratitude, Theodore pressed Mary's hand.

ARRIVAL IN PHILADELPHIA

At last, after a voyage of ninety-two days, the ship reached the city of Philadelphia. Hardly had it cast anchor at the foot of High Street (now Market Street) than many persons came aboard seeking workers and to prosecute the above-mentioned people business. Mary, whose father had paid freight for the whole family in Amsterdam, could land in freedom. Benz hastened to the captain so that he might pay him and go with Mary. As the young man stepped into the cabin and told the captain that he wanted to pay for his freight, putting a hundred fifty guilders on the table, this person became so angry that he called him a swindler who had had the money already in Amsterdam, feigning poverty and passing himself off as a redemptioner; he would not let such a swindle pass. And if Benz did not pay him a pound sterling more, he would see to it that he would not pass from the ship until he had found a buyer for him!

So Theodore, intimidated by the raw sailor, again took the money from the table and sped to the deck to give Mary the sad news. He soon found Mary, who was getting ready to leave, and who was busy conversing with a gentleman in clerical garb. When she saw her dear friend approaching with a sad and disconsolate face, she stepped toward him and anxiously asked him what had happened. In brief words he told her how the captain had treated him and what more he was demanding of him. Laughingly Mary drew out her purse and wanted to give her friend the money. The gentleman in clerical garb, who had heard the young man's complaint, held back her hand that was passing over the money and asked the young man to follow him into the cabin.

The kind words of so honorable-appearing a man led Theodore to follow his wishes. When both of them had entered the cabin, the clergyman asked the young man to put the one hundred fifty guilders on the table again and then asked the captain in a quiet but firm tone whether the money there on the table would or would not satisfy the freight-debt of the person present.... As the captain grasped the strong words and recognized the speaker as one of Philadelphia's most respected preachers, his face reddened with an angry flash, and without more ado, he took the money and gave Benz back the contract made in Amsterdam. With this both men parted.

After the young people had heartily thanked the reverend gentleman, he called a man over and asked him to take these two persons, with baggage, to Mrs. Kreider's guesthouse on Sassafras Street (now Race Street), the hotel of the "Golden Swan," and to say to the good woman that he was sending these two young people to her. Turning to Theodore and Mary, he said, "Prove that you are industrious and honorable, and God be with you." With these words he passed to other immigrants. This reverend cleric was none other than the at-that-time highly regarded German Lutheran pastor Henry Melchior Muhlenberg, who in those times received poor immigrants in Philadelphia with much self-sacrifice. Whenever a ship cast anchor nothing could keep him from speeding to it, even though bad sickness raged upon it. He brought help and consolation to the poor, sick, and miserable. He was a true servant of the Savior of the world, and his memory should be revered to latest times.

Theodore and Mary, with thankful hearts, followed the good man with their eyes. Then they left the ship upon which they had known such need and woe, quietly thanking the dear God that they were quit of it. They soon came to Mrs. Kreider's and were welcomed by her in a most friendly way. Mrs. Kreider was an honorable and devout woman who, after her husband had died of yellow fever—a sickness that often prevailed in Philadelphia— had to support herself by hard work, being ever good-spirited and diligent, and, although her means were limited, she still helped in a friendly way those immigrants who were sent to her, and many were lodged and boarded by her without obligation.

When, upon the recommendation of Pastor Muhlenberg, Theodore and Mary had been received into her house, they acted decently. And when Mary had told her sad tale, the widow felt drawn to her in a special way. She kissed Mary, and with tears in her eyes, the good mother said, "Console yourself, dear child! If you stay here, you will find in me a second mother.... First, you stay here. You can help in the kitchen and bedrooms until I can find a decent place for you.... And this one here"—she reached out her hand toward Theodore—"soon will find place with a farmer, for that is his spot.... And if he is industrious and honorable, he soon shall be an independent farmer in blessed Pennsylvania."

Theodore and Mary did not remain long under one roof, for on the third day after their arrival at the "Golden Swan" a German farmer from Oley, one of the most fertile regions and then a part of Berks County, came to Mrs. Kreider's hotel, where he always stayed when he visited Philadelphia, for he was always well received by the honorable widow. After he had greeted his old friend heartily, he said that he had come to find a young German farmer who would find good wages and treatment with him. He also promised that if he would serve him for three years, he would help him get a piece of good land on which he might establish his household.

Joyously overcome, the good widow Kreider reached forth her hand and said, "Mr. Frederick Leinbach"—so was the farmer called—"you needn't go far to find the right man. I have him here in the house. But before I bring him to you, you must promise me that you will treat the young man well. You can depend on his being industrious, and he will serve you well. He was a farmer's son and he seems to be a willing, well-intentioned person, not afraid of hard work." "Thank you! Thank you, Mrs. Kreider!" Leinbach called out. "I give you my promise that the young man will be well accepted by my family and me."

The widow hurried out and soon returned with Theodore and introduced the well-built and strong young man to the farmer, who was impressed by his fine build. He gave the young man a friendly hand and declared that he had come here to look for a good *Knecht* for his farm. He had a fine large farm in Oley with good rock-free soil where work was not too heavy as on other farms, and if Theodore were to take service with him and remain three years, fulfilling his duties well, he would pay him fifteen pounds sterling for the first year, along with clothes and good food and lodging. Mother Kreider had given Theodore a good recommendation, and, if he was satisfied with the deal, he should tell him now whether he would accept the position.

"Certainly," the young man called out and stretched his hand to the farmer. "I shall serve you well according to my best abilities, and I hope that neither of us shall regret that we have found each other." To the conditions named, he had to add that he be allowed, when farm work was not too pressing, to come to Philadelphia once a year, for an absence lasting no more than three days. Leinbach gladly agreed to this condition, drew out his purse and gave the young man some pocket money, as was then customary. He said he would take Theodore along the next morning; he should be ready very early, as the roads were new in many places, through forests, and, if no misfortune befell them, they could make it home in two days.

As the time for the noonday meal had come, Mother Kreider invited Leinbach to be her guest. He, not to be outdone, hastened to his wagon in the courtyard; took two turkeys, a sack of apples, and a can of butter; and carried them into the kitchen that he knew well. There he saw Mary, simply but cleanly clothed, at work. She aroused his curiosity. Soon, in bright good humor, they sat at the noonday table, where Mary dared not be absent. And when the farmer had observed the clean, nimble maiden waiting on the table, he, turning to his hostess, opined that if Mary wanted, he would take her along to the farm; she would be useful to his two daughters of nine and twelve, and he would reward her service well. But Mrs. Kreider immediately answered and said that that was impossible, that she would not fit on a lonely farm, as she had had so much bad luck. "Be satisfied, Master Leinbach," she continued quietly, "with this young man, and if he pleases you, it yet may happen that Mary shall come to you."

The farmer understood the wink and was silent. That the parting between Theodore and Mary was not easy can be understood. Each young person loved the other with upright heart. Theodore promised Mary, who was quite disconsolate, that he would send a letter by every opportunity through farmers who came to Philadelphia from Oley, and that she was to employ the same means to answer him, as postal connections from the interior of Pennsylvania were then unheard of. After harvest, however, he would himself come, when he could recount his experiences and desires for the future. With tears in their eyes, and with heavy hearts, the two young people parted, in joyous hope of seeing each other soon again.

As day broke the next morning, Leinbach's wagon rolled out of the courtyard of the guesthouse "Golden Swan" and drove before the house, where Theodore already stood waiting with his few belongings and next to him good Mother Kreider, from whom he now took heartfelt farewell. Then he climbed up on the wagon, where Leinbach already was sitting holding the reins, and soon it quickly went out of the City of Brotherly Love toward the new home in Oley.

The journey from Philadelphia—about sixty miles with a team of horses—lasted a full two days—that is, if no misfortune befell them along the rough road, or no other delays ensued. One had to put up not only with poor roads but sometimes with wild animals and also the dangerous marauding Indians. Luckily, our travelers had no accident. No wild animals or Indians came into view. And on the evening of the second day they happily arrived at Leinbach's farm, where they were received in a friendly way by the family as well as by some neighboring farmers. As a result, already in the first hours Theodore felt at home and firmly decided, by diligence and good conduct, to win the love and regard of his new companions, and to keep them.

As he was led to his clean bedroom to yield himself to rest, he sank down on his knees before the bed to thank the eternal Creator of all good for the blessings He had given to him. He also asked, as a dutiful child should, that He would protect his dear parents and brethren in the old world, as well as all who had favored him. Tired, he climbed into bed and soon was fast asleep until the sun's first rays awakened him.

The day after Theodore Benz had left Philadelphia was Sunday, and quite early Mrs. Kreider stepped into the kitchen and asked Mary whether she would go along to the church where the young Pastor Muhlenberg was preaching instead of his honored father. With her face beaming with joy, Mary came to the good mother and thanked her with hearty words for allowing her the great pleasure of attending church. Her parents had been devout people and they never missed church on Sunday, and she had hardly learned to walk when her mother had taken her to church and had taught her to pray. So when Mary had finished her chores, she went to her room to dress for church, and soon she stood by Mrs. Kreider, with whom she was to go.

With much devotion the women heard the words of the young preacher, who took his text from Jesus Sirach 14:14, which said, "Do not forget the poor when you have good days; then shall you know the joys that you desire." Then he said that we should not hang on to earthly goods; that we should help needy and sick people according to our abilities; that avarice and greed are great sins; that the avaricious and greedy clamor for the earthly, and that Heaven is not for them, and so forth. Properly edified, the women returned home.

Two weeks had passed since Theodore had parted from his Mary when Mrs. Kreider, with a cheerful face, came into the kitchen and announced that the Reverend Pastor Muhlenberg had sent for her. She could drop everything and let things stand. She was to hurry to the parsonage as fast as she could, and she should not be afraid, as he only had good news to announce. At that time Pastor Henry Melchior Muhlenberg lived in a board house on Mulberry Street (now Arch Street), not far from the church on Third Street. He lived there quite well with his dear wife and children, quite simply, without ostentation, with good management—eager and prosecuting his heavy tasks with much blessing in such sad times. Not only did he proclaim the Savior of the world, but he gave evidence everywhere that he followed the same in strict conscience.

When Mary entered the house of the reverend man, she was greeted in a friendly way and Pastor Muhlenberg introduced his wife, daughter of the celebrated German Indian agent, Conrad Weiser, to the young girl. Mrs. Muhlenberg offered her hand and said, "My husband has told me of your misfortune and sorrow on the journey to America, which has moved me deeply.... I wanted to ask you whether you would work for us for suitable wages and good treatment?" "Certainly I will," Mary said. "I shall serve you truly and well according to my best abilities, for I owe the reverend pastor so much for what he has done for me."

Pastor Muhlenberg asked about Theodore Benz, and when he was told that he was in the service of farmer Frederick Leinbach of Oley, he was much pleased. He said that he knew Leinbach well, that he had been a member of his congregation when he had served at the Trappe church. Leinbach's farm lay more than twelve miles from Trappe; yet Leinbach and his family had not missed one Sunday service. Mrs. Muhlenberg took over the conversation and said, "Since you have accepted service with me, it would please me if you could start tomorrow, for right now we have much work, especially for the needle, which you, as Mrs. Kreider assures me, well know how to use. My son, Peter, will soon marry and take a church in Virginia, so there is plenty of work."

"Mrs. Kreider praised me too much," Mary replied. "Still, I shall take pains to give you satisfaction. But let me speak to the good mother, as I still have much to do there and I do not want to have her think me ungrateful. I shall quickly go there and make sure I can come tomorrow at the proper time." "Go, dear child," the pastor's wife answered. "I trust you, and it is good that you leave the house of your second mother, who has done so much good, in honor." Mary left the parsonage and sped to the guesthouse of Mrs. Kreider, who already was standing in the doorway. Mary joyously hastened to her, embraced her with strong arms, pressed a long kiss on her mouth, and, with tears in her eyes, told her that tomorrow she must leave the house where she had found so much good. Still, she comforted herself that it was the good mother's wish that she serve in the parsonage.

At the appointed hour the next morning, Mary entered into Mrs. Muhlenberg's service. Soon she was sitting diligently sewing at a small window in the back room of the parsonage, so that she might finish the linens for the pastor's son in good time. Peter, the young minister, could not wait for the time when his household things were ready. Overall, the younger Muhlenberg was a disquieted spirit who, from early youth, had given his father trouble. Peter Muhlenberg had been born while Pastor Muhlenberg still was serving the German Lutheran congregation at Trappe, now in Montgomery County. Peter hardly had entered kindergarten when he made the acquaintance of some young Indians who at that time still roamed about the settlements. They taught him the Iroquois language of the savages and took him hunting and fishing, even though his father strictly had forbidden him going into the wilderness. The settlers just called him "Muhlenberg's wild Peter."

In ripened age, when Peter had calmed down, he became, as history tells us, a circumspect minister, but his patriotism for his native land and his passion for freedom led him to leave the ministry and trade it for a soldier's life. His noble, brave deeds are known to every American, and it is enough to say that he was General Washington's warm friend. His bones rest in the Trappe cemetery next to those of his father.

While Mary thus was busily occupied in Philadelphia and every day gaining more respect and love from the Muhlenberg family, our Theodore Benz also was hard at work in Oley, helping in the fields and making himself useful on the farm. By his good conduct, diligence and good spirit, he too won the hearts of the whole Leinbach family. Leinbach had four children: two boys of fourteen and seventeen years, George and Frederick, and two girls of eight and ten years, Maria and Elizabeth, who loved Theodore as a brother.

Great order ruled in the Leinbach family, and the parents managed a good education for their children. They were strict with them when they had to be, yet in such a way that the children's love for them was not destroyed.

The children learned how to pray quite early, and as soon as they were grown they were instructed in religion, learning to know the blessings of the Almighty Creator as well as the teachings of the World-Redeemer who shows the way to eternal life and blessedness. At that time parents held it to be a weighty sin to abuse the education of children—how different today!

At Leinbach's farm parental orders were diligently and dutifully carried out by the children. No one ventured contradiction. So blessing came over Leinbach's family and property. There still are in Reading, Womelsdorf, and elsewhere descendants of Frederick Leinbach, merchants, preachers, farmers, who have the best vocation. Thus one may say of Leinbach: "The Lord has blessed you to the third and fourth generation."

FIRST VISIT TO PHILADELPHIA

Fall had come, and work on Leinbach's farm was light and it could be done by Father Leinbach and his two sons. Theodore went to the farmer and asked him whether he could go to Philadelphia and spend a few days there: for he was curious to know if news of his dear parents and brothers, for whom he still had love in his heart, had come to Pastor Muhlenberg's; as there was no post between Oley and Philadelphia, he had all his letters addressed to Philadelphia.

When he entered the farmer's house to present his request, the farmer was sitting at his table, writing. Becoming aware of Theodore's presence, he arose and, in a friendly manner, asked what the young man wanted. "I want," he answered, "to ask you, Father Leinbach, whether you will let me go to Philadelphia and spend several days there?" "Surely, my son," was the good-hearted man's answer. "You have served me well so far. You are industrious and prudent, and more, you brought my boys, who were inclined to mischief, to take joy in work, to adopt everything with diligence, so that I have to praise you and give you thanks. Go, with God. And be assured that if you go on serving me well for some time yet, you need not be sorry your entire life. You may go to Philadelphia, if you wish. And you may spend an entire week there. When do you wish to leave?" "Friday morning, if it be possible, very early. For I want to reach Philadelphia early Sunday morning. It still is two days before my departure, and I shall use them to get the harvest work on the farm done so that the boys, who are still somewhat young, will not have it too hard." "Good," Leinbach said. "Come to my room Thursday evening, and I shall pay you your salary up to the day of your departure. For when you get to Philadelphia you will have all sorts of needs for which you will have to have money, and no one is going to be able to say that I sent my *Knecht* to

Philadelphia a beggar." Moved, the young man took Leinbach's hand and thanked him with heartfelt words.

The morning that Theodore had chosen for his departure was one of the more glorious days that, at this time of year, the end of October, are to be found anywhere in the world; these days and those of early November are called "Indian Summer" by the people. The young man was already prepared for the journey, as he had taken leave of his friends the evening before, and he wanted to put a goodly piece of road behind him by evening. Longing drove him toward Philadelphia, where he hoped to be received with joy. With a dry hickory stick, and a bundle under his arm, he started down the footpath that led over a hill behind the barn when a voice called out, "Stop! What's the hurry?"

Frightened, Theodore turned and recognized Frederick, the farmer's older son, who had disguised his voice somewhat, and who beckoned him with a wink to return. He followed the gesture and approached Frederick at the barn door. Frederick admonished the approaching one with his finger, saying, "Theodore! What do you think? Do you believe that Father and Mother and all of us would let you go, sack under arm and hickory staff in hand, to Philadelphia, where Father has so many friends? No! Dear friend! That will not do, and it would be a shame!" Saying this, he opened the barn door and led out the loveliest of the farmer's horses, finely saddled and well packed.

Astonished, Theodore had nothing to say. But Frederick did not let words come forth. He drew him to the horse and, pointing to it, said, "Here in this bag you will find a pot of our best butter that you will give to Mother Kreider. And over here," he continued, pointing to the other side of the horse, "you will find two of our best hams, which you will give to the pastor's family. And in the pack on the saddle you will find a piece of cloth that my two sisters have spun from flax and carefully bleached, to give to good Mary. And finally, here next to the saddle you will find a small sack of eats that Mother has put up for you so that you will not be hungry on the journey.... Now, climb up, ride off, and may the good Lord be with you on your journey!"

As one in a dream, with tearful eyes, and speechless, the young man climbed on the horse, firmly pressed his young friend's hand, and was about to start off out of the yard when the whole Leinbach family came to the door and waved goodbye, wishing him Godspeed. Theodore rode along the road with a concerned heart, sitting on his horse as in a dream. The horse stepped along briskly until all at once he stopped short, frightened. Theodore awoke from his dream and saw himself in a thick woods, and he grew aware of a frightful howling of wild animals, who, as it seemed, were slaughtering one another. He held the handsome horse firmly by the reins and it kept standing quietly, although quivering. In several minutes a pack of wolves stormed out of the thicket following a wildcat, which was running past no more than two hundred paces away into a small hill.

Then Theodore rode without further adventure onward until, as darkness began to fall, he came to an inn which stood invitingly by the road. Here he and Father Leinbach had spent the night on their previous journey. The inn, I have been assured, still stands, but now not along a lonely road but nearly in the center of the lovely town of Norristown. Mine host greeted the traveler with friendship, as he recognized the young man who had passed the night there about half a year earlier. As soon as Theodore had unpacked his horse, he led it to the clean stable and gave it good provender. After he had eaten his supper and drunk a glass of good cider, he gave himself over to rest, for he was quite weary. And soon he was sleeping until the day began to gray. He dressed quietly, looked after his horse, drank a cup of coffee, saddled his horse and took leave of his kindly host. Today he did not need to drive his horse, as he had already put more than half of the road behind him and easily could reach Philadelphia by afternoon.

The bell of the Philadelphia State House already was striking the third hour when Theodore stopped before the "Golden Swan" on Sassafras Street. Mother Kreider was standing at the door, and she was surprised when the handsome rider on the proud horse came to a halt before her place. She soon recognized him, calling out with a strong voice, "A thousand times welcome, my dear son!" She rushed over to him and offered him her hand, and when he asked whether he could spend several days with her, she, not answering his question, called the house servant and ordered him to take the horse into the stable and to provide the best. But Theodore did not want this. He rode into the courtyard, in order to look after the good and handsome animal entrusted to him. With the servant's help he soon had unsaddled the horse. Then they carried the things that he had brought along into the reception room of the hotel.

Until now the young man had no chance to ask Mother Kreider about Mary, for the woman was busy preparing the evening meal. Of course, he had received letters from Mary that had come by opportunity with Oley farmers and neighbors, and he had answered in a similar way. As soon as he had eaten the meal that the good woman placed on the table, he followed her into the sitting room (then called the parlor) and with an anxious voice asked about the girl. "Ja! Ja!" said the woman in Swabian dialect. "The good girl is well…. She is as she was in the springtime, and she is as busy and as honorable as the sainted Martha. The Muhlenbergs, especially the pastor's wife, are crazy about her, and she is loved as one of their own children, and they will not let her go away."

Mrs. Kreider said that in a short time the young Pastor Peter Muhlenberg and his lovely wife Anne were going to move to Virginia, where a German congregation in the Shenandoah Valley had called him to be their pastor. He had asked his mother whether he might take Mary with him. But she replied that this was impossible, as Mary was a necessity in her old age when her body was beginning to weaken, and because Mary had proven to be not only a good housekeeper but also a good worker. He could look elsewhere among German girls in Philadelphia; she would not let Mary go from her side unless Mary herself decided to go—and to Virginia! "Really, what do you mean? … Mary will not go as far as that! I well know that Oley is the magnet that strongly draws her, so that her journeys will be in that direction." So Peter would have to move away without Mary.

The good Mrs. Kreider continued, "Also, I have noted that when I visited Mary from time to time, and when we came to speak of you, many a sigh flowed from her breast and they all sped to Oley, for she knows that you were well taken care of. Now, are you satisfied with my account?" "Certainly," answered Theodore, pressing his old friend's hand, giving her hearty thanks. Now the young man unpacked his gifts, giving Mother Kreider the can filled with the finest butter, saying that this was a gift from the Leinbach family. Well pleased, the woman carried it into the kitchen. As it was already late, Theodore Benz did not wish to visit the Muhlenbergs, so he wandered about Philadelphia until it was time for bed.

The next day was Sunday. In the country Theodore had had little chance to go to church, so his first place today was church. He remembered the promise he had made to his dear parents never to miss a chance to go to church; he recalled how on this day his parents and brethren were devoutly attending church in the old homeland. Surely he would remember them in his prayers. So he dressed in his best for church, and when he came out of his room the Widow Kreider was prepared, and they went together to Saint Michael's Church at Fifth and Cherry Streets, where Pastor Muhlenberg was holding worship.

The pastor took his text from Exodus 20:12: "Honor your father and your mother that your days may be long in the land which the Lord your God gives you." Then he spoke of the great sin parents commit when they do not bring up their children well, keep them from school, and fail to train them for work from the earliest years. It is mostly the fault of parents when children are faithless and mischievous. To the youth, however, the pastor said, "A child that does not honor his father and mother, as long as they live, is a shame to mankind, and Heaven will not open to him and he shall be cursed already on earth." Then he gave examples of the good fortune that comes when parents and children live together peacefully, in unity, as the Almighty watches over them, and how the blessings of Heaven stream over them. After the sermon, the congregation sang the noble hymn of Gellert:

> How great the good God's blessings are,
> Let us by them be moved!
> E'en he with hardened mind and heart
> By gratitude is proved.
> To plumb the deeps of holy love
> Is my life's duty plain.
> The Lord forgets me nevermore,
> Recalls my heart again.

After the pastor had pronounced the benediction upon the gathering, the church doors opened and all went to their homes. Theodore went with dear Mrs. Kreider, still somewhat withdrawn and pensive, toward her home at the "Golden Swan." As no afternoon church was held, Mrs. Kreider suggested that Theodore visit the Muhlenberg family and Mary, saying that she also would send some gifts along with the house servant. This advice pleased the young man. When the bell struck the second afternoon hour, he went to the pastor's house, where he received a most friendly welcome.

With heartfelt words he thanked the good family for all the kind things they had done for Mary and him. At the same moment the house servant of the "Golden Swan" brought in the gifts, which Theodore then gave to the pastor's wife, saying, "Father Leinbach sends you two exceptional hams with his wishes that you are pleased to accept them and to let them taste good. The Leinbach family," he continued, "remembers the pastor with love. It is a very honorable and devout-minded family." And Theodore added that he was grateful that the pastor had sent him to Leinbach's, where he was being treated as a son and brother.

Pastor Muhlenberg bade Theodore to thank the Leinbach family heartily for the splendid gift and suggested that when he again got to the Oley region, where he had so many friends, he would visit the families Leinbach, Guldin, Keim, Yoder, Bertholet, Griesemer, all of whom were members of his congregation.

"Are you still happy in Oley?" was the girl's first question. "Certainly," Theodore answered, "for I am treated as a son and brother." He added that he had earned it by trustworthiness and diligence. "I keep no secrets from these good people, as you can see."

He took the package in which the linen cloth was wrapped and gave it to the young woman, asking her to open it. She did. Everyone present was astonished when they saw so glorious a piece of linen, so white and fine. "The two young daughters of my benefactor send this gift to you with the heartfelt wish that it may please you and with the request that you visit them sometime," said Theodore. After Mary had given thanks for the lovely present, she asked the pastor's wife to keep it for her, which she said she would do. Then Pastor Muhlenberg invited Theodore to stay for the evening meal. Afterward he could visit with Mary and satisfy her concerns. The young man accepted with thanks.

Soon, in good fellowship, the whole Muhlenberg family, with Theodore and Mary, sat at supper. The pastor was especially good-spirited, for he had a letter from his son, Peter, in the Shenandoah Valley that said the German Lutheran congregation there had received him most warmly and provided a well-built, imposing parsonage in a good location for him and his family, "to be his forever." At his installation service the church, which was larger than Saint Michael's in Philadelphia, was overfilled, and they had to open the windows so the many persons who could not find room within the church might hear the sermon outside. The Shenandoah Valley was a wonderful, lovely and fertile region, settled almost wholly by Germans who farmed prudently and industriously and were rewarded by good harvests. They were honorable, unspoiled people, clinging to their faith in love. He thanked God, who had led him there, and said he would strive to do his duty.

When the supper had been eaten, Mrs. Muhlenberg, her oldest daughter and Mary busied themselves bringing everything in the dining room and kitchen to order so that Mary could be given time to take a walk with Theodore in the city, where so many new buildings were being built. Meanwhile, in the parlor the pastor, his two sons Ernst and Christoph, and Theodore were discussing the work in and progress of German Pennsylvania. Soon the women were finished with their work. After Mary had dressed to go out, the pastor's wife brought her into the room where the men were sitting and asked Theodore to take his intended through the city and then to Mother Kreider's, who would be pleased to see them. Theodore immediately said he was glad to fulfill the pastor's wife's wishes. The couple departed with the bidding, "Have a good time."

They left the parsonage, soon reaching Chestnut Street, where a part of the State House was being built. Then they crossed to Fourth and Cherry streets, where construction was beginning on Zion German Lutheran Church. And finally they came to the "Golden Swan," where Mother Kreider was expecting them. She had prepared a little snack in her room, and she wanted the young people to share it with her. It came from a good heart and she would be happy if it tasted good. The lovers kept no secrets from her, and they spoke of present and future relationships. Theodore was of the opinion that if he served Leinbach for several more years, he certainly would keep his promise and help him get a piece of land where he might settle down and farm for himself. Mary was still to work for the Muhlenbergs and to save something for the start of housekeeping. Later he would come to Philadelphia again and have Pastor Muhlenberg marry them; then he would take her to his new home. Before then he would come to the city several times, and they could decide what they wanted.

Mother Kreider found the plans excellent, and Mary gave her hand to Theodore and said that he had expressed her own wishes. Then the hostess of the "Golden Swan" arose and said, with a commanding tone, "Children! I say to you that the wedding will be celebrated by me, and nothing is going to change that!" "Certainly! Certainly!" the two lovers said at once. "In sorrow and in joy you are our only mother! May Heaven help us to repay you in your old age, to reward you for treating us so maternally."

The Gift of Land

After Theodore had done his errands precisely as Leinbach and the other neighbors had asked him to, he took leave of his Mary, the pastor's people, and the good hostess of the "Golden Swan." He climbed up on his handsome, well-rested horse and quickly rode along the Ridge Road toward Oley. And on the second half of the second day he reached Leinbach's, where he received a loving welcome. He went back to work industriously, busying himself in the fields, with animal husbandry and with practical improvements, so that Leinbach gave him full confidence in the management of the entire farm. So passed about two years of his service time, during which he was permitted to visit Mary and his Philadelphia friends several times.

One day Leinbach said to his wife, "Dear Anna! Since we have had Theodore on our farm the blessings of God have come upon us every day. Theodore has kept both our boys at work and also maintained good order, making them knowledgeable farmers, and now it is time that we think of the good man who has brought so much good fortune to our home, making our farm one of the best in the neighborhood. What do you say if we were to sell the fine piece of land of 175 acres lying at Motz's mill, which I am unable to farm, and which my cousin Jacob DeBenneville Keim often has told me should not be idle?

"Our own farm is large enough to feed two families already. This our two boys may share when our eyes have closed. For our girls we have two large tracts of valuable land near the city of Reading on which commodious buildings can be built. Now, how would it be if we were to give this piece of land to Theodore? Then our cousin, Jacob DeBenneville Keim, would get a good neighbor, and Theodore could establish a home, bring his Mary there and be thankful to us frequently, often visiting us to see whether our boys are doing well."

"I agree with pleasure," Mother Leinbach said, "and our children likewise will not oppose it, since they love him as if he were a dear brother."

THEODORE'S BIRTHDAY

[Then Father Leinbach said,] "I shall ride over with him and show him the land, and, if he likes it, he may have it. I shall say to him, 'See, dear young man, we are giving you this piece of land on which you can build a good house. And then you can bring your Mary as an honorable housewife, and to this we ask the dear God to give you blessing.'" With these words tears welled in the good wife's eyes, and she went over to her husband and said, "Frederick, you are a good man. Almighty Goodness will further protect us and our house."

That same evening Leinbach called his servant, Theodore, to the sitting room and asked him to take a seat, directing the following words to him: "Theodore, you know that all of us are glad to have you with us. We know that tomorrow is your birthday. So I thought to myself that we might let all the farm chores go and ride over to our cousin Keim at Motz's mill. You have never been there. Some good farmers are over there, too." Theodore accepted thankfully this invitation that aroused his curiosity about the region itself, and to know better its fertile land, of which he had heard so much. The next morning, very early, both riders, Father Leinbach and Theodore Benz, sprang out of the yard and speedily went over to Keim's. There they were greeted by the entire family in the most friendly manner and, as it was noontime, were also entertained.

After they had spoken of the day's news for a brief time, and especially of the deep dissatisfaction of the people of the colonies with England—finally agreeing that under British rule the colonists were being treated tyrannically—Father Leinbach asked them to go with him to take a look at the 175 acres that belonged to him at Motz's mill. He was eager to learn from his administrator, Theodore, what the land was good for. When they had come to the piece of land Theodore gave it his full attention, examined the soil here and there, found a fully adequate spring, admired the fine woods on the hillside with hickory, oak, and chestnut, and then said that this piece of land was as fine as any in the whole region, and also that he was astonished that Father Leinbach had let it lie for so long. "It could be worked easily and a diligent farmer, with some help, could make a highly productive farm of it."

"Dear Theodore," Father Leinbach answered, "I have found him! This land shall be yours! And my wife and children wish you good luck with it! In a few days I shall give you the documents that shall show you to be the rightful owner. You have earned it by trustworthiness and diligence. I rejoice that Cousin Keim will get so fine a neighbor." Theodore stood there for a while like a stone. Then tears rolled down his cheeks. Dumfounded, he pressed his benefactor's hand. "Now I understand," Cousin Keim said, pressing the young man's hand and continuing, "Theodore! Now we are neighbors. I promise you that as soon as you take possession your neighbors will help you to build a log cabin on it where you can bring your little wife. Since I already knew my cousin Leinbach's plans, I have spoken to Miller Motz and also to the able carpenter Bertolet. They have kindly promised to direct the building of the house, as they heard you were such a good farmer and, more than that, a religious, peace-loving man."

After this conversation they visited Miller Motz, who greeted the visitors most warmly, rejoicing that Theodore was visiting there. Again the situation between England and the colonies was mentioned, and the same conclusions were reached as at Cousin Keim's. The afternoon was well gone when the riders left Keim's and came home again.

THE REVOLUTION

In a few days Theodore had taken care of the most pressing chores on the farm, and, as there was nothing special to be done, he asked Father Leinbach to let him journey to Philadelphia and give the good news of the gift of land to his Mary. Father Leinbach gladly consented, since he had several errands to be done there, for, as he gathered, things were restless in Philadelphia. The earlier Theodore saddled the horses, the better, Leinbach opined. Theodore promised to take care of everything right away, and early the next morning he rode off from the farm for Philadelphia.

As always when he came to the city, he was heartily received by good Mrs. Kreider, by the Muhlenberg family, and by Mary, for he had grown into a handsome, good-looking man from whose deportment one could not guess that he worked at farming and husbandry. He told his friends how he had been treated by Father Leinbach. He showed them the deed for the piece of land that was to be his future home. All were overjoyed, wishing the young people the best in their new home. Then they again talked about the wedding, deciding that Pastor Muhlenberg should solemnize the marriage in Philadelphia and that Theodore should bring Father Leinbach and his good wife to Philadelphia for the wedding festivities. Still, the wedding should not take place until a log house had been built on the new land and Mary had provided for the furnishings, in which the pastor's wife and daughter (later to be the wife of Pastor Kuntz) and Mrs. Kreider wanted to help.

Theodore and Mary were more than fortunate, and they looked with finest hope on the future looming before them. Only it was to be different. Man proposes, God disposes! At this time ever-darkening clouds came over the colonies. Ever more the British government burdened the North American colonials. And more and more did bitterness against the oppressors mount. Had the people of Boston not thrown the highly taxed tea overboard from the ships, other disputes would have arisen between the colonies and the British soldiers.

This is why the noblest men of the land had gathered in Philadelphia to throw off the British yoke. They called the men of the colonies to arms, pitting force against force. Daily hundreds showed up enthusiastically to join. In Philadelphia an especially disturbed life raged. Everywhere one heard curses against the British government and its arbitrariness. Able speakers fanned the fires until they raged in bright flame. Even Pastor Muhlenberg, otherwise a Christian man, declared himself disgusted with the British government and openly said that the British king wielded his power over the colonies without conscience.

Now we leave the events (which are known to all) that took place in the struggle for the freedom and independence of these United States, and return to our story.

In Philadelphia Theodore accidentally met a young farmer's son, Isaac LeVan, from near Reading, who had visited Leinbach's farm several times and with whom Leinbach's older son, Frederick, was friendly. Young LeVan often had invited Frederick and Theodore to visit his father's place in Alsace near Reading. However, they had not yet been able to keep their promise to do so.

The two young men greeted each other joyously. LeVan told Theodore that he had come here at the request of Joseph Hiester of Reading in order to see how things stood with the rebellion, and in what way they could help, for in Reading and Berks County generally people were determined to take the play away from the British in freeing the colonies. Especially was Hiester, a young man glowing for liberty and independence, eager to learn how things were going with General Washington's army. Hiester was planning to raise a military company from among the young men of Berks County and to place it under the command of the brave Washington. Furthermore, LeVan said, he had visited Benjamin Franklin and Thomas Jefferson and had assured them that with energy and acceptance of sacrifice, such as Washington displayed, they would win out in the end, although after a hard struggle.

Both of the leaders rejoiced that the Germans were so eagerly taking up the cause of freedom. In Bethlehem and Lancaster, Germans were gathering to volunteer for freedom in no small numbers. Jefferson had given Hiester, whose father he knew, a special charge that he be highly enthusiastic for the cause of independence, as well as heartily to greet all who wanted to enter into the struggle for right. "Consider, my good young man," Jefferson added, "the time when we shall be able to say that this grand land is ours, belonging to its citizens, who want to and can rule themselves! What blessings shall come for us and all mankind!"

"Now, friend Theodore," LeVan continued, "I shall return to Reading and tell what I have heard from the good patriots, for we shall eagerly go about forming a military company and, as soon as it is full, move to Washington's camp. I shall go along too, as it is one's holiest duty to fight for freedom and for country. I enter the struggle joyously."

When LeVan had ended his story, Theodore stood in thought for a while. Then he raised his head, stretched out his hand to his friend, and said, "Isaac! Believe me. Like you I am committed with body and soul to freedom and independence! And what I learned from good Pastor Muhlenberg about the British persecuting and tyrannizing with fire and sword those colonials who seek righteousness gave me such anger that I wanted to strike a blow. But when the pastor told me that his son, Peter, had cast off the surplice and girded himself with the sword in order to drive the oppressors from the land, I could not rest anymore. And now I'm glad that I found you. I will help drive the robber band back to England. I had firmly determined this already, and although I am about to establish a good home, and to take a lovely maiden as my wife, still as a good patriot I say: It is a man's holiest duty to fight for freedom and country."

He continued, "Now, LeVan! Your way to Reading passes close by our farm. I shall ride with you. You stay with us, tell Father Leinbach what is happening, and, since I know how much he bears hatred for the oppressor, he surely will not oppose it if I join up with the Berks Countians and go along to war. Still, before I leave Philadelphia, I want to go to Pastor Muhlenberg's and tell him my decision and get his advice. You, LeVan, meanwhile go to Mrs. Kreider's and await my return. And then we shall ride together."

"Don't make it long," LeVan answered, "or else we shall not get to Norristown today, stay overnight, and reach Father Leinbach's farm tomorrow evening."

Now Theodore hastened toward Pastor Muhlenberg's parsonage, and when he entered the house he found the whole family, Mary included, in the pastor's study. All was in great agitation, for the pastor had just received the following letter from his son, Peter, which he read aloud:

> Dear Father, Mother, and Brethren!
>
> The Tenth Virginia Regiment, consisting mostly of Germans, whose colonel I have been named, is now fully appointed. My people are eager and ready to move into the struggle for right even today. May God protect all of us, and may you only hear good from me. I leave a dear wife, a dear child, but the fatherland calls us and it is my duty to follow that call.
>
> All of you live well.
> Yours,
>
> Peter Muhlenberg
> Colonel, Tenth Virginia Regiment

Encouraged by this news, Theodore informed the pastor's people that he also had decided to enter the service of his country and to join in the military company then being formed in Reading, if Mary did not take it too hard that he forsook her just when so fine a future loomed before them. When Mary heard these words, tears rolled down her cheeks. But with a firm step she went over to him, gave him her hand, and said, "My dear Theodore! Earlier today you promised to establish a good home and to take me there as your bride, by which I was greatly pleased, and I looked forward to that time with much longing when we should be joined together, one with the other.

"Yet I cannot hide from you that ever and again a dark premonition filled my heart that the longed-for time would draw further away. And I see that this premonition is true, as I see already many men forsaking their wives and children to enter the holy struggle, even as Pastor Muhlenberg's son has done here. And so I say to you, dear Theodore, keep true to the death to your fatherland and to your love." She pressed a hearty kiss on the young man's mouth and left the room.

Shaken and white from Mary's words, Theodore stood among the pastor's people, who also were taken aback by what she had said. Then quickly he went to the pastor's wife, reached forth her hand, and asked her to take care of the poor maiden, to try to console her, and to let her marry him before he went to war. Pastor Muhlenberg and his wife promised to take the place of parents with Mary, and they also agreed to try to get Mary to marry him before he went off to war.

After hearty goodbyes from the good family, he sped to Mrs. Kreider's, where he found LeVan waiting, and soon the two young men were astride horses, speeding along toward Oley, to the farm of Father Leinbach. They reached it the next noon without accident and were received most warmly by the family. Theodore told them all that had passed in Philadelphia without exception. He told how he had found LeVan; of the great disturbances then dominating Philadelphia; how every brave man felt obligated to enter the fight for freedom and independence. Even men of ripened age had forsaken wives and children and had taken up arms in the righteous cause.

"My friend LeVan here," he continued, "is a good patriot too. He has joined the volunteer military company in Reading, and I thought, after having counseled with Pastor Muhlenberg and Mary, that if you—Father Leinbach— had nothing against it, I would go to Reading with LeVan and join the company and enter the fight. For it would be shameful if a sturdy young man should avoid the fight when he sees men forsaking wives and children to take arms in order to chase the tyrant from the land." He added that Mary herself had said to him, "Go forth and keep true to the death to your fatherland and to your love."

When Father Leinbach heard Theodore's words, he rose up, tears rolling down the cheeks of an otherwise unemotional man, and said with deep feeling, "Theodore! The fatherland, the right cause calls you! Go forth into the strife! The Lord guides you in all your ways and brings you safely back again. Now go and rest. Tomorrow we have much to do."

As it was already late, the two young men gave themselves over to rest. But hardly had the day begun to gray when Theodore already was consulting with Leinbach's older son about how the future work of the farm would be guided. The son thought that now he could not leave the fields, but when the harvest was done no one—he said—could prevent him from going along to give the British a good licking. He would seek out the Reading company, he said, even if it were standing under fire. Stirred, Theodore shook the young man's hand.

After Father Leinbach also had joined the young people, it was decided, since the fall harvest already was in, to take care of most of the winter work, as far as possible. Young LeVan then joined them; things went quickly, and by evening all preparatory work in the barn, stalls and wagon shed was accomplished so that they could finish the tasks without Theodore. Night came. Tired out, they went into the room where a meal for the workers had been prepared. After eating, Leinbach spoke, praising the young people for their decisions and giving them the best advice. He decided that his son should ride along to Reading and bring back Theodore's horse, as he would have use for it.

Thereupon they went to sleep, and hardly had morning broken forth than the young men were on their feet preparing for the journey. When they came into the room an excellent breakfast already was served, and Father

Leinbach invited those present to partake of it. After breakfast, Mother Leinbach gave Theodore a package of necessary linens and Father Leinbach
pressed a well-filled purse into his hand without being able to say anything.
The farmer was so deeply moved that he had to go to another room. Theodore
now said goodbye to the rest, and soon they hastened from the farm—
Theodore with a heavy heart, for perhaps it was the last time that he would
see the farm and his dear ones.

March to Washington's Army— Joyous Reunion—The Wedding

The warrior sallies forth to war
To fight for country, freedom, right;
He passes his beloved's house,
To take a final lingering sight;
O, weep not red your son-owed eyes
As if no consolation were above; I shall remain true unto death
To fatherland and to my love.

In a few hours, after a brisk ride, the young men reached the small village
of Reading, at whose marketplace (now the square on Penn Street between
Fifth and Sixth) stirring business was going on. One heard rolling drums and
saw men and boys with guns on their shoulders, gathering, preparing to
march away. Captain Joseph Hiester stood on an elevation and was about to
address the troops when he saw LeVan and his companion coming down
Penn Street.

He quickly left his place, turned to LeVan, and asked him to tell him
how things stood in the matter of the Revolution and how things looked for
Washington's army. LeVan said that volunteers were coming in by the hundreds to enter the fight; that Washington now had a small, brave band which
in brief skirmishes had beaten the British; that many Germans from Hesse
impressed in the British army already had come over to the American army;
and that Washington had his camp near Princeton. Hiester sped back to his
place, raised the banner and gave the news to the crowd, whereupon a thun-
derous shout of joy filled the air. When the first cheer was over, LeVan introduced his comrade, Theodore Benz, as a new recruit from Oley. His words
were received with cheers.

That same day, precisely as the clock struck noon, the Berks County
Volunteers moved out of Reading. After a march of three and a half days,
they reached the city of Philadelphia. Along the way the volunteers picked
up a number of farmer's sons, and it was quite a considerable column that
entered the City of Brotherly Love and was jubilantly received by the popu-

lace. When Hiester's people had been taken into quarters, Theodore Benz hastened to the captain and asked his permission to visit Pastor Muhlenberg, as he had important personal matters to attend to. Hiester agreed to the young man's request. Theodore then sped to the pastor's house, where he was welcomed by members of the family and by Mary. They discussed the main business—the wedding—and, as Mary was agreeable with everything, they concurred that the wedding should take place at six in the evening in Saint Michael's Church on Fifth Street, near Cherry, and that Mother Kreider and other friends should be invited. When the time arrived, the little church was filled with invited guests and the curious, among them the good Mother Kreider, LeVan, Captain Hiester and Captain Graul, and many others.

The pastor's sermon to the bridal pair, and his prayer to the Almighty for their welfare, was so moving that not even a sigh was heard in any part of the church, and tears stood in the eyes of the fiery soldier, Captain Hiester. Only Mary's and Theodore's eyes were dry. When the wedding ceremony was over and the minister had pronounced the benediction, he announced that the hostess of the "Golden Swan" invited all those present to partake of the wedding feast that had been prepared, and that they were to leave the church in procession. Soon the procession was moving. Captains Hiester and Graul came first, next LeVan; then followed the newlyweds, Pastor Muhlenberg and his good wife, Anne; next came Mother Kreider and the pastor's daughters; and then the rest, pair by pair.

This wedding procession was imposing but quite silent, more like a funeral procession than one for a wedding. Soon the hotel was reached, and the astonishment of those who came was great when they saw all the windows, the main door, and the steps decorated with evergreens and flowers. On the right side stood a husky man, and on the left side a lovely woman. These people were Farmer Leinbach and his true wife, born a Guldin, who had been invited to the wedding by Mother Kreider but who arrived too late to attend the ceremony. As soon as Theodore and Mary recognized their benefactors, they went over to them and embraced them, kissed them, and then heavy tears came into the eyes of the pair.

When they had stepped into the dining room, the newlyweds were given many well wishes, whereupon they sat down at the table that was covered with all the kinds of delicacies that Mother Kreider could get together. Bright good spirits ruled the gathering. The time passed with joyous conversation until a late hour. When midnight struck most guests already were gone, excepting Muhlenberg, his wife, Father Leinbach, his wife, and the soldiers who remained. Then Theodore went over to his Mary and gave her the deed to his land, his certificate of naturalization and a letter to his parents. "Dear

Mary!" he said. "These documents are better with you than with me. You are now my wife and what belongs to me also belongs to you. And if by good luck I return, then shall my love and joy be great, and then you may be proud of your Theodore, who was a true fighter for freedom and independence."

Then he pressed a kiss on her mouth, promised that he would visit her in the morning, and thanked the pastor's people and the Leinbachs for sharing his good fortune, and with his comrades he returned to the soldiers' camp. It stood in the field that now is Franklin Square, one of the loveliest parks in Philadelphia. However, it turned out differently than the good Theodore had envisioned. He had parted from his beloved forever.

Hardly had the day begun to break than the drums roused the camp and the sharp command was given that the recruits march immediately to the Delaware River, where a ship already was waiting to take them to the Jersey side. They were marched there with all speed. The ship bore them across. Soon they had landed in the province of New Jersey, where more officers of Washington's army were waiting to receive them and to supply them with guns, ammunition and other necessities.

After a few hours the forward march began toward Trenton, a place that at that time already was quite a town. There they were ordered to march to Elizabethtown, where they were to train until they were ready to be incorporated into the regular army. Reaching that place, the Berks Countians were divided into companies, the first under Captain Hiester and the second under Captain Graul. Then the young soldiers continually were trained by drillmasters in the manual of arms as well as in various marching formations.

One day Theodore stood guard with several comrades on a height, somewhat distant from the camp, from where one could look out over the whole region. He saw a group of men coming from the direction of Trenton, marching toward the camp. When they had come near enough for hearing, Theodore called out, "Halt! You are not allowed to proceed until you have stated what your business is!" "To become soldiers like you, Theodore," a resounding voice called out. One can imagine Theodore's surprise when he recognized the caller as his friend, young Frederick Leinbach. He hastened over to him and vigorously embraced him.

Leinbach took over the conversation, pointing to the young men who had accompanied him, and said, "These are my friends, Samuel Guldin, John deTurk, Samuel Bertholet and Jacob Yoder, all from Oley, who want to be enlisted in Hiester's company, and you will introduce us to Captain Hiester." "Certainly," Theodore replied. "But first, Frederick, have you brought any news for me?" he asked somewhat anxiously. "Yes," answered Frederick. "First, my parents and brother greet you, then a thousand greetings from your lovely wife, and many from Mother Kreider and the pastor's people. All hope and wish to see you soon again. Your good wife sends you a silver ring that she found among the things left by her father. You are to wear it with love."

The young men had to stay with Theodore until they were released. Then he took them to Captain Hiester, who received his Berks County compatriots with much joy, enrolling them in his company and commending them to the drillmaster in a friendly way. Theodore, who had contracted a kind of homesickness, felt himself quite fortunate to have found a dear friend in Leinbach, with whom he might share fraternal joys and sorrows. He learned from Captain Hiester, when he introduced the young person to him, that the next morning an army boat was going to Philadelphia, and if he wanted to communicate anything, he had a good opportunity.

Later that evening Theodore wrote to his dear wife and Frederick to his parents. They told, among other things, how they had found each other, and how only death could part them. The letters reached those intended and spread much joy among relatives and friends.

SAD NEWS

Meanwhile, Hiester's and Graul's companies of Berks County Volunteers were ordered from Elizabethtown to Long Island, where they were incorporated into Washington's army. It was not long before skirmishes took place between Americans and British in which Berks Countians were wounded and killed. And soon after, when the English had hastily gathered themselves, they attacked the Americans. They killed many and took prisoner Captain Hiester, with other officers and many soldiers. The prisoners were incarcerated on the notorious prison ship *Jersey.* Through the bad treatment the prisoners received, many of the brave fighters for freedom and right fell sick and died. After those who remained had spent some months in this frightful prison, they were brought to New York, where things were not much better.

Frederick Leinbach, who had escaped the clutches of the enemy and was mustered into another regiment, wrote his parents at the first opportunity after the battle on Long Island. He told them that since the unexpected attack he had lost sight of Theodore and had heard nothing about him since. Apparently, with Captain Hiester, he also had been taken prisoner. The tragic news of the loss of the army came to Philadelphia too. When she had heard Father Leinbach's account, Mary was overcome by deep sorrow and the premonition became strong: "I shall never see my dear Theodore again."

Neither the consoling words of the minister nor those of Mrs. Muhlenberg could comfort the young wife. She did her work quite precisely, but no

An engraving of the original (1858) painting by Alonzo Chappel (1828–1887) depicting the Battle of Long Island during the American Revolution. Mountain Mary's fabled patriotic husband was allegedly lost after this battle, and she subsequently retreated into seclusion. Chappel, an American painter, was born in New York City and was well known for his paintings depicting events from the American Revolution and early 19th-century American history. Prints were created as early as 1874, and high-resolution TIFF images of Chappel's works are available for the public to view via the National Archives and Records Administration in Washington, D.C.

laughter came to her face anymore. Her otherwise blooming health wasted, and each day she more and more sought consolation in religion. Pastor Muhlenberg took exceptional pains to learn something about Theodore's fate. He wrote friends in New York, then turned to the quartermaster of the army—all to no avail. No one knew anything about the missing. Finally, when Captain Hiester was freed from captivity and exchanged, he informed the pastor that Theodore had been transported out of the prison ship *Jersey* to New York with him; he said that Theodore had been severely wounded and looked very bad. In New York he himself had been sick, and he was hardly recovered when he was exchanged. He had heard and knew nothing more of Theodore Benz.

Pastor Muhlenberg kept this news from Mary, as he did not want to make the sorrowing more sorrowful. Daily he consoled her by saying that Theodore was in all likelihood still a prisoner. Years passed; the Americans won out over the oppressors. Peace was concluded. The country was free.

Then the victors returned to their homes, among them Frederick Leinbach. He came from Yorktown, where he had been honorably discharged from the army, and took the road to Philadelphia, where he hoped to learn something from the pastor or Mary about Theodore. But, alas! No one could tell him anything.

Although Pastor Muhlenberg had seen fit to make a list of the captured and dead defenders of the fatherland, he found Theodore's name only on the rolls of Captain Hiester's company. Frederick still was talking to the pastor when Mary entered. The young soldier stood shaken and speechless when he saw Mary's sad countenance as she approached to offer him her hand in greeting. Where was the blooming, friendly face? Where were the graceful movements of the maiden? Deeply disturbed, he asked Mary whether, for the sake of her health, she would move into the neighborhood of his father's farm. Surely there she could recover quite quickly, and if Theodore still was among the living, he certainly would come to Father Leinbach's farm! But Mary thanked him and said she had to remain at her post, as good Mrs. Muhlenberg was quite sick and she had to take care of her.

THE RECLUSE

He, who lets the good Lord rule and hopes on Him with every day,
Shall be maintained remarkably in every need and every way.

Mary did not have long to serve good Mrs. Muhlenberg. Only a few days after Leinbach's departure from Philadelphia, the cold hand of death destroyed the life which had been so helpful to humanity. The pastor, who had known great bitterness in his time, and who was much weakened by age, was so shattered by the death of his true life companion that he decided to give up his household and move to his daughter's. Mother Kreider died soon after the pastor's wife, and the early remains of the one who had been so helpful in life were given over to the cool earth. Mary let many tears fall on her grave. Then Mary decided to move to Leinbach's farm, and she soon departed with Muhlenberg's blessing.

Her reception at the farm was heartfelt. She was caressed by the mother and daughters. She was assured that she would be held in no other way than as a member of the family. Old Mr. Leinbach spoke consolingly and asked her not to give up hope of being reunited with her husband. Mary, though, pointed toward Heaven with her finger and said, with a quivering voice, "Yes! There beyond the stars!" One day, when Father Leinbach again had spoken consolingly to her, she said, "Father Leinbach! If you love me and would please me, then let me build a cabin on the land of my dear Theodore. Then you will have no more bother with me. My intention is to work out something good there, to do some kind of work that will take my cares away!"

To these firmly spoken words the good man made no objection but said meekly, offering his hand to the young woman, "Your will be done!" Early the next morning, Leinbach and some workers went to the land in Pike Township that he had given to his brave servant. According to Mary's wish, they built her a small cabin near a spring at Motz's mill. It was at the beginning of the month of March that Mary, with the blessings of the Leinbach family, moved into the cabin, where she was protected from storm and cold. A mighty chestnut tree shadowed it.

After Mary had arranged everything inside, she went to the door and looked out at the lovely hill country, where here and there in the forest green leaves were already sprouting and on the farms the trees were beginning to blossom. Then her heart filled with love and gratitude for the Creator who had made so lovely a world, and she resolved to cease bewailing her fate and to become useful to mankind.

Soon the neighboring farmers saw the quiet, wan lady dressed in black passing through the forests, seeking healing herbs whose natures and curative qualities were described in a book that Pastor Muhlenberg had given her as a present with the note that "in the country everyone has to be his own doctor." After Mary, during the springtime, had gathered all kinds of herbs, she asked on her travels among the farmers whether they knew of any sick persons, because she wanted to offer her good help as comfort and consolation during suffering.

Mary's offer soon was known throughout the region. All kinds of people came to the cabin seeking help, and she sought always to help them conscientiously. The herbs and ministrations that she gave to the sick generally had good results, and when these no longer helped, she sat for many a night at the bedsides of the sick and dying, offering consolation. From all sides came the warmest greetings; whenever she went out, she was at home. Many revered her as a saint. She was known far and wide as MOUNTAIN MARY, and many sick persons came from afar seeking help and consolation from her.

Although this work and activity markedly eased her pain, still now and again sadness and trouble came over the poor woman. Death finally came to her friends Pastor Muhlenberg, Frederick Leinbach, and his good wife. They also rested in the bosom of the good earth.... She heard nothing more of Theodore. Thus, Mary lived in her cabin near Motz's mill, Pike Township, Berks County, for thirty years, until the year 1819, when she blessed the eternal with the temporal and was freed from her misery, care and concern.

News of her passing plunged the whole region into deep sorrow, and men and women came from great distances to see again the face of one who had done so much for humanity. The funeral procession was the largest that had taken place in the township until then. There was no one in Oley or the neighboring townships who did not send representation. Mourners came from afar, riding in carriages and on horseback, to pay Mary her final honors.

The casket was adorned with the loveliest wreath of flowers. When Pastor Conrad Miller gave the eulogy, no eye was tearless. The gravestone still is well kept. And, as the inhabitants of Pike Township have assured the writer of this history, it is visited by many admirers of the departed.

A gentleman of Oley who knew the story of poor Mary wrote the following epitaph:

> *Here beneath these stones There rest the placid bones of Mountain Mary;*
> *All her life and heart*
> *Were given Glory the start of her devoted story.*
> *Meekly she dwelt withdrawn Till thirty years had flown, A solitary life;*
> *The pattern of God's grace was etched upon her face, Blessed in sorrowed strife.*
>
> *When she had passed away a joyous peace did stay upon her countenance; So, fullest joy and love, Like sunlight from above, were seen in her glance.*
>
> *Now she has passed away: With God shall she now stay, Beyond this vale of tears! Upon the heavenly mead With Jesus shall she feed, Freed from earthly fears.*

Appendix: Will of Anna Maria Jung (Young)

I, Anna Maria Young of District Township in the County of Berks and State of Pennsylvania, Single Woman, being weak in Body but of Sound and disposing Mind, Memory and Understanding, do make and publish this my last Will and Testament in manner and form following, Viz

In primus—My will is that my Body be decently buried, my funeral expenses and all my just debts speedily paid out of my Estate by my Executors hereinafter Named.—

Item—I do order, authorize and empower my said Executors to Sell my Tenement and Tract of Land whereon I now live, Situate in District Township aforesaid, Containing forty Two Acres more or less, adjoining lands of

Matthias Motz, Daniel Oyster and George Jocler, either by public or private Sale, as to them may seem meet, as soon as Convenient after my decease, and to make or execute a Legal Title to the purchaser, or purchasers for the Same, and also of all my moveable property whatsoever, my Books and Manuscripts only excepting which I do dispose of as herein after mentioned, the proceeds or money arising from the Sales, Together with all my other Personal Estate, I do Will and dispose of as follows.—

Item—I give and bequeath the Sum of Two Hundred pounds to my Niece Maria Elisabeth Schneider, Daughter of my Sister Anna Elisabeth Schneider, deceas'd, and further I give to my said Niece all my Books, having her Name written in them,—the same to hold to her, her Heirs and Assigns forever.—

Item—I give and bequeath the Sum of three pounds to my Brother-in-law John George Schneider, Father of the aforesaid, Maria Elisabeth Schneider, if he be living, but in case he is deceased, I give the said Legacy of three pounds to his Daughter, my before named Niece—And further my Will is that in Case my afore named Niece, and her father, or their legal Representatives do not personally apply for their respective Legacies within the Term of One Year next after my decease, producing unquestionable evidence of the Legality of their Claim, It being unknown to me whether either of them are living or not, Then and in Case of such non application within the Term aforesaid, my Executors Shall pay the Same to the Children of my Deceased Sister Maria Catherine Noll, or their Legal Representatives in equal Shares or division, Namely, John Noll—Henry Noll, Elisabeth Helm, and Anna Maria Noll, the same to hold to them Severally and respectively their Heirs and Assigns forever.—

Item—All the rest, Residuary and remainder of my Estate, not herein before Be-queathed my Will is shall be equally divided between the last named Children of my Said deceased Sister Maria Catherine Noll, or their legal Representatives, the same to hold to them, and each of them, severally and respectively, their Heirs and Assigns forever.—

Item—I do hereby order and direct that in case either of the Legatees herein named, or other person claiming Heirship, Shall be dissatisfied with this my last Will, and oppose my Executors in the Legal execution thereof, Such Legatee, or other person claiming Heirship, Shall be excluded and forever debarred from any Share or part in my Estate, and such offender's Share be divided among the other Legatees, at the direction of my Executors.—

Lastly—I do hereby Nominate, Constitute and appoint my Trusty friends.—Daniel Joder, and Thomas Lee Executors of this my last Will and Testament, Hereby Revoking all former Wills by me made, Ratifying and Confirming this, and no other, to be my last Will and Testament—In witness whereof I have Hereunto set my Hand and Seal this Thirteenth day of March in the Year of our Lord One Thousand eight Hundred and Thirteen—1813.

Signed, Sealed, pronounced delivered by the said Anna Maria Jungin to be her last will and Testament, in the presence of us, who at her request, in her presence, and the presence of each other, have subscribed our Names as Witnesses hereunto.

Hanes Bechtel

Heinrich Levan

Author's Summary: In Wollenweber's moralistic story about hard-working immigrants who through their Christian fellowship helped each other to survive in the North American wilderness (and during a period of time when Indian savages took their sick and afflicted loved ones to the base of the Sacred Oak to be cured by a tree god), much of Mary's good fortune comes from neighbors and Christian tavern owners like Mrs. Kreider, who introduced her to Oley farmer Frederick Leinbach, who in turn gave her husband, Theodore, land to start a farm in the Oley Valley. However, the tragic loss of her patriotic husband following the Battle of Long Island forced Mary into seclusion, with no one to turn to but God. Thanks to a gift from Reverend Muhlenberg, she learned to use native herbs to cure illnesses among her neighbors in the Oley Hills, many miles from Reading or any other city.

Having adjusted to life as a hermit, living in seclusion, Mountain Mary supported herself with the aid of a milk cow or two and the friendship of neighbors who marketed her butter and cheese goods when they went to nearby farm markets. But having been cheated out of love following the death of her beloved Theodore almost as soon as she arrived in America, she was more than a Christian healer to anyone who sought her assistance in healing an affliction. As time went on, her powers to heal people of even serious afflictions became famous.

Thus, the power of positive thinking was a healing power that worked on her behalf, besides the powerful personal ability of prayer. Having lived more or less alone in God's natural habitat for so many years, Mountain Mary had aged in such a way that the country people believed that she should be canonized as a saint. The Mother Nature ambience that she possessed was perhaps the bygone personality she retained from the 18th century—humility in Christ Jesus that only true believers know. The legend of Mountain Mary (also called "Berg Maria") is also an excellent example of the tie between the people of the Oley Valley and the citizens of the port city of Philadelphia during the American Revolution.

The Pennsylvania Dutch immigrants of the Oley Valley were some of the most dedicated farmers in the nation, and this romantic early American love story has never died out among older generations who were told the stories (and perhaps read the original novelette) or younger generations who became acquainted with the English translation. Whatever the case, Mountain Mary continues to spur devotion to God and country in the Oley Valley.

According to what records are available, Berg Maria (Mountain Mary) died alone on November 16, 1819. Coincidentally, the infamous faith healer John George Hohman, who practiced "Braucherei," published his most well-known book, *The Long Lost Friend*, a year later in 1820.

16

John George Hohman, Berks County's Christian Wizard

Much has been mentioned in previous chapters about the compassionate John George Hohman, mostly in connection with his publications (for details, see chapter 14, "Frontier Faith Healing in the Pennsylvania Dutch Country"). But the purpose of this chapter is to take a more precise look at how far reaching his influence has been on other parts of the world's occult practices, outside of the Pennsylvania Dutch Country, and to look at other recorded findings of folklorists in the field. Hohman truly was an amazing Braucher, though nowhere near as revered locally as Mountain Mary (one might wonder why). His impact in the realm of black and white magic in the region of the Pennsylvania Dutch Country has no equal, and he compiled an impressive catalog of publications and imprints, as well as an amazing success rate in his cases. But true to his mysticism, Hohman died in relative obscurity, his physical form essentially vanishing in records to historians and folklorists alike.

One of many German immigrants who arrived at the port of Philadelphia in 1802, Hohman became an indentured servant to a farmer in Springfield Township, Bucks County, to pay for his passage to America. His wife, Catherine, was indentured to a Newbold family in Springfield Township, Burlington County, New Jersey. A German Catholic, Hohman eventually joined the Church of the Holy Sacrament at Bally, Berks County, built in 1743 (the oldest Catholic church in the county). Hohman seems to have paid off his indenture by printing and selling German hymns and broadsides, and he published a catechism in German for use at the Bally church in 1819, the same year he wrote *The Long Lost Friend*, and aforementioned Mountain Mary died.

A learned person, possibly a journeyman printer, Hohman was undeniably industrious, publishing an early Himmelsbrief (and possibly helping his wife to purchase her freedom over in New Jersey by such means). In 1820, his sympathetic medicine book was published by Carl Bruckman in Reading, Pennsylvania. Titled *Der lange Verborgene Freund*, and translated as "The Long Lost [or Forbidden] Friend," it consisted of a hundred pages, some of which dealt with Braucherei (known today popularly as Powwowing). Hohman's first book (a general medical arts book for local farmers) had been published by the same printer in 1818.

Widely known for practicing sympathetic medicine (i.e., faith healing), John George Hohman peddled and illuminated Pennsylvania German birth certificates for illiterate farmers and their families, for whom he wrote in the vital statistics. The Reading *Adler* print shop listed his home as Rosedale, Alsace Township, in 1805, but he was known to have frequented and lived on the Pricetown Ridge as far east as District Township. He once gave his residence as two miles north of Pricetown near Fleetwood and was a publisher of the Ballad of Susanna Cox, as well as other religious tracts meant to teach Rhineland immigrants the straight and narrow path to God.

Traversing the wilderness of the Pricetown Ridge, Hohman served the needs of a variety of religious people and sects, but he seemed to be at home with the local Brethren farmers. A man of modest means, he bought land from Jacob K. Boyer in 1819; however, when he was unable to pay back his debt to Boyer, Hohman's Alsace home was auctioned off on Christmas Eve 1825. Joseph Smith of Reading purchased the property, but Hohman may have continued to live there. The last German book he published was released in 1846, and it is believed that he and his wife migrated with other Pennsylvania Dutch out to the Ohio Territory to heal the sick and afflicted thereafter; however, a son, Caspar, listed on the Alsace tax rolls may have remained in Berks County.

Arriving in 1802, after the American Revolution, and before more Pennsylvania Dutch were wounded in the pending War of 1812, Hohman was an opportunist who sold a great many baptismal certificates and broadsides for print shops he had aligned himself to. One of Hohman's many occult copies found its way down to North Carolina, where it was used in a faith healing practice known as "Using," possibly taken there by one of the local Moravian missionaries at Bethlehem, Pennsylvania. However, Hohman's *Long Lost Friend* was reprinted in English down south as early as 1855 by a printer at Westminster, Maryland.

Noted folklorist Dr. Alfred Shoemaker stated in 1960 that, at an American folklore meeting, he met a person studying human behavior in the West Indies who asked him what he knew about Hohman's *Long Lost Friend*. Shoemaker was informed that the book was used among the Islanders in local rituals, and it may have been brought there by Moravian missionaries. Not

$\mathfrak{Hohmann's}$

Lang Verborgener Freund,

enthaltend

Wunderbare und Erprobte

Heil-Mittel und Künste

für

Menschen und Vieh.

Herausgegeben von

Johann Georg Hohmann.

Gedruckt bei Theo. F. Scheffer.
Harrisburg, Pa.

A later printing of John George Hohman's *Long Lost Friend* (again, note German spelling: Hohmann, as well as the variation on the title), this version was pocket sized and made its way south for a practice similar to Powwowing called "Using."

exclusively a book of sympathetic folk medicine and faith healing incantations, Hohman included occult recipes in his 1820 volume taken from the German book *Egyptian Secrets*, supposedly written by Albertus Magnus and surviving from the medieval period.

Dr. Alfred Shoemaker made it his mission to record our Americana civilization for future generations, so that they might rejoice in the freedom that the Old World pioneers enjoyed in William Penn's land of milk and honey. The early success of the Pennsylvania Folklife Center and the nationally attended Kutztown Pennsylvania Dutch Folk Festival had a lot to do with Shoemaker's amicable personality. He wanted to share with America that even though the Pennsylvania Dutch might seem different, they remain a unique part of America's history and versatility (photograph late 1950s).

John George Hohman served the 1743 Roman Catholic Church mission of Father Theodore Schneider at Bally, Washington Township, by printing an 1819 German Catholic catechism for the spiritual community, whose members were as far away as Maxatawny Township. His catechism was copied from an earlier German one. Local Bethlehem Moravian missionaries, who had also established an early church (1748) and boarding school in Oley Township, sought converts in Berks County as well and were part of this pioneer religious mix.

According to researcher Wilbur H. Oda, Hohman was a "true believer" in Jesus Christ and the Catholic Church, and he became a noted German faith healer in Berks County.[1] It is very probable that Moravian missionaries shared his German book of faith healings and carried some of his religious practices south on the American frontier. The Moravian church (1741) at Bethlehem founded several Pennsylvania frontier communities, from whence these missionaries read Hohman's German imprints and spread Berks County folkways to Moravian Salem, North Carolina, and possibly to missions in the British West Indies.

Maria Jung (Mountain Mary), a pious immigrant German Protestant folk healer practicing in the Oley Valley, used native Rhineland arts and herbs before Hohman's time, and she was thought to be a saint. Her miraculous Christian healings near Hill Church, Pike Township, elevated her among the Pennsylvania Dutch—in contrast to the commercialism of Hohman, selling his occult books upon Mary's death in 1819 to support himself.

17

Catholic Church Holidays
Kept Alive by Pennsylvania
Dutch Pioneers

Although an overwhelming majority of Pennsylvania Dutch people have long been and are of Protestant, Lutheran, and German Reformed faiths, this chapter focuses on a religious minority group less mentioned in the Dutch Country and its influence on the culture's folk calendar. During the early years in Pennsylvania, there were few Catholic churches to serve the pioneers on the frontier. The Roman Catholic Church of the Blessed Sacrament at Bally, Berks County (founded in 1743 by a Jesuit missionary, Father Theodore Schneider), was one of the first German Catholic churches in America.

Although some Protestant and non–Catholic Dutchmen have long associated Catholic worshipers with only large, urban city parishes, they are mistaken if they believe there were not a considerable number of Pennsylvania Dutch Catholic farmers in the Oley Hills and the rest of Berks County. Dr. Alfred Shoemaker, a celebrated ethnologist, frequently spoke of the Pennsylvania Dutch underground Catholics among the Pennsylvania Dutch Protestant, Lutheran, and Reformed families, who, in breaking away from the Roman Catholic Church in Europe, did not forget their German Catholic Church holidays, which they celebrated in the New World, adding to William Penn's religious freedom vision.

The Bally Church of the Blessed Sacrament, whose members went beyond the immediate Washington Township area, reached far into the Oley Hills to farm families in the remote countryside, including such members as the famous John George Hohman. In fact, as noted in the previous chapter, the celebrated Catholic faith healer printed a Catholic catechism in 1819 for his neighbors and made numerous visits to heal individuals along the Pricetown ridge that led to the city of Reading, where he published several religious tracts besides his Powwow faith healing book, *The Long Lost Friend*.

Thus, in frontier times, priests and various clergymen had congregations that extended beyond the immediate neighborhood, requiring them to travel a number of miles to see their flock. Certainly the German press of Pennsylvania was crucial for printing Bibles and necessary religious documents to support German dialect teachings by numerous religious sects and churches in a time when education for the common man was almost nonexistent.

Those who could read and write used colorful drawings, known as *fraktur* folk art, to instill in non-readers the religious message they were trying to get across. These early 18th- and 19th-century decorated birth and baptismal certificates were highly cherished and handed down by each family as a record of their American experience. However, sometimes after the death of an individual, the family might instruct the minister to bury the religious

Popular motifs in Pennsylvania Dutch folk art, be it on fraktur or dower chests, are the North Carolina parrot, tulips, (bulbous) flat hearts, distelfinks, and (good luck) unicorns. In this printed and hand-drawn fraktur birth certificate, North Carolina parrots, tulips and hearts have been incorporated. The work was done by Friedrich Krebs (southeastern Pennsylvania, active from the 1790s to the early 1800s) notably in 1776.

(and sometimes colorful) baptism certificate with the departed in their respective coffin as a sort of passport to Heaven, proving the individual was indeed baptized. One need only research prestigious auctions' past sales to see that this early folk art form in America can bring tens of thousands of dollars for the most unique examples.

In meeting a number of Pennsylvania Dutch people in the hinterland of Berks County over the years, and specifically in the Oley Hills, I was often told that two of most devoted and well-known Catholics in the area were famed potter Russell Stahl and his wife, Alma Stahl, who operated the Fredericksville Hotel. Practicing Christians, they set a good example for all their neighbors, running the remote Fredericksville Tavern in the isolated back-country of District and Rockland Townships, and they were not alone, as there was a sizable Irish Catholic contingent nestled within the Oley Hills.

Alma was particularly fond of Allie Day, an Irish neighbor, who in his senior years benefited from Alma's cooking and companionship; she often took

Interior, in the 1950s, of the Fredericksville Hotel when Russell Stahl, part of the famed Stahl pottery family of Powder Valley, Lehigh County, Pennsylvania, owned it. Russell's wife, Alma, is seated on the left observing a card game, most likely "Haas and Pfeffer," a popular Pennsylvania Dutch game, translated as "Pan Rabbit."

Charles Day, brother to Allie Day (who lived at Fredericksville), could be seen walking with his tall walking stick as he made his way from his Five Points intersection home, west of Fredericksville. In this early 1970s photo, he passed one of the early American circular stone smokehouses built by Irish stone masons after the American Revolution in the Oley Hills.

him along to Shupp the butcher in the 1950s and 1960s on Crow Hill down near Bally, where Alma's parents lived.[1] Her parents, Frank and Mary Miller, had been long-time members of the Bally German Catholic Church from the early 1900s, and their children naturally grew up under the denomination.

Living in the remote territory of the Oley Hills, one might think that Alma's Catholic upbringing may have worn thin, but her faith in God allowed her and Russell to survive in this rough hinterland. Never one to shy away from work, Alma liked to play bingo, but she never missed a chance to enjoy a friendly game of "Haas and Pfeffer" cards with villagers Allie Day and George Hilbert to while away the time in the Fredericksville Hotel. She was known as such a good friend and caring Christian to others that nontraditional Catholics among the Pennsylvania Dutch would even attend one of the historic Catholic church services with her to meet more of her kindhearted Pennsylvania Dutch friends.

18

Famous Stahl Pottery Works Fired "Ferhext" Redware Pie Plate

Dutchman Russell R. Stahl (a Catholic, as mentioned in the previous chapter) was the last of five generations of Pennsylvania Dutch potters (dating back to the mid–1800s) of the famous Stahl Pottery Works of Powder Valley, Lehigh County, Pennsylvania. Surviving well into the 20th century, the techniques used at Stahl's pottery were the same as those followed in the 18th century. Later in life, Russ also became known for dabbling in Hexerei. But the subject of this chapter is an ambiguous experience Russ had with an unusual piece of pottery thrown and fired by him at his pottery works but decorated elsewhere by an artist from Huff's church at the Oley pottery in Lobachsville.

On occasion, a very close friend of Russel's, Irwin P. Mensch, would decorate an earthenware plate in the sgraffito style (which involves scratch carving a design in the clay through the slip covering that had previously been brush-painted on, thereby showing the motifs or design in the red silhouette underneath), and he would then ask Russ to fire his masterpieces. Mensch was a well-known Pennsylvania Dutch fraktur artist born in nearby Rockland Township, Berks County, Pennsylvania, and he only did a few pieces. This unusual plate turned out to be Mensch's last and has been referred to as the "plate of flame."

This sgraffito decorated plate was given extra care, since Irwin and Russell were good friends, and in the process of setting or stacking the large stone kiln, Russ picked a special place for the plate "so all would come out well." The plate was intended for a special friend of the artist, and Mensch had spent a lot of extra time on the sgraffito work. Russ was said to have valued this plate more than any other piece of pottery he had taken out of the kiln to date.

The Mysterious Plate of Flame

As Russell saw it, his artist friend was not supposed to have this plate, and that was his simple answer, or "justification," for the ultimate misfiring of the piece. If one studies the plate, one can see in its center a swan with birds etched around the edge. And in looking closer, one can see a name and other traces of designs. So what happened to the plate? Russ had built special sackers around it, since it was an oversized plate, and after he set the plate inside the kiln, he said to himself that it was "strong enough to build a house on." When Russ had finished setting up the kiln and walling up the doorway with bricks and clay, as was the custom, he was sure of success.

The next day, Russ started the firing of the kiln; the firing process went very well, and the weather was in his favor. After 27½ hours of continuous wood-firing, Russ was tired, but he remained sitting outside, smoking his corncob pipe while the kiln cooled off, and the plate often came to his mind. Russ was sure that the plate and the other pottery pieces would come out well. After a week of waiting for the kiln to cool off (yes, that's how long those large stone kilns took), he started to remove the bricks from the kiln doorway. He could hardly wait to retrieve the plate; however, when he finally began emptying the kiln, he knew something unexpected had happened.

"The Plate of Flame" (left) was a sgraffito decorated plate by well-known fraktur artist Irwin P. Mensch, fired at Stahl Pottery Works in 1950. Not recognizable in the picture are the swan and the name "Laura" in the center. Russel Stahl threw and fired a second plate on the right, also decorated by Mensch, but due to Mensch's untimely death, the artist never saw the finished redware plate he had designed.

Two visitors to the famous Stahl Pottery Works were fellow potter James Christian Seagreaves and his wife, watercolorist Verna Seagraves (1913–2000), who loved painting the East Penn Valley landscape. Her memories of the day's visit to the family-owned kiln were parlayed into her painting. Since her passing, her more popular scenes have fetched $1,600–$1,850 at prestigious auction galleries.

Piece by piece, he removed the sackers and wares with flawless colors and perfect pieces, until he came to the plate. In the darkness of the kiln, he could not see much, so he took the decorated redware pie plate in his hand and carried it outside "to get more light on it." However, once outside in the sunlight, he still couldn't see any design through the glaze. Russ was puzzled and couldn't understand it. He just "looked and looked" and knew that the plate "went wrong!"

The next day, feeling terrible (even sickened) about the plate, he called Mensch; he apologized and explained that the plate went wrong in setting the kiln. He then went to the pottery shop and got the plate to show him, to which Mensch shockingly responded with laughter.

Perhaps not taking into account a possible ferhext, Mensch said he would just make another one. Russ, though relieved, told his friend that he didn't like what had happened, since he had been very careful, but Mensch patted Russ on the shoulder and said, "Russ, you worry so much! You make me another plate and I will decorate it; they can't all go wrong." Two months or so later, another plate was ready to be decorated, but Mensch never got the chance to see it, as he had passed away.

Ferhext Plate Not Potter's Fault

Sitting alone in his shop at his potter's wheel, Russ thought of Mensch and the plate he had just thrown. He went to the shelf to take down the original plate, which he had hidden from his sight. After studying the plate "for hours" and walking around in the shop, something came to his mind. Sitting back again in his chair, smoking his trademark corncob pipe, the mystery of what went wrong with the plate became as clear in his mind as if someone had told him.

If Russ had just examined the plate more thoroughly at the time, then he would have found that Mensch's artwork was consumed by a fiery red flame. Just about every design was covered by the swirling flame, including the name of the woman it was intended for as a gift. "Laura," the mysterious recipient, was said to be a woman whose relationship with the artist was in question, and with Mensch's untimely death, it occurred to Russ and other area folks that Laura was never to behold Mensch's God-given talent. The potter did not make a mistake in the setting of the kiln; the plate was "ferhext!"

Russ wasn't the only Pennsylvania Dutch potter to use the same techniques followed in the 18th century by Rhineland immigrant potters. James Christian Seagreaves (1912–1997) was known for the ultra-Germanic redware birds and whistles that he created to the delight of children and area collectors alike.

A learned scholar, James Christian Seagreaves utilized the best of Pennsylvania Dutch folk art motifs, including the North Carolina parrot, the flat heart, and the tulip. Among his most unusual pieces were his grotesque voodoo jugs.

James's true gift in the field of free molding pottery objects lay in his ability to take a true life form, such as a bird, and innovate its features as true German folk artists did, and then take it one step further to accentuate its positive features in clay. Since it was impossible for antique pottery collectors to find authentic pottery dogs, birds, face jugs, and other clay animal forms of their pottery collections, James did a thriving business in press molding all types and sizes of free-standing birds and animals.

However, one of his rarest creations, now eagerly sought out for the finest redware collections, are grotesque voodoo jugs, complete with horns and embossed with hex signs on the backside. Prices on the auction block have been in the thousands for the most unique jugs created by this contemporary potter. But not to be forgotten in this contemporary class of Pennsylvania Dutch Renaissance potters were Ned Foltz and my friend, the late Lester P. Breininger (1935–2011), mentioned earlier in this book in connection with his humorous acquisition of a rare Helfenstein book. Lester considered himself a student of Russell Stahl and created pottery for 45 years (and, much like his teacher, he was somewhat peculiar himself). Ned continues on in creating beautiful redware pieces in a career spanning over 50 years.

Part IV

Folklore Derived from 18th- and 19th-Century Beliefs

Pennsylvania Dutch Weather Lore of the Early 20th Century

Although laws have been formulated to explain many forces and phenomena of nature (such as Newton's laws of motion, Kepler's laws regarding the movements of the planets, and Galileo's laws concerning falling bodies), no such unalterable laws have been found to explain weather phenomena. Nor will there most likely ever be, for the actions and seemingly wild inconsistencies of the weather are far too unpredictable. To be sure, the modern Weather Bureau, with the aid of thermometers, barometers, anemometers, pluviometers, hygrometers, and other measuring instruments, does announce intelligent forecasts well in advance of given weather systems, but even these are not always accurate.

While we still fall short in weather knowledge, a great deal of weather lore is available, and perhaps no other group of people in this country has a richer fund of weather folklore than the Pennsylvania Dutch. They have predictions, forecasts, and prognostications of the weather based on every phase of the moon, on every phenomenon of nature, on every condition of the sky, and on many of the actions and habits of birds and animals. It should be noted, however, that much of this weather lore is neither original to these people nor indigenous to Pennsylvania.

Many of the beliefs that have been handed down from generation to generation among the Pennsylvania Dutch are part of a common heritage from the great Germanic races that once occupied the immense expanses of northwestern Europe as far as Ultima Thule (the northernmost region of the habitable world as imagined by ancient geographers).However, many of the same ideas and predictions are found in other languages, notably in French and Italian.

Occasionally, these weather predictions were referred to as superstitions, because many people for several decades thought of the Pennsylvania Dutch only in terms of superstition, Powwowing, and witchcraft. However, the Pennsylvania Dutch did not care for the designation of "superstition." Aside from the unwarranted remarks and supposed silly talk, there was no more superstition in these predictions than there was in the scientific forecasts vocalized by the Weather Bureau at the time. To refuse to sit down to the dinner table with twelve other guests for fear of ill luck is certainly superstition, as is the idea that if you cut baby's fingernails before it is a year old, it will turn out to be a thief, but to say that wild geese flying southward in the autumn foretells a cold wave is not superstition at all. My point in this chapter will be to discern between these two concepts.

Folklore embraces the traditional beliefs, customs, tales, legends, traditional knowledge, and popular superstitions of the common people—that is, the people en masse. Weather predictions are a subdivision of that folklore, as opposed to a subdivision of superstition. Nearly all of our German ancestors were tillers of the soil, and farmers are, of all industrialists, the worst

According to tradition, a Native American weathervane was a good luck symbol among Pennsylvania Dutch farmers who shared their harvests with the native Indians. For example, Mrs. Trexler, whose husband founded Trexlertown in 1760, fired up her bakeoven on Fridays, as was customary. The local Lenape Indians, seeing the smoke from her oven, came to sit near her farmhouse; according to Mrs. Trexler's neighbors, they did not cause her any trouble. Being a Christian woman and an excellent baker, Mrs. Trexler shared her weekly allotment of bread with her Indian friends, as one of the white man's culinary treats.

"gamblers," as they take great risks when they proceed with their planting (and if their gambles do not pay off, they may not recover enough seed to repeat the operation in the following year).

Historically, the success or failure of farmers' harvests, which regulated their livelihood, depended on the conditions of the weather. Nothing was more important than the probable state of the weather, not only for the morrow (near future) but also for the next day and the next. The only instrument available to the modest Pennsylvania Dutch farmer in the early 1900s looking to obtain a probable weather forecast was the weathervane (also called a "weather cock") perched on some outbuilding or post to indicate the direction of the wind. Even thermometers were not reliable before 1714.

Consequently, all people, and farmers in particular, scanned the earth, sky, and air for signs that might indicate the condition of the weather for at least twenty-four hours. Keen observation was a noticeable German trait, and by observing certain weather conditions a sufficient number of times, and then noting their effect on crops and cattle, the Pennsylvania Dutch collected a large amount of lore that served a useful purpose until more scientific means became available (i.e., until the Weather Bureau developed a better understanding of meteorology and better equipment was established). But even then, predictions based on local folklore were often just as accurate as those of the Bureau in the early 20th century.

One cognizant auctioneer realized this early Americana weathervane was a one-of-a-kind item made by a local Dutchman. In this case, the tin weathervane was made by Charlie Haas when he was a young man for use on a barn. At auction this unique piece sold for an outstanding price of $2,500!

Some of these weather predictions were simple, trite sayings; some attained the merit of proverbs, while others were open to ridicule, and some have lost their potency due to the discovery of scientific methods. Still others were dismissed as idle talk. However, many were based on the actions and peculiar habits of numerous animals. It was long believed (and still is by some) that animals have a keener sense of the changes of temperature, atmospheric pressure, and humidity than humans (although in prehistoric times, before they started wearing clothes, human may have been equally aware of these changes). It was almost imperative that animals should have this sensitivity; otherwise, they might not have survived. Along those lines, many Pennsylvania Dutch believed that the "untutored" Native American was better able to detect such changes than his civilized neighbor, and his sense of direction was surely uncanny.

Furthermore, even though humans have a more highly developed cerebral cortex, in many ways their development is lower than that of other animals. After all, if dogs had abstract thoughts, they might think we know little of life and of the world, given that we know so little of the world of smell. The dullest of all our senses is the keenest in all other animals. It is hardly a secret that all dogs possess a keen sense of smell, and the hunter who goes

The more than 500-year-old Sacred Oak of the Oley Valley is about 1.3 miles south of the village of Oley. It is the oldest yellow oak in the United States and also used by local Lenni Lenape Native Americans for religious ceremonies.

in search of deer knows perfectly well that he must keep on the leeward side of the animal in order to be successful. It is also worth noting that a horse will not drink out of a smelly water trough or bucket.

Behavior of Animals

The number of Pennsylvania Dutch prognostics based on the actions and behavior of animals, both wild and domestic, is countless. The most conspicuous animal to pose as a weather prophet is the groundhog. Here, in Pennsylvania, we have the well-known Punxsutawney Phil. A popular and fanciful idea is that if this creature comes out of its hibernating place on February 2 (popularly known as Groundhog Day) and unfortunately sees its shadow, it will go back into winter quarters and stay there six weeks longer; in consequence of such actions, we are supposed to have six more weeks of winter. How it ever happened that this creature chose to peer out of its winter home on the religious Candlemas Day (February 2), no one has ever been able to find out. Many prognostics are based on this day in Pennsylvania Dutch literature, such as the following:

"Ist's zu Lichtmess hell und rein Wird ein langen Winter sein."
   (It will be a long winter if it is clear and bright on Candlemas Day.)

"Scheint zu Lichtmess die Sonne heis
Kommt noch sehr viel Schnee und Eis."
   (There will still be much snow and ice if the sun shines on Candlemas Day.)

"Wenn es sturmt and schneit
Ist der Fruhling nicht mehr weit."
   (But spring will not be far away if it snows and storms on Candlemas Day.)

DOMESTIC ANIMALS

If cattle in winter kick and jump in the field or barnyard, and snort and sniff the air with extended nostrils and tails erect, or if they act the way Bossy did when she jumped over the moon, then stormy weather is brewing (as anyone who has been much around cattle has observed). If dogs bay or howl at the moon, cold weather will follow, and if they eat grass, there will be rainy weather. If a cat basks in the sun in February, it will have to go back to the stove in March. A cat sleeping with its head lower than the rest of its body indicates the coming of a storm. It is also a sign of rain if cats "wash" their faces with their paws.

The croaking of a tree frog ("Laubfrosch") can be regarded as a sure sign of rain. Weather lore also states that fish bite more readily, are more active, come closer to the surface, and may even leap out of the water just before a rainstorm; those with a fish pond may have noticed such behaviors. A thunderstorm is also indicated if snails and slugs are found in garden beds.

Feathered Creatures

Birds and fowls of every kind serve more extensively as weather prognosticators for the Pennsylvania Dutch than perhaps any other creatures. According to the local lore, chickens take great pains to preen their feathers just before a rainstorm, and if chickens run for shelter when it begins to rain, then the rain will not last long; by contrast, if chickens slop around in the rain with their tail feathers down, then the rain will continue indefinitely. If chickens molt early in the fall, winter will set in early. If roosters crow before 10 o'clock in the evening, it will rain the next day. If the peacock that once strutted proudly about many a barnyard spends the evening on the ridge of a wagon shed (or on some other rather tall building) and utters a shrill, piping cry, one can expect rain for the next day.

Clear weather can be anticipated if a robin perches on the topmost tree branches and sings, but when it sits on the lower branches, rain is coming. Likewise, if the owl, reputed to be the wisest of birds (but in actuality one of the dumbest), sits high and hoots, one may expect fair weather, whereas the opposite should be expected if it sits low. If swallows fly low over autumn fields, meadows and ponds, it is a sure sign of rain. Some other birds act in a similar manner; for example, if domestic geese fly low, propelling their ponderous bodies some distance through the air, and shriek, then stormy, blustering weather is sure to follow. Any restlessness among many feathered creatures, like the querulous cawing of crows and the noisy quarrels of the English sparrows, has always been considered a sure sign of rain.

The flying of wild geese southward in the autumn foretells a cold wave. (These regimented flyers of the upper air are among the most reliable weather prophets.) The plaintive cooing of the turtledove indicates rain. There will be a change of weather if the rooster crows on the manure pile in February. Unfavorable weather is predicted if crows fly high up in the air. If crows fly in a certain direction in a more or less steady stream, there will be stormy weather within ten hours. A screech owl hooting in winter portends a thaw; in summer, it means rain. The congregating, screaming and cawing of crows on the south or summer side of a hill indicates rain, but snow should be anticipated if they congregate on the north or winter side.

If geese waddle in mud between Christmas and New Year, they will do so every month of the winter season. (This prediction sounds similar to another one—namely, if the frost comes out of the ground in December, it will come out every month of that winter.) If geese and ducks flop and splash their wings in the water, it will begin to rain in a very short time. If pigeons take a bath or splash in a little pond or in a water trough, one should get ready for a rainy day. It will be an early winter if migratory birds leave early in the fall (this sounds more like common sense). The singing of birds early before sunrise is a sure sign of rain before sundown.

INSECTS

Even insects are considered worthy weather prophets. If hornets build their nests high in the trees, the winter is sure to be long and severe. There is rain in the near future if wood flies are persistently pestiferous (bothersome) to man and beast. If grasshoppers hop upon the snow, a mild winter may be expected. (Of course, this would surely be a strange sight, but it is nonetheless recorded in the folklore of the Pennsylvania Dutch.)

Cobwebs spun on the grass or between fence rails indicate fair weather everywhere, and it has been noted that bees work twice as hard just before a rain—much like the busy housewife who tries to get the wash from the line before the shower descends. If bees have stored up a large quantity of honey, the winter will be long; however, it would seem that the quantity they can store up depends more on the weather conditions of the preceding summer.

In sum, whether animals have an innate weather sense may never be found out fully, but surely some of these observations can be considered decidedly dependable.

Phenomena of Nature

Some weather predictions are based on aspects of nature. If trees shed their leaves early, then winter will be early. If silver maple, willow, and aspen trees turn up the white undersides of their leaves, rain will follow in a very short time. If the husks on the ears of corn, the skins on onions, and the hulls of hickory nuts and walnuts are close and tight, a very severe winter may be expected.

It is also said that if the bristles on hogs are long, and if the hair on horses and cattle is long and shaggy in the fall, a long winter is to be expected. However, this prediction may need modification, because at this time of the year, the coats of these animals look the most uncouth because of the long unkempt and disheveled hair (the result of growing heavier coats for winter); it is a natural condition of things, and the prophecy does not mean much unless the hair is unusually long and straggly.

Much fog in autumn indicates a snowy winter, while late roses indicate nice weather and a mild winter. Heavy, thick fur on fur-bearing animals indicates a severe winter. If the milt (spleen) in hogs is thick and short, there will be a corresponding short winter.

Occasionally some of the above predictions fail, as many did a century or more ago. For example, in the fall of 1890, the goose-bone man from Maine predicted a severe winter. Hunters returning from the chase reported that all fur-bearing animals had very thick and heavy pelts. Fallen apples also had a hard, rough, and cracked skin, like the green tops seen on ripe tomatoes, and the cracks "were deep enough to sink an ordinary sized knife-blade into." All these signs indicated a severe winter; yet, despite the predictions, my great-grandfather vividly recalled in notes written on old farmer's almanac pages that he was plowing (turning over soil) between Christmas and New Year that year, among other things. He also "wore a straw hat and was in his short sleeves."

Such mild winters continued for three years, as he recorded, and the ice crop was virtually a total failure. Yet in 1888, two years prior, the year of a great March blizzard, he had helped to "cut ice eighteen inches thick, strong enough to bear the run of a freight train." This sudden and unusual change in atmospheric conditions was attributed to a change in the course of the Gulf Stream, which for some reason had suddenly swung closer to the Atlantic coastline. This shift naturally brought about milder weather, but the reason for the change remained unknown. In this way, nature sometimes accounts for freakish occurrences.

Illogical or Unnatural Lore

Some weather predictions can be classified as innocent prattle, idle talk, and superstition. One example of this category is the notion that if all the dishes on the dinner table are emptied at mealtime, there will be fair weather the next day. Additionally, the appearance of a polecat in winter indicates a thaw, while in summer it means rain. A day on which a murderer is hanged is always rough and stormy. And even if the weather is threatening, one can still undertake a planned trip or voyage if there is a speck of blue sky as large as the seat of a pair of trousers, for then the sky will ultimately become clear. (This folk belief also exists in Massachusetts and Ohio, where the speck of blue sky "must be as large as a woman's apron").

Further examples of illogical weather lore from the Pennsylvania Dutch culture include the following: If the base of the tea kettle is white when it is removed from the fire, one may expect a snowstorm, but it is a good sign of rain if the tea kettle boils over. A load of barrels or a crowd of women on the street in the morning foretells wet weather, and goose eggs will not hatch if it thunders on Sunday.

Other Bases for Predictions

Some predictions were based on the atmospheric conditions on specific days of the month. For instance, the winter will be mild if the wind blows from the south on September 29, and the apple crop will be heavy if the sun shines brightly on January 25. If the wind blows from the south on November 16 and 19, the coming winter will be mild, but it will be a cold winter if the wind blows from the north or west.

Other forecasts were based on the prevailing weather conditions on certain days of the week. In this way of thinking, a beautiful sunset on Friday will bring rain before Monday, and the kind of weather prevailing on the last Friday of the month will determine the kind of weather one can expect for the following month. If it rains on the first or last Sunday evening of a given month, it will rain the following three Sundays. If it storms on Friday, a second storm will follow before Monday. Some forecasts might have contained a certain amount of reasoning; after all, if similar conditions brought about similar results often enough, then, by means of a little inductive reasoning, a general rule or principle could have been formulated.

The following incident, though not exactly applicable, perhaps best illustrates the point of a Pennsylvania Dutchman's stance when accepting lore as fact. Some years ago, members of my family attended a large exposition of livestock; among the exhibits was a pen of Poland-China hogs. The hogs of this breed, which they had seen before, were typically black and white, but these hogs were entirely white. So they asked the keeper of the pen about the reason for the different coloring. He replied by saying that "the 16th litter of inbreeding will establish the strain, a new strain, not a new breed."

In this area farmer's defense, if it rains or snows regularly, consecutively, and often enough every time, there is surely a ring around the moon; likewise, if the rain never lasts long whenever the chickens scurry for cover, what could be wrong with pinning such observations down as an established rule, or law, as was done with the 16th litter of the inbreeding of those pigs? It was only plain common sense and a little inductive reasoning.

Some predictions were based on sound, and on the sudden appearance or disappearance of water. If one heard the whistle of a locomotive or the rumbling of a train in the distance, or a fog horn miles away, rain was certainly on the way. If the water disappeared suddenly in the puddles, ditches, and rills in the meadow, especially after a shower, more rain was sure to follow. By contrast, if these spots, after having dried out, suddenly become moist or show the presence of a small amount of water, a good rain is to be expected.

However, there might be a physical reason for such conditions, as the following story illustrates. My great-great-grandparents' old 19th-century homestead was located at one angle of an equilateral triangle, and there was a large mill dam at each of the other two angles. These properties were roughly a quarter mile apart. In these days, before there were any railroad facilities in this extensive community, and when everything had to "be hauled on the axle" (an expression the old folks used when they meant to say that the hauling had to be done by heavy teams), my forebears, like others in their community, would hitch up a four-horse team in "the wee hours in the morning" and drive long distances for coal, lumber, or slate. Occasionally, they would observe that the upper mill dam was running over—this was an indication that they could expect to encounter unpleasant weather. The implied prediction may have been based on the sudden increase of the flow of water or on the direction from which the sound came. Regardless, they certainly weren't the only people who depended on a mill dam as a "weather prophet."

Church Calendar Days

Some predictions were based on atmospheric conditions on certain church calendar days: Much rain on Easter Sunday will bring about a good crop of corn, but little hay. The weather on Ascension Day will indicate the weather for autumn. A rainy Easter will be followed by seven rainy Sundays. If it rains on Whitsunday (Pentecost, or "Pfingsten"), six weeks of rainy weather will follow. The weather on Shrove Tuesday (popularly known as "Fasnacht Day" in the Dutch Country) will last until the end of Lent, and the sun will not shine clearly before 9 o'clock on the morning of Good Friday. There will be snow at Eastertime if there is green grass on Candlemas Day (February 2). If it snows on All Saints' Day, one might find it necessary to have a fur coat close by.

Quite a few "saint's" days enter into these predictions as well: If it rains on St. Swithin's Day (July 15), it will rain for forty days. If it rains on July 2, when the Virgin Mary goes over the hill, there will be rainy weather for six weeks, or roughly forty days, but August 15, the day of her return, will be fair. But if it is fair on the day she leaves, the opposite may be expected. The chestnut crop for the year will be small in quantity and poor in quality if it rains on John Huss's Day (July 6), and acorns will spoil if it rains on St. James's Day. Likewise, the harvest will be wet, and nuts will spoil, if it rains on St. John's Day. One should not set a hen on St. Valentine's Day, for the young chicks will be either blind or lame, or else they will soon die off in some way. If geese stand on ice on St. Martin's Day (November 11), they will walk in mud on Christmas Day. Bees that swarm after St. John's Day are not worth "bagging."

Still other prognostications are based on the aspect of the sky. If the horns of the shell of the New Moon point upward, thus forming a bowl, there will be no rain, for the water cannot spill out of the bowl. But if the bowl stands upright with the horns perpendicular, there will be rain, because the bowl can no longer hold any water. (This is sometimes called the *farmer's moon* in Pennsylvania Dutch weather lore.) A ring around the moon indicates rain or snow, and the number of stars within the ring indicates the number of days before "falling weather" began.

There will be a good crop of grain if it thunders in June, but if the moon is in Cancer, the hops will suffer damage. If it thunders when the moon is in Capricorn, there will be much rain, and seed in the ground will rot. The rain will last for fifty days if it rains when the moon is in the Virgin (Virgo). If it rains "into" a rainbow, rainy weather will continue for three more days. If it rains while the sun shines, it will also rain the next day. A rainbow in the morning indicates foul weather, but one in the evening points to fair weather. A star in front of the moon promises fair weather; one in back of it means foul weather. A thunderstorm in spring is invariably followed by a spell of cold weather; however, a thunderstorm in the autumn will be followed by warm weather.

And then we have the rattling of soot down the chimney, the sweating of walls and cellars, of glasses and pitchers, and the "watery" salt shaker—all of which are supposedly signs of rain. Perhaps the most common predictor mentioned today is the poor rheumatic, whose aching joints foretell a change to rainy weather: "He feels it in his bones." Some predictions have taken on the importance of proverbs, while others are expressed in weather jingles, such as the following:

Peter, Paul
Macht der Frucht die Wurzel faul.

(On Peter and Paul's Day [June 29]
The roots of the grain begin to decay.)

En nasser April and kihler Moi
Bringt viel Frucht and viel Hoi.

(A wet April and a cool May
Bring forth much grain and plenty of hay.)

The condition of the sky at sunrise and at sunset is a fairly reliable indicator of what the weather will be like in the next twenty-four hours. The substance of it all is couched in the following rhyme:

Evening red and morning gray
Speed the traveler on his way.
Evening gray and morning red
Shed rain on the traveler's head.
Morning red makes cheeks red
Evening red brings dry bread.

(Morga rot rnacht Backa rot
Owet rot bringt drucke Brot.)

Stretches of thin, long, drawn-out clouds (called "cow tails" regionally) were also forerunners of rain; such a sky was also called a *mackerel sky*, as illustrated in the expression "Mackerel sky, not twenty-four hours dry."

Other Sources of Weather Knowledge

The Pennsylvania Dutch farmers of the early 20th century and prior had two other means of obtaining a little foreknowledge of atmospheric conditions (and their possible effect on farm life and all its activities) before the advent of modern weather equipment: the ruling planet for the year and the *One Hundred Year Almanac* (or *Farmer's Almanac*). There were once many people (now only perhaps an isolated farmer) who eagerly awaited the arrival of the new almanac to find out which of the seven planets would be the governor of the elements of nature, in all its manifestations, for the ensuing year. The ruling planet once determined the character of the weather in the Pennsylvania Dutchmen's eyes, the bountifulness of their harvest, and, most important, the health of the community.

20

Goose-Bone Prophets
of the Dutch Country

Mary Shade, a longtime resident of Lobachsville, was best remembered for traveling about on foot carrying her trademark umbrella. Being such an oldtimer, she was always prepared for any type of weather. As a folk personality, Mary was well known for her faith healing until she was taken ill and died in 1970. She lived in seclusion, similar to folk legend Mountain Mary a century and a half earlier, for many years atop the locally known "Chimney Rocks Hill." Ms. Shade was very much at home with Mother Nature and subscribed to most of the folk wisdom about the weather, even consulting her pet rooster when in doubt.

This modern world has long been built around the premises and traditions of the old, some of them mightily romantic and delightful. Take, for example, the detailed account later in this chapter of a turn-of-the-century (early 1900s) meeting of eighteen local "experts" who reported their findings based on rural folk beliefs to the World Meteorological Organization. Scientists have long recognized that barometric pressures and weather affect people's health and, furthermore, emotional well-being, and we as a people seem to be returning to a deeper sense of appreciation of what weather may do (or not do) to the human system.

The Native Americans, for instance, realized that if the caterpillar wore his fur long and thick, then they should prepare additional supplies for the winter. Scientists also understand that weather, be it extreme hot or extreme cold temperatures, may be a deciding factor in determining the sex of an unborn child. Even the turn-of-the-century meteorological gathering described reported that during a summer thunderstorm more people seem to be born, come down with disease, sustain injuries, or even die than if the weather had remained normal. These reports are intriguing because they prove that our forebears were not so far off in placing their faith in the winds, rains, and small native animals who could warn them about what to expect.

Mary Shade was a Christian faith healer who lived outside Lobachsville atop "Chimney Rocks Hill." Mary (a widow) was considered something of a sage; her merciful compassion for the sick and afflicted was witnessed by Jacob Moyer, a Pikeville storekeeper who was a recipient of her healing gift.

Lobachsville Weather Prophets Assemble

I must begin by admitting that I'm not quite certain whether the old *North American* newspaper aimed to pull its readers' legs a little bit when it reported on this scientific conclave at Lobachsville in 1912. The newspaper made its annual report of the congress of weathermen each year, claiming that they met in seminar at Lobachsville, where these men discussed the prospects for the season ahead. Whatever the *North American* intended, the records indicate that some serious discussions took place in the old general store of William Hessig on the subject of the weather.

Public records verify that the following men, named by the newspaper, could well have driven to Lobachsville (each in his own carriage), remained overnight at the old hotel run by Zacharias Miller's wife, and in the morning stepped over to Hessig's store at Lobachsville to hold their session. Leaving aside questions of accuracy or sincerity, in September 1912, the *North American* avowed that these men conducted themselves in the following manner:

> The weather prophets of Berks County, who have forecast the weather for many years here, held their annual convention at Lobachsville, and by a two-thirds vote it was agreed that the coming winter will be an unusually severe one. Whether prognosticators from all sections about Lobachsville were represented at the meeting and exchange their views on the subject. Many are closed followers of the goose bone weather Prophet, Eliza Hartz. Those in attendance did not hesitate to express their views. Some are guided in their theories by the actions of small animals such as reptiles; others pay close attention to the trees and shrubbery.

Ever since colonial times, wayside inns, halfway houses, and country taverns of the Pennsylvania Dutch have been treating the American traveler to a regional hospitality that has come to be one of the most colorful in the nation. Pictured here is the Yellow House Hotel, similar to the Lobachsville hotel/general store (site of the 1912 goose-bone prophets' meeting) as it looked at the turn of the century.

Below are some of the more interesting examples of weather folklore recorded and, based upon their folk beliefs about weather and observations, predictions formulated by these goose-bone prophets:

Henry Walers, of Seisholtzville, said, "Farmers are preparing for a hard and long winter because the red squirrels and chipmunks have become very busy digging deep in the ground and preparing their nests for storage of the food."

H.H. Brown, of Exeter, said, "My great-grandfather used to say that when there was a good crop of persimmons that 'Indians' would provide themselves with a good supply of buffalo meat, for they were sure of a long and severe winter. The persimmon crop is a prolific one this year and we can look for a hard winter."

Cyrus E. Hessig, of Palm, said, "I am unable to make a prediction until after November 23 and 24. If on the former day it is blustery and cloudy, then January and February and March will be severe months. If it is clear on

November 23, the weather will be mild. If it is blustery on November 24, the winter will extend into April and May."

Cyrus Delp, of Grill, said, "A dry summer is invariably followed by a winter with lots of snow. This year the rainfall exceeded the average, and I predict that there will be but little snow and that winter will be mild. A wet fall means an early winter."

Jackson Peger, of Hill Church, said, "Fifty years ago Ember Day weather was very closely watched by every household in Berks and even to this day there are many persons who have faith in those old-time prognostications. The belief is that if it rains on Ember day, there will be a great deal of rain in October. If, on the contrary, the weather is fair, the outlook for October will be fair with hardly any rain, and a cold winter will follow."

John S. Fritz, of Reading, based his predictions on the planets, claiming that the coming winter would be a mild one. He was recorded as standing in front of the window and looking out toward the old chair factory while "tugging on his beard," saying, "From September 29 to October 10, as we approach the full moon, we will again be approached by a warm spell. As Jupiter is predominant for three years, the weather will accordingly be warm. Next summer will be featured by a drought and intense heat. Jupiter embraces an area of 1000 miles, which territory is affected as the planet moves."

I am not positive of accuracy of these prognostications, but I am willing to venture the guess that they were more accurate than not. Bill Becker, who was the longtime owner of the general store formerly run by Mr. Hessig in the old days, allowed very few modern changes to enter into the scene up to recent times, so that this great store remained a delightful gathering place for many years. If Bill had only possessed a good tape recording of those old seminars as they took place around the turn of the last century, he could have forgotten all about merchandising and sat back on the porch rocking chair with his trademark Pittsburgh stogie (cigar) and just listened to his audience comment upon his great Pennsylvania Dutch folklife show.

The location of these seminars about the weather, Lobachsville, is itself an intriguing subject. An early American hamlet founded in 1745, Lobachsville comes with very interesting folklore, because the settlement never developed into a metropolis larger than it was at a point in time 200 years ago. Industrially, it actually slipped, but that very lack of modernity is the source of its great appeal for overcrowded humanity. In variety and qualities of the human equation, it has always excelled. A hundred and fifty or more years ago, though, among the Pennsylvania Dutch pioneers of the Oley Hills, there existed some strange impulse to outdo all others in the matter of playing host to tramps (foot travelers) and vagrants roaming the hill slopes. Some generous households held an open house on the Sabbath for all who came to the door requesting food; others fed them every evening throughout the year, vying with one another in an unofficial competition to establish a record for having prepared and distributed the most free meals among the numerous townships. Such activities no doubt provided a curious reward when these folk could later read about themselves as the magnanimous benefactors who had turned away no one during the long winter.

21

Appalachian Powwowing among the Pennsylvania Dutch

When President Lyndon B. Johnson launched his war on domestic poverty, the federal government discovered pockets of poverty that existed among the hill folk of the Appalachian Mountains. Affluent city folk, with their push-button modern living standards in the 1960s, could not believe that contemporary fellow citizens did not share equally in the modern U.S. standard of living, though others were not at all surprised at the inequity.

In researching the Pennsylvania Dutch practice of Powwowing (known in the dialect as "Braucherei"), folklorists had come to know the unfortunate plight that some economically disadvantaged people faced while living in some of the depressed wilderness territories of Pennsylvania that had not rebounded significantly from the Great Depression of the 1930s. Having interviewed many hill folk and recorded existing folklife practices and folklore for nearly twenty-five years on Berks County's Pricetown Appalachian Ridge, I knew that some of these oldtimers were hard pressed to make a living, as were parts of my own family, and they had continued to make extra money (albeit illegally) through moonshining long after the Prohibition period was ended.

Living on land too poor to cultivate, Powwower Raymond Sterner was a very crafty, yet enterprising, individual; when his faith healing practice was low on patients, he would get in his old touring car and head deeper into the Appalachian Mountains. According to an older informant who went along for the ride, if they were lucky, they found poor souls in need of Sterner's Powwowing skills who paid him off in foodstuffs and goods, bartering for his unique services. There is no doubt that Doc Sterner was a very charismatic individual; he wore a silver dollar charm around his neck on a dog choker's chain, which evoked curiosity in everyone who met him, who wished that his services would turn their bad luck into good fortune. Sterner's personal

This silver dollar hex charm was used by Doc Sterner, living near Fredericksville, Berks County. He could both break evil spells and cast them, according to his neighbors (photograph c. 1960s).

age-old wisdom gave him insight to cure his ailing victims, who were ignorant of their real human faults and problems!

According to Allie Day, Ray Sterner was very good with animals, and in traveling from farm to farm, there was usually a farmer in need of his services. There are numerous cases documented or told of how sometimes the cows would refuse to come back to the farmer's stable at milking time; Doc Sterner would then offer his assistance to charm the wayward cow to follow him into the stable for the grateful farmer, who would subsequently reward him for his assistance. Some farmers in Appalachia, who were almost destitute, blamed bad farming habits on witchcraft spells.

Redware potter Lester Breininger (mentioned in previous chapters) liked to tell a story about the Powwower who was asked to cure a ferhext cow for a Dutchman in his Bernville, Appalachia, area. The cow was certainly wasting away and was in desperate need of help, so the crafty Powwow doctor confirmed the farmer's diagnosis and, after repeating an incantation in the Dutch dialect over the victimized cow, told the farmer that in order to break the hex, he should feed the cow three certain size scoops of feed each day in the name of the Holy Trinity (God the Father, the Son, and the Holy Ghost). Since the farmer was broke, this was more daily nourishment than the animal normally received. Unsurprisingly, the cow made a remarkable recovery once the unfortunate farmer started feeding her more. The astute Powwower was given credit for invoking the Lord's Sacred Blessing on the beast, but any veterinarian would have told the farmer that the happy outcome was due not to the secret German incantation pronounced over the cow but the insistence by the outsider that this critter be fed a normal diet instead of starving her!

Further setting back the hill folks' way of life was the soaring cost to medical doctors in setting up new practices in the remote Appalachian wilderness; as a result, few people could pay the high bills they charged for their services. Thus, there was a resurgence of traditional Brauching, with practitioners dispersing age-old folk remedies among the Pennsylvania Dutch people, since the payment for the Lord's healing was not usually made in cash but in a bartering of in-kind favors to reimburse the Powwow practitioner.

One of the first medical doctors to set up a practice in these backwoods, north of Fredericksville, was Dr. William Weisbecker from Philadelphia

Irish immigrants migrated to the Oley Hills in the post–American Revolutionary War period and built their fieldstone homes in the early 19th century. The most prominent Irish immigrant family who settled in the Fredericksville area and became assimilated into the Pennsylvania Dutch culture was the Day family. Above is one of the descendants, Jonas Day, called "Uni" by his Pennsylvania Dutch friends, continuing in America's melting pot theme and William Penn's vision of religious freedom. Here, Uni points to a rosette-type hex sign he painted on one of his outbuildings as an example of his family's assimilation (photograph c. 1973).

(1954). He was a neighbor of the Wetzel family, and one of the only modern medical practitioners in the territory. At first, he had to overcome the Pennsylvania Dutch language barrier of his patients in order to communicate modern medicine, and then he had to avoid the superstitions of the hill folk. The Wetzel family members were the first to admit that his modern medicine was superior to age-old Powwowing techniques, and in regard to setting broken bones and mishaps, Weisbecker quickly gained the respect of hill folk far and near. But since he could not speak Pennsylvania Dutch fluently with the local Appalachian folk, their trust in age-old Braucherei faith healing remained an underground practice as long as the Pennsylvania Dutch language was spoken fluently in the area up to the 1950s.

Another of the area residents was Mary Bieber Hilbert, who had inherited 70 acres of woodland forest on the Rockland Township side of the Fredericksville Hotel, which was very close to a group of poor inhabitants that the town folk called "Little Korea," mostly because their housing was substandard by the norms of the 20th century, but also because the area essentially became a warzone if any *Auslander* (outsider) came in looking to steal or cause harm. Mary's husband, William Hilbert, learned the German incantation to bless away pinkeye affliction, as some were able to learn in the region, but after he moved to Allentown in the 1940s from Rockland Township, his new urban neighbors no longer needed this ability, so it was kept within the family as a personal cure.

Life must have been difficult among the early Appalachian Dutch families prior to the 1950s, and if not for the compassionate religious Brauchers who followed Christ's teachings and healing arts, there would have been less chance for survival. True Powwowers or Brauchers were humanitarians providing the necessary care until medical doctors and hospitals were in place by the 1950s.

22

Historic Kutztown University
Its Interaction with the Occult and Its German-Speaking Community

Nowhere were the innate feelings of ethnic enculturation, particularly in retaining one's Old World language, more evident than in the one-room schoolhouses and the colleges of the early Pennsylvania Dutch as the American assimilation process entered its final stages. By the 1980s, however, modern education had all but extinguished the local German dialect, and there was hardly a trace of its colorful accent left among Berks County children (a situation that continues today).

There is, however, a collection of interested accounts from up to the 1960s, when the second language of Kutztown was undoubtedly Pennsylvania Dutch, and a new men's dormitory (Rothermel) was dedicated on the campus. Some bizarre, yet true, accounts were documented in connection with this student housing, where ancient sympathetic medicine from the Rhineland was used by native Kutztownians. At the time, most townspeople spoke the German dialect fluently, and some college students not commuting or housed on campus were fortunate enough to find a local family with whom they could board. One particular student-boarder, whose name was not collected or remembered by my mentor, provided an account of the people with whom he lived during his time in college. As recounted by my mentor:

"He was an out-of-state student who had no knowledge of Pennsylvania Dutch culture. Since I started researching folklife studies with Dr. Alfred L. Shoemaker, who had his office on Main Street, the student's roommate at Rothermel Hall asked me to interview this informant for posterity. Luckily, the young man, who had boarded with a middle-aged couple who lived downtown for a few years near the early folklife offices, was also able to confirm his experience and divulge much more information about his account."

The kind housewife who hosted this student was an exceptional Pennsylvania Dutch cook, and the student-boarder enjoyed their hospitality very much. But, since most conversations with this couple and their friends were in the local German dialect, English was limited, and there were times when the student felt at a disadvantage. After the first year, sensing her boarder's discomfort, the bilingual wife, who spoke English very well, took him aside and confided in him her husband's mysterious, yet amazing, gift. She explained to the young college student that her dialect-speaking husband was one of the few living Powwow natives who could cure a human affliction known as *Wildfeier* in the German dialect (called erysipelas among physicians)—an ugly, red skin inflammation. Pennsylvania Dutch people from all around who suffered from this condition would come to their residence seeking the man's unique ability, since he was an oldtime Braucher. He had the power to cure them by using an ancient German incantation, taught to him years ago by another wise Braucher, who had passed her power onto him.

The ritual was as follows: After the initial contact, the *Wildfeier* victim was to go home, and, on a certain week designated, they were not to lock the doors of their home. Without the victim's knowledge, the faith healer would secretly pay a visit to the house during that week, entering through the kitchen or cellar, where a stove or furnace was located, in which fire was made. Here, he would stand and recite the ancient German *Wildfeier* incantation or blessing, and when the Braucher left the house, he would mysteriously draw off the disease from the victim. In a few days, the inflammation would slowly disappear, never to come back. These events took place during the modern age of the 1960s, and, for the out-of-state student, the fact that this secret incantation worked among many of the afflicted was only dramatized by the fact that local doctors were unable to cure this condition.

Others (eventually including the student) eagerly passed the name of the "Doc" on to patients who still believed in this folk practice and used it as a last resort. After learning of his landlord's abilities, the student no longer wondered why so many people came to his landlord's residence speaking the local dialect or why he left the house at odd hours of the night. The Braucher, a pious man, was never doubted by the college student again, who kept his knowledge of the healing practice a secret until urged by his roommate in earnest to reveal this wonderful healing to my mentor.

In elaborating, sometimes a "red string" and a shovel of hot coals was used in other local sympathetic *Wildfeier* cures, but, most likely afraid that she would jeopardize her husband's powerful gift, the wife did not divulge that information to the student-boarder; however, it did explain the reverence and respect his callers had for him.

During the decade of the 1960s, it was common for social science students to stop in at the Pennsylvania Folklife Office, opposite the Eagles Fraternity Hall on Main Street, to have academic discussions with Dr. Shoemaker. Samuel Himmelberger was one of those people, a college commuter whose family had a general store at Seisholtzville near Kutztown. He also became intrigued with Powwowing, and, while student teaching in the Kutztown Area School District that same year, Sam approached the subject with his social studies students. One alert lad said the doghouse of his farm was protected by a Powwow incantation. The next day, the boy returned with the incantation written on a piece of paper sewn within a small triangular muslin bag. The rusted tacks were still clinging to the cloth where it had been fastened to the inside wall of the doghouse. At the time, it was a normal Pennsylvania Dutch custom to name one's watchdog *Wasser* (water), according to Dr. Shoemaker, since people believed that witches and evil spirits were repelled by water. Therefore, Dr. Shoemaker believed that this amulet, a marvelous surviving artifact, was meant as an extra precaution to protect the watchdog in his doghouse.

Being an avid collector of Pennsylvania Dutch books, imprints, and historic broadsides, and having extensively studied such, I knew from attending Berks County auctions that such items as religious documents and prayers were to be found that protected our native folk (as well as their houses and well-being) from harm or misfortune. Among several German occult books, which listed sympathetic folk medicine formulae and incantations, there were numerous

Partially removed from its secret hiding place, the folded paper bearing a written incantation was sewn inside this three-cornered muslin bag and nailed inside a Kutztown-area doghouse to protect the watchdog from evildoers (photograph 1960–1961).

household broadsides like "Himmelsbriefs" (letters from Heaven) that were saved in old German family Bibles; people believed that these items would protect a Christian home and its occupants from disaster (a concept discussed thoroughly in later chapters).

One of the archived German specimens is the famous "Kutztown Fire Brief" or charm, which was printed near the college in the mid–19th century. This rare incantation broadside, intended to be purchased by homeowners to protect their dwellings and barns from conflagration, was copied from earlier Rhineland originals. Printed in the German language, above the body of the text are three crosses representing the Holy Trinity. This talisman also carries the initials C. M. B., which stand for the Three Kings or Wise Men (commonly known as Casper, Melchior, and Balthazar) who visited Christ shortly after his birth.

The community of Kutztown at one time was a religious printing center among church groups in Berks County, and its German press published late

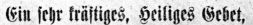

This copy of the "Kutztown Fire Brief," printed in the 19th century by the German press at Kutztown, like its earlier Rhineland examples, was intended to be purchased by householders to protect their homes.

into the 19th century, notably with the bilingual German and English weekly, the *American Patriot* newspaper, published in 1874. The *Patriot* only stopped printing in German at the turn of the century, when it began printing exclusively in English, and it is still run weekly today. Although the Pennsylvania Dutch were never a minority within Berks County and surrounding counties, enterprising politicians had bilingual political cards printed by the German press that listed candidates in both English and German, along with the office or position for which they were running. Regardless, the Americanization process, which involved learning English and becoming a functioning citizen in mainstream society, was the ultimate goal.[1]

Recent presidents of Kutztown University, such as Dr. F. Javier Cevallos, are faced with further challenges in assisting Berks County citizens to achieve bilingual English competence as the Spanish population grows and requires further educational opportunities, like so many native Pennsylvania Dutch in the past. In Dr. Lee Graver's centennial history of Kutztown State College (as the university was once known), *Beacon on the Hill*, he paid particular attention to how Germanized the community remained when its famous native son, Dr. Nathan C. Schaeffer, was appointed superintendent of public instruction in the state of Pennsylvania (1893–1919) and, furthermore, how he occasionally conducted his meetings at Harrisburg in the Pennsylvania Dutch dialect, in addition to writing his reports in the German language when appropriate to reach the vast number of teachers in eastern Pennsylvania still speaking the dialect.

Professor Graver's interesting account states that in the boarding school years of the Keystone State Normal School (the earliest incarnation of Kutztown University), "the trustees counted themselves fortunate if they could find teachers who did not have a heavy German accent." Consequently, they also conducted the board business in the German dialect. Reverend Abraham Horne, Normal School principal (1871–1877), however, did think that teachers of Pennsylvania Dutch heritage well trained in English were more effective in teaching Pennsylvania German children than were non–German teachers.

Longtime sociology professor Mary E. Rickenbach (1892–1984), also dean of women, told how, in her early days at the college, she would travel by horse and buggy to nearby one-room schoolhouses in the backcountry around Kutztown to supervise young teachers: "The Pennsylvania German accent of local children was so outrageous and grammar so poor, it did seem impossible to teach them good, proper English in such an environment." But Mary, who was reared near Leesport, led by example in upholding educational excellence throughout her life.

Furthermore, Dr. Nathan Schaeffer (1849–1919), a distinguished author and outstanding educator, had used his knowledge of Pennsylvania German to his advantage, and he also became president of the Pennsylvania German Society. He kept his local pronounced accent and earthy humor until the day he died. Almost all the principals of the earlier Keystone State Normal School (first established in 1866) were ordained ministers, and Pennsylvania Dutch folk medicine, like Braucherei (dubbed the "ecclesiastical underground"), remained an occult practice in the German Reformed and Lutheran churches of the region.

In 1934, Dr. Quincy A. Rohrbach (1894–1988), appointed president of Kutztown State Teachers College (as the Normal School became known following 1928), like other administrators, was concerned about the influence of the local German dialect and its accent on the student body; he therefore preferred that his support personnel of locally employed custodians not speak their German dialect in college buildings. This taboo was heeded, but the dialect "echoed there after midnight when he was not around." Dr. Henry Ryan, in the department of teacher education, stated that "when state colleges were allowed to specialize in foreign languages by the Commonwealth, he thought Dr. Rohrbach purposefully chose the Russian language over German for Kutztown State, because it was contrary to our native German culture." The horrors of World War II also aided in silencing the Pennsylvania Dutch dialect from being spoken publicly.

As several native Pennsylvania Dutchmen attested, it appeared at times that Dr. Rohrbach was embarrassed of his own roots. However, whether Dr. Rohrbach knew it or not, his Pennsylvania Dutch avocation as a weaver did portray his human side to all who knew of it, and once a year during his presidency, overwhelming numbers of native German descendants would invade the college to hold the annual Berks County Pennsylvania Dutch *Fersommling* banquet in his formal Georgian dining hall. This exclusive dialect-speaking get-together renewed the county's German heritage and did more to promote the public relations of the college than any other event in recruiting Berks children and grandchildren as potential students. Thousands of families had visited the campus, until this event became so huge that it had to be moved to the Leesport Farmers' Market Hall, twelve miles away.

Although Dr. Rohrbach was a graduate of Franklin and Marshall College, the institution that established the Kutztown Pennsylvania Dutch Folk Festival at the local fairgrounds in 1950, he was not an active supporter. Suffering from a Pennsylvania Dutch inferiority complex, he did not encourage Kutztown State professors to be academically associated with Franklin and Marshall's Pennsylvania Folklife Office downtown either, but a few recorded contributed anyway.

Only near the end of his administration did Dr. Rohrbach have a Pennsylvania Dutch scholar appointed to the faculty, but this distinguished author, Dr. Arthur D. Graeff, should have been appointed long before that. After the Pennsylvania Folklife Society had severed its ties with Franklin and Marshall College, having a substantial Dun & Bradstreet (D&B) rating for its Kutztown Folk Festival, it searched for another academic institution with which to be affiliated, and since Kutztown University had a dysfunctional acceptance of its grassroots Germanic culture and limited ability as a state-operated institution, the society sought a more germane tie with Ursinus College, a traditional German Reformed Church institution. There, in the Myrin Library and the Berman Art Museum, were for many years a multitude of files and a magnificent folk art collection of Kutztown's outstanding Pennsylvania Folklife Society, which in its early days published the *Pennsylvania Dutchman* magazine, which evolved into *Pennsylvania Folklife*, with the last issue released in 1997.

Dr. Rohrbach's successor as president of the college in the 1960s was an articulate Italian man named Dr. Italo L. DeFrancesco (1901–1967). He became the first non–German headmaster in the institution's history and was distinguished for art education, but also for publishing a Pennsylvania German folk art portfolio, which endeared him to the local folk. DeFrancesco was considered a liberal thinker who even engaged a member (John Stinsmen) of the notorious campus Heidelberg Philharmonic to give the benediction at the dedication of the new Rothermel Men's Hall. And so our story comes full circle to the 21st century and to the historic borough of Kutztown, its university, and the Pennsylvania Dutch culture, whose people still make an everlasting impression on the American scene.

23

The World-Famous
Hex Sign Folk Art ... Myth!

While an overabundance of material has already been written on Pennsylvania's world-famous hex signs, one more attempt will be made to discern their meanings (or lack thereof). As a 10th-generation Pennsylvania Dutchman and avid antiquarian, I should begin by saying that this form of folk art, which is most commonly associated with the Pennsylvania Dutch people, by no means advertises the occult or has any occult affiliations. Activities dealing with the occult are a personal, private, undercover, whisper-type affair, which people do not publicly acknowledge, much less broadcast on their barn fronts or forebays.

As a surprise to most, these barn decorations are rather recent, the practice having only spread within the past century and a half. Roughly 90 percent of all originally decorated barns lie within a 40-mile radius of Kutztown, Pennsylvania. The architectural style of the barns in this area produces a great expanse of uninterrupted barn front or forebay, perfect for such embellishment. Typical barns in the Lancaster County area have long sloping roof lines on the front, which produces a deep forebay but severely reduces the broad area of the front of the barn or broadside; the Plain People or Plain Dutch, such as the Amish and Mennonites, do not participate in this vanity art.

Because the Kutztown type of barn front was available, it provided a place for individuality and artistic expression, besides breaking up the monotony of this large surface. Decorations certainly appeal to the Pennsylvania Dutchmen, evidenced by past folk art over nearly three and a half centuries of occupying this part of the New World; their love of color and design is apparent and seen in museum pieces today. The patterns chosen for hex signs were generally simple, with a compass and straightedge easily completing the job. There was a myriad of star forms, ranging from rosettes to six-, eight-, and twelve-pointed examples to "swirling swastikas" or whirling pinwheels, sometimes even five-pointed stars.

Religiously devout farmers of Berks, Montgomery, Lehigh and other Pennsylvania Dutch counties celebrating their freedom in the New World promoted this fraktur art form of Christian symbolism by painting their barns and some houses.

The above is said to be the "Most Beautifully Decorated Barn in America." Nowhere is there a greater difference between native East Penn Valley farmers and Plain People than in their treatment of their barns. Plain Dutch who purchase Berks County bank barns with multicolored hex signs on their broadsides will not repaint them, but they generally favor the Lancaster County tradition of painting the entire barn white.

Most likely a deliberate, or at least ignorant, misinterpretation of these six-pointed stars (or, in the Pennsylvania Dutch dialect, *sech-spittich-schtona*) led willing believers to question the signs' status of witchery and protection against the same. The sturdy farmers who had their buildings decorated in this manner certainly had no Hexerei in mind, although the designs, which had a natural appeal to these rural folk, may have had ritual significance in pre–Christian Europe or Asia. We are, after all, less than 100 generations removed from the European Stone Age and may have many customs, superstitions, and perhaps even personal traits left over from these times.

Similar geometric designs were used prolifically on Pennsylvania Dutch textiles, fraktur, tombstones, and decorated blanket chests or dower chests.

One of the romantic tales told by farmers when asked why they painted white arches over the doors on their barn forebays was that they wanted to trick the witches into bumping their heads when they entered the barn at night to cause trouble to the animals! Here, Johnny Claypoole paints these hex signs directly on the barn.

Nowadays, of course, one can buy jewelry, placemats, and silkscreen or hand-painted hardboard or masonite with all kinds of authentic symbolism, including the shamrock for "Irish Dutchmen" to hang on an outbuilding or shed. Even modern farmers purchase these things to liven up other buildings that would never have called for such things. Traditionally, though, they were meant for barns. Dr. Don Yoder, a Pennsylvania Dutch folklife scholar, stated that "the current hex sign revival with its fake symbolism for suburban garages is something entirely tangential to the culture." Nonetheless, large four- to six-foot hex signs painted directly on barns (authentically) have become popular for the Pennsylvania Dutch farmer in retaining tradition and breaking up the monotony of his forebay, as most of the oldtime hex sign artists who would climb up on tall ladders and paint directly on barn fronts have passed away, including Claypoole (pictured).

The design of four flat or Dutch hearts once painted on the old barn of the Jacob Keim homestead (now washed away from the elements in Chapter 10) was the adopted symbol of the American Folklife Institute and serves as its trademark. The original design was found on an old door of the stone cabin on the Jacob Keim property, shown in chapter 10. As many of the old designs are quite decorative, a do-it-yourself project is quite possible (although many find it difficult to understand how to properly use a compass as part of the process).

Elusive Sunbursts: A Contemporary Study

The heyday of frakturism (circa 1775–1820) paralleled the period of time in which Dutchmen built grandiose architectural barns with English Palladian forebay windows and, later, hex signs during the antebellum period of the young republic, or so we thought. In 2007, when folk art researcher and author Dr. Donald Shelley's rare 1780 decorated Pennsylvania Dutch dower chest was sold for more than $140,000 at auction, folk art experts recognized its unique relationship to gable-end (side of the barn) hex signs recently discovered on a handful of early 1800s barns, including the 1801 Oscar Bieber barn at Kutztown, Pennsylvania.[1] This 1780 Hanna Eister decorated dower chest, done in the twin heart motif school of Jacob and John Bieber, had geometric pin-wheel stars similar to the Oscar Bieber and 1819 Snyder hex sign barn medallions near Kutztown, uniquely built into the barns' gable ends.

The most enchanting feature Dr. Shelley's dower chest in relation to later barn folk art was the

Dr. Donald Shelley's rare decorated dower chest provided a link to folk art and hex signs found on barns in the Pennsylvania Dutch Country.

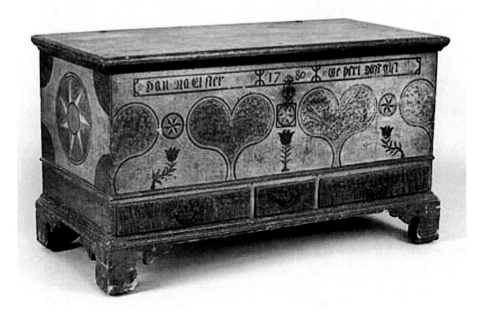

Made in Oley Township for Hanna Eister in 1780, the chest is a superb example of the Bieber flat heart motif with free-standing tulips and hex signs.

unusual seven-pointed hex sign stars, or large sunbursts, painted in yellow and red-orange on each end, with bold orange centers. Most assuredly, this was the sunburst-type design that author Frances Lichten had attributed to the original archeological sun cult idea of hex sign motifs she had seen overseas in the Rhineland Valley. The stylized Bieber flat hearts (an Alsatian design from Europe), outlined in red paint, did not have star designs in each lobe, as later Bieber dower chests did. Instead, they reminded the author of the demure twin flat hearts inscribed at the bottom of the historic 1783 David Hottenstein mansion date stones, just outside of Kutztown on Route 222, once known historically as the Great Easton Road.

Located along the nearby Kutztown-to-Bowers road, south of Kemp's historic tavern at Kutztown (where President John Adams once stayed), the 1801 John Bieber Farmstead (owned later by Oscar Bieber) was a familiar part of rural Kutztown.[2] Among numerous Pennsylvania Dutch folk artists who known to have scribed exceptional compass folk art designs in the colonial days of Berks County were the father and son team of Jacob and John Bieber, Oley relatives of the Kutztown Bieber families. Their folk art–crafted dower chests proved that they or another member of the family would have been capable of designing Oscar Bieber's sunburst gable-end barn medallion.

Dower chests attributed to the Jacob Bieber (1731–1798) clan were usually laid out with a compass technique and included large, flat hearts with compass stars in each lobe of the heart, continued by son John until 1825.

Built by master carpenters, the farmhouse on the Oscar Bieber farm is a high fashion English-Georgian type. Familiar with medallion circular boards incorporated in the stone gable ends of English homes and barns in the Oley Valley territory, the Biebers may have been the originators of the unique gable-end masoned hex signs that are found in the greater Kutztown area. Jacob Bieber and his son operated a pioneer sawmill near Lobachsville and supplied wood for building Berks County's early homes and barns.

Sunbursts or hex sign designs may have originated among emigrating Rhinelanders watching the mariner's compass star aboard 18th-century ships heading for America. These eight-pointed compass ship stars with black sawtooth-edge triangles in their circumference allowed sailors to navigate their ships and very likely served as an everlasting image for immigrants who were inspired to paint barn stars on their homesteads when they finally arrived in good health on the shores of the New World after a tedious and difficult voyage.

The hex sign medallion with a pinwheel center on the gable-end wall of the Snyder barn near Lenhartsville,[3] several miles north of the Bieber barn,

The Oscar Bieber family farm, dating back to 1801, features a unique eight-pointed hex sign with a sawtooth border recessed in the stone masonry of the barn's gable end. More astounding is the fact that the current owner, Moses Zimmerman, a historically minded Mennonite, spent 30 arduous hours repainting this rare gable-end hex sign in traditional ochre yellow and black colors.

The similarities between the medallion painted on the Snyder barn and the hex sign of the Bieber farm are certainly striking, though there are noticeable differences between the two.

appears similar. Dated "SK 1819 MK" for the original Kistler owner and wife, the owners were as proud of their barn as they were of their formal farmhouse. A few other rare gable-end medallion barns are found elsewhere in the county (though these are best saved for another discussion). However, the remarkable similarity of the Bieber-style sunburst hex sign to the Kistler hex sign (on the Snyder barn) with a pinwheel center leads to the conclusion that they may have been done by the same artist, and I am in agreement with Frances Lichten, in her 1954 book titled *Folk Art Motifs of Pennsylvania*, in that the earlier Bieber barn design, with a bold, black, sawtooth, circular border, does look more like the symbol of the sun, without which no farmer's crop can grow!

Hex sign–decorated Swiss bank barns are only found in the Pennsylvania Dutch Country of the Worldly or Church Dutch, not the Plain Dutch (Amish, Mennonites, or Brethren in Lancaster County and elsewhere in the Dutch Country), making Moses' restoration unique. The Church Dutch have always decorated their barns, homes, and furniture with rural folk art that has evolved since the early days of colonial immigration. The fraktur designs penned by folk artists on rare birth certificates with geometric star and sun shapes most likely inspired these rural people to extend their colorful geometric designs to the forebays of their otherwise mundane barns. But it was most unusual for a Mennonite couple to spend so much time restoring vestiges of a local Kutztown barn heritage, possibly the oldest one in the Dutch Country, as the Zimmermans did in tediously repainting the Bieber medallion.

One must recall, historically, that during the time of the Louisiana Purchase (1803) and thereafter American agriculture was prospering, and farmers became flamboyant in their building habits. The practice of industrious farmers putting architectural hex signs on their barns might very well be a legacy left from the republic's antebellum days of agrarian wealth. Academically speaking, in 1924, when New Englander Wallace Nutting coined the term "hexa-foos" (witch's foot) for Pennsylvania Dutch hex signs, he did not know anything about this traditional geometric American folk art. The colorful folk art images displayed by the religious-oriented Pennsylvania Dutch impressed this New Englander as being quite bizarre, yet significant enough to be included in his 1924 book, *Pennsylvania Beautiful* (eastern edition)— "a sort of demonic lightning rod," said Nutting of the barn designs.

Had Nutting written his book ten years later, he would have observed that the Pennsylvania Dutch fraktur practice of medieval hand-scribed illumination of native birth certificates with geometric designs had become the rage at national museums in the 1930s, as this art style was now recognized as early American folk art. Not being privy to the religious practices of Church Dutch congregations, Nutting's interpretation of the decorations as "witch's foot" was peculiar from the very instant he recorded it.

Dr. Alfred Shoemaker, in his extensive study *Pennsylvania Hex Marks* (1950), discovered that nowhere among the Pennsylvania Dutch in America or Rhinelanders in Germany was there any occult magic associated with the Germanic folk art symbolism linked to these popular barn stars or hex signs: "This hex sign myth was only popular among the uneducated or tourism writers who exaggerated the historic truth. I suppose there is always a percent of parents who scare their children into behaving righteously by using the fears of the Devil or witches to have their children follow proper farming practices or behavior."

Nonetheless, there may be no better Christians than the Pennsylvania Dutch, whose religious fraktur documents are illuminated with positive folk art, including the swirling swastika or, more politically correct, a whirling pinwheel design that was actually adopted from the native North Americans. Hex signs, correct in term but not in literal meaning, represent the overwhelming, enduring sense of pride in God and country that best defines the Pennsylvania Dutch, born of the soil and subservient to the Lord.

Part V

Amulets and the Lord's Protection from Evil

24

"Deivel's Dreck" and Other Rural Devices to Ward Off Evil

Witchcraft on the Farm

Most of the witchcraft lore discovered on the farm was employed either to prevent bewitchment or to break spells that had already occurred. In almost every instance, the means by which the farmer wished to break or prevent witchcraft was hidden from view or not very noticeable (unlike the hex signs painted on the barn fronts or forebays of so many of Pennsylvania Dutch barns, which were created purely as attractive decoration). To find real evidence of a belief in witchcraft among the Pennsylvania Dutch, one must look inside the decorated barns on the rafters of barn roofs, the lintels of doorways, and the less obvious peg holes. Hexerei, being an occult art, cannot be as readily noticeable as a six-foot barn star painted in gaudy colors on a forebay for the entire world to see.

There are doubtless many different Hexerei formulae that were used on the different farmsteads, and the methods may have varied considerably. Listed below are several types of formulae, both the exclusive and the commonplace.

WITCH BALL

In the Pennsylvania Dutch Country, farmers often selected for butchering the poorest of their milk-producing cows. In this way, they would build up a herd of only very good milkers. However, on occasion it was discovered after butchering that the cow had been bewitched and a large ball of hair had been shot into its stomach by a witch. This ball of hair (a hexballa) was of course the cause of the cow's limited milk capacity and the delight of the witch.

Hexa-Foos

To prevent witches from entering the barn to perform evil deeds, farmers sometimes drew or scratched a small five-pointed star on the door frame or sill, hidden from view.

Hex Letter

In all parts of the Pennsylvania Dutch Country, hex letters were written (often by hex doctors) and hidden in barns to prevent witches from entering and doing harm to the animals. Usually these letters were written in High German and concealed under boards in the rafters, or else they were put in peg holes. The following is a translation of a hex letter discovered at Macungie, Lehigh County, Pennsylvania, in 1935, which was hidden under a board:

> *Demon Head, I forbid thee my house and premises, I forbid thee my horse and cow stable, I forbid thee my bedstead, that thou mayest not breathe upon me, breathe into some other house, until thou hast ascended every hill, until thou hast counted every fence-post, and until thou hast crossed every water. And thus dear day may come again into my house, in the name of God the Father, the Son, and the Holy Ghost. Amen.*

Mercury Sacks

If the farmer discovered that several calves had been stillborn, he might suspect that the cows that bore them had been bewitched. In order to break this spell and continued bad luck, small muslin bags filled with mercury would be hung over each of the cow stalls. Subsequent calves would then not be expected to be born dead.

Devil's Dirt (Deivel's Dreck)

Similar to the above method, if a farmer discovered that his animals were bewitched and not behaving well, he would hang muslin bags of Devil's dirt (asafetida) above the stable doorway through which the animals would pass. Often, to prevent sickness in the Dutch Country, this herb was hung around a child's neck in a bag until the danger period was over.

Ferhext Horses

To prevent witches from hexing horses, a person would urinate in a pot, add oats to it, and feed the oats to the horses. Afterward, no witch would be able to put a spell on them.

ANIMAL BLOOD

To keep witches from entering the barn, the blood from both hogs and cows was mixed together and smeared over the top of each entrance to the stables.

POSSESSED ANIMALS

Animals that were possessed by evil spirits, and were a constant source of trouble, could only be killed by being shot with a silver bullet.

Witchcraft in the Home

Besides the bewitchment of people and farm animals, there is a considerable percentage of occult lore associated with the home and chores. Often, when a farmwoman found that she was having unusually bad luck, she would curse the woman she believed to be the witch who was causing it. For example, if the cider in the barrel would not turn to vinegar, the names of three suspected witches were shouted into the bunghole. It was believed by many folk that witches took great delight in making household chores difficult and in tormenting the farmer's wife and her helpers. The following selections show cases of bewitchment and solutions for stopping or preventing witchcraft in the home.

BEWITCHED CHURN

When butter would not churn, one had to put a red hot horseshoe into it. That would burn the witch out and bring the butter.

SILVER BALLS

When three small balls with silvery luster were found in the family dinner pot, that family had been bewitched. To break the spell, the silver balls would be shot into a white oak tree.

BROOMSTICK

To prevent a witch from entering the house, a broom would be placed across the doorway; no witch could then step over it.

SILVER BULLET

If one's butter churn was bewitched and the cream would not churn, a gun had to be loaded with silver and fired into the churn to kill the witch. If the milk was bewitched, the gun would be fired into the milk crock.

STOLEN PROPERTY

In the event of something having been stolen, three twigs from a tree would be placed on the axle of a wagon. Then the wagon wheel, with the twigs caught between the axle and the hub, would be replaced on the wagon. If the thief did not return the stolen property within one day, the wagon wheel would be turned around slowly; if this did not work, the next day the wheel would be turned faster and faster. Eventually, the thief would appear and sit on the tongue of the wagon, and he would be unable to move until the owner released him.

HAZEL SWITCHES

Should a butter churn be prevented from operating because of witchcraft, the churn would be lashed with hazel switches; after that, the witch would let the butter be churned.

REPULSING A WITCH

If one suspected a person of being a witch and feared that they would do harm, the next time one was in their company one would say (under one's breath), "Kiss my ass." This would certainly make the witch uneasy, and she would not be able to cause harm.

TESTING FOR A WITCH

If a person was believed to be a witch, when they came to call, a broom would be placed in the oven. As the broom became hotter and hotter, the witch would suffer and have to leave the house. If, however, the suspected person did not become restless and leave, they were safe and not a witch.

Furthermore, almost everyone who comes across Pennsylvania Dutch homemade cooking savors the food, but a few oldtimers remember Pennsylvania Dutch homemade recipes that were used to protect young children from catching deadly illnesses when going to an old-fashioned one-room schoolhouse. The folk tradition once followed in the 1930s and 1940s, practiced by the Pennsylvania Dutch in the Dutch Country, called for parents to protect their young with a small bag of asafetida, worn around the neck, when they went off to school.

Undoubtedly, in the winter months, children attending crowded schools were more apt to share contagious germs, which were more easily passed on in close quarters, especially one-room schools that were not heated sufficiently by old-fashioned pot-belly stoves. In an age without antibiotic knowledge or modern medicine, there were a number of individuals who blamed illnesses on Hexerei (evil causes); therefore an individual's illness was the work of the Devil or his associates.

Parents wishing to protect their children from illness in crowded quarters would and could go to a drugstore and order some asafetida, which had a terrible smell. Called in the Pennsylvania Dutch dialect "Deivel's Dreck" (Devil's dirt—a nice way of saying excrement), the asafetida was then bagged in muslin cloth bags. Worn around the neck, like an addition to one's undergarments, this secretive piece of apparel was used to ward off anyone who might get close enough to cast an evil spell, since the smell was really repulsive. In addition to keeping witches at bay, the end result of wearing these bags was that someone who had a contagious disease would probably not want to get too close either, meaning that you were safe from contact with this person and would not be a victim of that disease. In jest, older people referred to asafetida as Devil's dirt, feces, or worse because it was so revolting.

In this time period, it was not uncommon for several area barns, including one belonging to my own family, to be protected by nailing a lump of Devil's dirt in a muslin bag over each cow's stall, so that they would not give birth to stillborn calves. But in times of national emergencies, when individuals might resort to any means to protect themselves from dangerous epidemics, pharmacists might be asked for more of this ancient mixture to protect their customers in case it did actually have abnormal power.

Aside from the practice of protecting rural animals with bags of asafetida over the lintels of their stalls, the occult practice of foiling a witch with a small bag of mercury was also used by the Pennsylvania Dutch. In 1961, the Pennsylvania Folklife group found several mercury bags in the cow stalls of a stable in Bareville, Lancaster County, built in the late 1700s.

In more contemporary times, Deivel's Dreck has fallen out of use. Perhaps the practice was already obsolete or in decline when, in the 1960s, at the Kutztown Folk Festival, folklorist Donald Roan of the Goshenhoppen Historians interviewed individuals about the past practice of wearing Deivel's Dreck bags when they were young children. To his surprise, this folkway had only been prevalent among rural Americans. This was a topic heavily researched by the American Folklife Institute as well, and I often asked myself what this commonly used drug of yesterday could be. And why did it have such a picturesque Dutch name? I'd also be asked several questions while out on field research; the most frequent were: Why in the world would anyone use it? And how do you spell it?

Sometimes upon hearing these questions, I would just hand the other person a bag and say that to truly understand the meaning behind the name, it was best to take a long, deep smell of asafetida and discover the surprising essence that has been described as a mixture of garlic, onions, limburger cheese, and old feet. From this pungent odor, the German language had derived the name *Deivel's Dreck*, or devil's filth, or (more commonly translated from the dialect by oldtimers) devil's "shit." However, a few Berks Countians would fewer chuckle when Deivel's Dreck was mentioned, because it brought to mind the common story of the English (non–Dutch) salesman who stopped at a country store to exhibit his wares. The storekeeper asked if he carried Deivel's Dreck. The Englishman did not understand the dialect and, when told of the translation, replied, "The devil didn't 'shit' yet." Perhaps not the best story, but tell that to an old Dutchman over the age of 75.

The most frequently asked question was "How do you spell it?" The name can be properly spelled in its Latinized form (asafoetida) and in the accepted English form (asafetida). Many incorrect spellings have been attempted, the most common being the English folk-dialect form of "asafed-ity" or "assafedity" and "asafetity" or any combination of the letters used above. The English name is derived from the Latin *foetidus*, meaning fetid or having an offensive smell or stinking—a proper and fitting name for this drug. The colorful German name kept its spelling easy for the Pennsylvania Dutchmen, but the English name did cause difficulty.

A common tale in the Berks-Lehigh County area tells of a little boy who went into the town drugstore and asked for a nickel's worth of asafetida. Upon receiving his foul-smelling purchase, he told the druggist to charge the purchase. "What is the name?" the druggist asked. "Monroe Bennawell Glingel-heffer," came the reply. "Take your purchase and go," said the druggist angrily. "I will not spell Monroe Bennawell Glingelheffer and asafetida at the same time and on the same line."

In order to establish what asafetida is, it was necessary to go to an old-time pharmacologist and his resources. The natural order of asafetida is *Umbelliferae*, or, to relate it to more familiar terms, it is a member of the parsley family. Asafetida is native to Persia and India, and it is a large perennial herbaceous plant from six to nine feet high. The official drug is a gum resin obtained from the living roots of mature plants.[1] The drug can be best described as being made up of lumps or small masses of varying size (from the size of a pea to the size of a lump of stove coal), opaque, and white on cutting. But after short exposure to air, it becomes yellow-brown to brown in color. Now that a particular description has been furnished, the reader can go into the field and search for asafetida plants. (As ridiculous as this seems, once the origin of the plant was known to locals, a number of area people in all seriousness said they had family members who spent many years looking for asafetida plants.)

Historically the plant was first used by the ancient Assyrians and has come down to us in medicinal texts from the Middle East. During the Middle Ages, it was used extensively in Europe as a medicine and has been recorded as being prescribed by Galen, the father of pharmacy, as a medicine for "cold in the stomach." "From the more strictly therapeutic view, the outstanding characteristic of the Middle Ages is polypharmacy, the use of an enormous number of remedies of a fantastic or distinguishing character in a single mixture.[2] ... The Germans have an expressive term, 'Dreckapotheke'—filth pharmacy." Asafetida was one of the most popular drugs in this "filth pharmacy," possibly because of its unique odor. As medicine progressed and enlightenment came, these drugs were relegated to the herbalist, the quack, and the occultist.

Filth pharmacy did have one important effect, as it codified and cataloged many cabalistic, astrologic, and herbalist medical remedies into charms, many of which were worn around the neck to prevent diseases and in which the common people placed great faith. It was from this medieval influence that we derive one of the most common folk-medicinal remedies of the past generation—the asafetida bag. Contrary to the ideas of many Dutchmen, the asafetida bag was not only a common experience for the children of our area but also quite prevalent in most parts of the United States.

Many records exist in the American Folklife Institute's archives of people who willingly shared their bag-wearing experiences over the decades, and it can be geographically established that, throughout the rural Northeast, the wearing of asafetida bags was quite common. In addition, the Midwest and South also had an exceptionally large population of bag-wearing residents, as confirmed by fellow folklorists of the areas. It is interesting to note that among the rural southern African American culture, the practice of wearing an asafetida bag was as prevalent (and almost as long lasting) as in the Dutch Country. The two geographic areas of the country where the fewest examples of bag wearing were found seem to be the Southwest and New England; however, I believe there is enough evidence present to support the argument that it was also common to New England.

Asafetida bags were worn throughout rural America mostly until the 1920s and in the metropolitan areas until after the turn of the century, with the exception of their revival during the great influenza epidemic of 1915–

1920. It must be understood that the concept of a foul-smelling bag hung around the neck to prevent disease and keep away germs was not unique to rural America. The city dwellers, to be sure, wore asafetida bags, but on a very limited scale compared to the rural residents. Rather than asafetida bags, urban residents instead wore garlic or camphor bags for exactly the same purpose. This practice was limited more to the foreign element but was applicable to all groups. The children of South and Central European families wore garlic bags, while the children of Northern European parents tended to wear the camphor bag.

The wearing of asafetida (or, for that matter, camphor or garlic) bags seemed to be primarily confined to school children, but there are many cases of adults wearing them for the same purpose. The greatest period of adult use was most certainly in the aforementioned influenza epidemic. People were desperate to protect themselves from this scourge, and they tried the remedies their grandmothers had used. Those who had never worn a preventive bag, but had only heard of them, constituted the bulk of living metropolitan residents who recalled such an experience in our archives. Children of the Pennsylvania Dutch Country probably wore these bags longer than in many other parts of the country, with examples having been recorded mostly up to the late 1940s.

The diminution of the one-room schoolhouse, combined with the advent of bus transportation and the central school, brought about additional reluctance to wear such a foul-smelling device in public. Of course, there was always reluctance on the part of the child to wear such a bag, but "Mother always insisted that it must be worn" to keep away disease. Throughout the Pennsylvania Dutch Country, there were tales of the reluctant scholar who would discard his bag at the mailbox before leaving for school and return it to his neck as he returned. How did one determine who wore an asafetida bag? Obviously, one took a deep breath and was immediately informed of who had one.

It is most interesting to read the recorded comments of the rural school teachers who had to put up with these foul-smelling bags. Their opinions can be summed up with such colorful descriptions as "putrid, horrible, terrible, and thank God for spring when the windows could be opened." This last comment was especially apropos when one imagines every child, twenty to forty in a room, wearing a bag next to their warm bodies in a warm, woodstove-heated school room.

Every fall it was customary to send a child to the drug store or the country general store to purchase a nickel or a dime's worth of asafetida. For a nickel, the traditional amount, one could purchase a chip of one of the pharmacist's lumps, about the size of a lead pencil mounted eraser. This lump would be taken home and sewn into a small square or rectangular bag approximately one to one and a half inches in size. Although muslin seemed to be the most popular fabric, any material would do, and frequently the bags were quite colorful. A string was tied to one corner or "ear" of the bag in such a way that it would hang around the neck without visual detection.

Asafetida bags have been recorded as being used not only for the prevention of disease and protection from germs in general but also as a preventive for specific diseases. As protection against smallpox, an onion, garlic, sulfur, or a bag of asafetida was carried on one's person. These contents were supposed, on the one hand, to absorb the disease and, on the other, to ward it away through the offensive odor. Whooping cough was also supposedly prevented by putting an asafetida bag around one's neck. However, tradition also held that carrying a lump of asafetida in one's pocket had the same effect as the bag. This seems to have been the form most adults took when they used the drug for its preventive purposes.

The practice of carrying a plain lump of asafetida was not as widespread as wearing a bag, but it was nonetheless an accepted method of disease prevention in the Dutch Country, as it was elsewhere. Other medicinal forms of the use of the drug have been recorded in the past; the following comes from the Lebanon County Historical Society Papers, compiler or author unknown: "Nearly everyone wore an asafetida bag. I do believe the germs were afraid to come near on account of the dreadful odor if there was any truth in its being a preventative; many made each member of the house eat a tiny bit for breakfast. Eating this foul smelling drug seems a repulsive thought, but it was nonetheless used in this manner."

The practice of consuming the drug has also been recorded in the Dutch Country, but perhaps the most interesting example came from Mr. Chris Shirk, a former employee of the Wernersville State Hospital, Berks County, Pennsylvania, a century ago. Shirk was interviewed in the winter of 1920 and stated, "Every patient at the hospital was given an internal dose of one-half ounce of asafetida (interval unknown) for the prevention of disease." Wilbert Gaul, pharmacist of Kutztown, Pennsylvania, told interviewers that he had an elderly customer living in Kutztown who at that time still purchased asafetida for internal use, documented around the 1950s: "She takes a pea-size piece and eats an onion for her breakfast every day. She has never been sick a day in her life to my knowledge." Mr. Gaul further explained, "Internal dosages of asafetida was frequently taken for a bad stomach." Most advocates of this form related that it did help digestion. Although the practice of eating the drug was not nearly as common as wearing it or carrying it externally, it was used internally as a home remedy by many people.

The practice had diminished by the 1940s, but it was still practiced on a limited scale throughout the Dutch Country in the 1960s, when it seemed to have almost disappeared elsewhere. Asafetida was used for many purposes in addition to its medicinal value. If taken internally, the drug acts as a carminative, producing stomach gas and, if consumed in larger quantities, intestinal gas. An old gentleman living in Lehigh County said, "When we were young, we were 'son-of-a-bitches' in school. We used to eat Deivel's Dreck in the morning before coming to school, so that we could 'fart' in school." At Lebanon Valley College in the 1930s, asafetida was given to prospective fraternity brothers in the morning—unidentified, to be sure—for the same purpose.

Related back to folklore in the rural areas, asafetida was also very useful to the farmer. Asafetida was a common remedy for a horse that had stomach gas from eating wet food, and it was given to the animal to create more gas and make natural passage possible. Fred Bieber, of New Jerusalem, said, "If a horse has too much gas in his belly, give him '*asafisic*' to make him belch." Another past use by farmers was for chicken lice, where finely ground asafetida was placed in the chicken feed to help keep down the lice. This was quite common in the eastern Lancaster County area and, furthermore, practiced by the Team Mennonites in the Kutztown area. The drug was an extremely common remedy for horse colic, just as it was in smaller doses a remedy for the same disease in humans. Again, as with the chicken lice control, it was placed in the feed of the animal.

Farm boys used the drug to attract pigeons, and lumps were placed on top of the barn wall, on the ledge that formed where the gable end met the wall, and on the rafters. The boys could then stand on top of the high-piled hay of the hay den and capture the birds as they landed, which proved to be a good source of pocket money. Asafetida was also used by outdoorsmen, and many fishermen used it to mix in with dough bait; one recipe called for a mixture of sugar and boiled cornmeal, which was a sure method of attracting and catching catfish. A wife of a county official in Lancaster County reported that her husband used it as skunk bait for trapping. The observation made here is that one stench must attract another, equally obnoxious one.

With a name like Deivel's Dreck, one must presume that this drug is associated with the occult of the Dutch Country. This assumption is correct and can be traced in part to John George Hohman in his *Long Lost Friend*: "To Prevent Evil Persons from Getting to the Cattle in the Stable. Take wormwood, black caraway, cinquefoil (five-finger grass), and asafetida of each three cents worth; take a hog's bean straw, the sweepings from behind the door of the stable, and a little salt, all mixed together and placed in a little bundle in a hole in the threshold where the cattle pass in and out, and plug the hole with lotus wood. It certainly helps."

One photo in my collection shows a Deivel's Dreck bag over the cow stable threshold on the Fred Bieber farm near New Jerusalem, Pennsylvania. This bag had been there for about sixty years, as the barn was rebuilt just after the turn of the century. The farm previously belonged to the Delong family, and Fred believed that someone was bothering the cattle by either stealing their milk or stopping them from eating; for this reason, the bags were placed above the door. It must be noted that generally every animal entrance was so protected, and Fred's bags remained in good condition, although the smell was no longer evident. Fred further explained that the Delong family had the "hexa-notion"—that is, they believed strongly in Hexerei. How prevalent this practice was in the past is very difficult to ascertain because of the easily destructible nature of the cloth and the organic matter within. However, it can be assumed to have been a common practice in the past, as were the rest of the Hexerei practices of the Dutch Country.

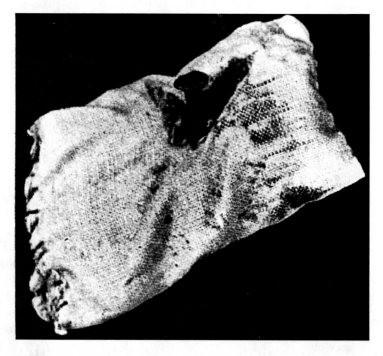

Discovered in the 1960s, this bag of Deivel's Dreck was found on the lintel of a cow stable in the Oley Hills and contains asafetida, the universal substance used by local residents to repulse witches; mercury was sometimes used for the same purpose (photograph c. 1962).

Those who believed in Hexerei said that if asafetida was carried on one's person, either in lumps or in bags, it would ward off evil spirits and keep one safe. An old gentleman who lived in Fredericksville, Pennsylvania, was given a "bag of Deivel's Dreck" by a Pennsylvania Dutch neighbor. He later avowed that he always carried his bag in his pocket, day and night, and for the first time in twenty years since his wife died, he was able to sleep the whole night through, as someone had previously been "bothering him" during the night.

Another excellent method of keeping evil spirits or persons away was related by an elderly informant living near Mertztown, Pennsylvania: take asafetida, bread, and salt and place them in a bag worn around the neck. The informant recalled wearing one as a child. He had eaten jelly bread at an old woman's house in the neighborhood, and after that he could not eat—a sure sign that someone was bothering him. His mother placed a bag around his neck, and his appetite was restored.

So what is the status of asafetida in the 21st century? It has been called an obsolete drug by pharmacists in the Pennsylvania Dutch Country, though it was still known or remembered by its local folk. It was still produced in its traditional form (lumps) by S.B. Penick and Company (a major supplier of raw drugs in the country at the time) up to the late 1970s. In addition, it was being produced in a pill form that had also succumbed to the 20th century, packaged as "chocolate covered pills." These pills were produced by the Eli Lilly Company, a national distribution company, and by such local companies as Park Brothers and Hance Brothers and White of Philadelphia. The following statement appeared on the label of the Lilly product (and was similar to that appearing on the other manufacturers' products): "These tablets are useful as a carminative for the relief of flatulent colic." Pharmacopoeias and dispensatories of the first part of the 20th century credit the drug as being a "stimulant and antispasmodic used in croup, hysteria, spasmodic nervous diseases of females, colic, and minute doses for increase of mammary secretion, and functional wrongs of the stomach." Later editions seem to have placed the drug in the background, although none of the earlier information was removed.[3]

A geographic check of the Pennsylvania Dutch Country in the American Folklife Institute's archives shows that the drug was widely available only in the first half of the 20th century, and after that mostly had completely disappeared, except for the random country store where it could be purchased up to the late 1960s. The towns of Intercourse and Strasburg, Lancaster County, reported that they have not carried it for decades, beyond the 1960s, as did Huff's Church and Lenhartsville, Berks County. Pikeville, in Berks County, carried it until sometime in the 1950s. Some merchants said that they kept a supply on hand for a few years after the demand stopped but eventually discontinued it. Schwenksville, Montgomery County, did not carry the drug in its traditional form, but it once had the pill form, with no sales or recollections having been recorded for the drug past the 1950s. Honey Brook, Chester County, reported carrying it only in the traditional form, mainly for an oldtimer who used it for fish bait. Strasburg, Lancaster County, reported no calls since the early 1950s and has not carried any in stock since then, but at New Holland, Lancaster County, it was purchased in the 1960s. Lebanon City reported that it had an account of the drug being purchased as Deivel's Dreck in 1963.

At Kutztown, Berks County, where the institute's offices are located, there are a few reports of vendors in the town carrying the drug in both traditional and pill form well over half a century ago. But a most vivid account of the status of asafetida in the early 1960s came from Wilbert Gaul's oldtime pharmacy in Kutztown, courtesy of a former employee, Roxie (Mosser) Reidenauer, before her death at age 94, as well as surviving members of Gaul's family who shared stories, old purchase records, Gaul's notes, and even photos retained of the family's early pharmacy. In examining the old, blurred photos, one can see that Gaul both stocked and sold the drug and even placed asafetida in a position of prominence on a shelf in the front part of the prescription room that was situated immediately behind the store.

It is also interesting to note that in 1963, when the pictures were taken, such raw drugs as sassafras bark, mace, sweet marjoram, aniseed, Spanish saffron, whole and ground flaxseed, powdered rhubarb, Pluto water, and dog oil were still obtainable and being dispensed. The Pennsylvania Dutch have long had a tradition of collecting medicinal plants from the woods, fields, and gardens, and these few drugs were among the most popular used sixty years ago or more. Although most of these drugs had fallen out of use and were no longer readily available in the 1960s, Mr. Gaul, and other pharmacists throughout the Dutch Country, still made it possible to obtain these "valuable" and "effective" remedies of yesteryear..

So, to answer the question about the use of asafetida, if it were available to purchase today, it would most likely be bought for such purposes as fish and animal bait and not to ward off evil or sickness. However, I am convinced that a very few from the oldest of generations in the area would still use it for either medicinal or occult reasons. Its use as a disease preventive in bags or other forms seems to have become antediluvian by the 1940s, but it is not impossible to find a bag or two in rural barns and outbuildings. And if you happen to come upon a bag in the Pennsylvania Dutch Country, take a good sniff and see!

Pennsylvania Dutch Traditions of the All-Seeing Eye (of Jesus Christ)

Among the oldtime traditions of the Pennsylvania Dutch people are the 18th-century broadside amulets that have been handed down from colonial times and that have become iconic good luck charms among devout Christian families who live in southeastern Pennsylvania, as well as French Huguenot pioneer descendants who live in New York State. Always written in the German dialect, these Himmelsbriefs, published in German, were amulets of religious folk beliefs and a reminder of native Christian folklife that protected each family from evil or calamity and unfortunate health hazards if practiced in conjunction with a Christian folklife.

Among the most popular Himmelsbriefs (letters from God) was the one dropped from Heaven at Magdeburg, Germany, in 1783. Many of the Himmelsbriefs feature an "all-seeing eye" at the top of the broadside or in some other prominent position. Almost every Pennsylvania German press was known to have printed one or two styles of Himmelsbriefs for the people of its locale. In order to save space and paper, some of the 18th-century letters from Heaven were simply titled "Ein Brief." Of course, these early artifacts in black ink were published in German for the Pennsylvania Dutch community; rarely did one find any early English briefs in the Pennsylvania Dutch Country dating to the 19th century!

More personalized "Ein Brief" German reprint letters were about seven by nine inches in size, made for soldiers to fold and carry secretly when they fought in wars. One such Pennsylvania Dutch soldier, who sought to verify his enlistment with Washington in the Revolution, used his worn "Ein Brief," which he carried for protection, as proof to claim his veteran's land benefit in the Northwest Territory. His "Ein Brief" now in the Washington, D.C., archives. During World War II (1942), the Allentown *Morning*

This 9" × 15" Magdeburg "Ein Brief" copy (dated 1895) was published by Jessie G. Hawley at 542 Penn Street, Reading, Pennsylvania. An all-seeing eye printed below the title persuaded believers of God's omnipotent power.

This European "all-seeing eye" amulet is a counterpart to the American ones, but the message is the same, reflective of an all-knowing God. Antique dealer Robert Merritt would bring these items to America from his treasure-hunting trips in Europe.

Ein Brief,

so von GOTT selbst geschrieben und zu Magdeburg nieder-gelassen worden ist.

Er war mit goldenen Buchstaben geschrieben und von GOTT durch einen Engel ge-sandt worden; wer ihn abschreiben will, dem soll man ihn geben, wer ihn verachtet, von dem weicht der HERR.

Wer am Sonntage arbeitet der ist verflucht. Demnach gebiete ich, daß ihr am Sonntage nicht arbeitet, sondern andächtig in die Kirche gehet; aber euer Angesicht nicht schmücket; ihr sollt nicht fremdes Haar tragen und sollt nicht Hoffahrt treiben; von eurem Reichthum sollt ihr den Armen geben, reichlich mittheilen und glauben, daß dieser Brief mit meiner eigenen Hand geschrieben und von Christo selbsten ausgesandt sey und daß ihr nicht thut wie das un-vernünftige Vieh; ihr habt sechs Tage in der Woche, darin sollt ihr eure Arbeit verrichten, aber den siebenten (nämlich den Sonntag) sollt' ihr heiligen; werdet ihr das nicht thun, so will ich Krieg, Hunger, Pestilenz und Theuerung unter euch schicken und euch mit vielen Pla-gen strafen. Auch gebiete ich euch, einen Jeden, es sey wer es wolle, Jung und Alt, Klein und Groß, daß ihr am Samstag nicht spät arbeitet, sondern ihr sollt eure Sünden bereuen, auf daß sie euch mögen vergeben werden. Begehret auch nicht Silber oder Gold; treibet nicht Bosheit; meidet des Fleisches-Lust und Begierden; denkt daß ich euch gemacht habe und wie-der zernichten kann. Freuet euch nicht wenn euer Nachbar arm ist, habt vielmehr Mitleiden mit ihm, so wird's euch wohl gehen. Ihr Kinder ehret Vater und Mutter, so wird's euch wohl gehen auf Erden. Wer dieses nicht glaubt noch hält, der ist verdammt und verloren. Ich JESUS habe dieses selbsten mit meiner eigenen Hand geschrieben, wer es widerspricht und lästert, derselbe Mensch soll keine Hülfe von mir zu erwarten haben; wer den Brief hat und ihn nicht offenbaret, der ist verflucht von der christlichen Kirche und wenn eure Sünden noch so groß wären, sollen sie euch, wo ihr herzlich Reue und Leid habt, doch vergeben werden. Wer es nicht glaubet der soll sterben und in der Hölle gepeinigt werden und ich werde am jüng-sten Tage fragen um eurer Sünden willen, da ihr mir denn antworten müsset. Und derjenige Mensch so diesen Brief bey sich träget, oder in seinem Hause hat, dem wird kein Donnerwet-ter Schaden zufügen, er wird für Feuer und Wasser sicher seyn; und wer ihn offenbaret vor den Menschenkindern, der wird seinen Lohn haben und fröhliches Abscheiden aus dieser Welt empfangen. Haltet meinen Befehl den ich euch durch meinen Engel gesandt habe. Ich, wah-rer Gott vom Himmels-Thron, Gottes und Marien Sohn. Amen.

Dieses ist geschehen zu Magdeburg, im Jahr 1783.

This individual-sized traditional 1783 Magdeburg Himmelsbrief (about 7" × 9") was printed in German by a Pennsylvania German press in the early 19th century. These versions were most likely printed for Pennsylvania Dutch soldiers for protection in wartime or on the dangerous frontier.

Call published the 1783 Magdeburg Himmelsbrief in English to protect native soldiers and their patriotic families. The Magdeburg letter from Heaven was the most frequently printed German brief by the local Pennsylvania German press.

The rarest of broadsides were the Pennsylvania imprints made by local German village presses like the one in Kutztown, Pennsylvania. Isaac F. Christ printed a 19th-century, post–Civil War 14" × 17" Magdeburg broadside with beautiful hand-colored borders in a period frame, decorated in red, white, and blue in a patriotic theme for patrons. Originally, in the early 1800s, sacred Himmelsbriefs were purchased by Pennsylvania Dutch families and merely

Printed in the 1860s by the native Kutztown German press, this broadside is in the original Victorian frame that its owner, Annie K. Feick, acquired while living in Berks County. The red, white, and blue colors were symbolic of the Civil War period.

tucked away in their large family Bibles. They were considered a good omen that would protect individual members of the family, as well as the household as a whole, from fire, flood, and pestilence. Thus, some of these early broadsides are often found with many creases from being folded and pressed.

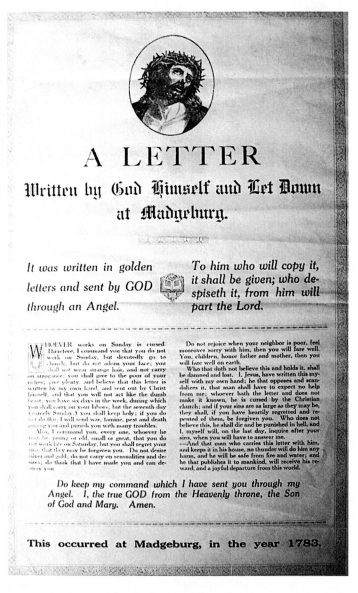

The most popular Himmelsbrief, the Magdeburg brief, can sometimes be found printed in an English translation, as seen here.

In the Victorian period, some printers published large "public copies" of the Himmelsbrief, as well as the Lord's Prayer, with artistic engravings to display on one's walls. But for the most part, these amulets were kept secret, hidden from view. As late as the year 2000, there was hardly a Pennsylvania Dutch family that could not remember some kind of folk belief legend in keeping a Rhineland Christian letter from Heaven in their home.[1]

According to Pennsylvania Dutch archivist Dr. Wilbur H. Oda (1892–1953), there were no less than eight such historic heavenly letters over the years. Oda was the head of the Modern Language Department of Philadelphia's Germantown Academy for twenty-five years and an authority on Pennsylvania Dutch books and broadside imprints; he resided near Huffs Church, Berks County. Of these various religious letters, most of them required that there should be no work done on the Sabbath, as that the day must be kept holy. "As far as a belief in heavenly protection that the Letter would ensure its owner, perhaps our sophisticated modern Christian times (with advancing medicines) have outgrown that type of assurance," stated Dr. Oda.[2]

These heavenly letters, nonetheless, were an integral part of the 19th-century psyche of the Pennsylvania Dutch people, whose religious beliefs were the heart of their moral communities. More than a few soldiers who survived the world war years carrying Himmelsbriefs into action would not doubt the efficacy of their mystical powers!

26

Folk Legend of the Pennsylvania Dutch "Himmelsbriefs" (Letters from Heaven)

Many times in field interviews with an old Dutchman, I will conclude the interview by asking if he is carrying a Himmelsbrief. Over the years (and even in the present day), I have chronicled several Pennsylvania Dutchmen carrying copies of *Himmelsbriefs* (translated as "holy letters" or "letters from Heaven") as something of a passport to Heaven, in case of unfortunate circumstances. Even into the 20th century these letters were carried by many a Dutchman in wartime, heavily promoted or purchased by Pennsylvania Dutch farmwomen worried for their sons.

Like the Pilgrims of New England, Pennsylvania Dutch people were a very religious lot, and wherever they settled they built churches or meeting-houses, which were the most important buildings in their communities. One need only look at a road map of Pennsylvania to notice all the biblical town names in the Dutch Country, from historic Moravian-founded Bethlehem, Emmaus, and Nazareth to the humble town in the Oley Hills known as New Jerusalem. Some typical Pennsylvania Dutch churches (for example, historic 1754 Salem UCC in Oley) still hold dinners for the public at large and the congregation made by their farmwomen consisting of age-old delights such as ham and dandelion.

In examining the agricultural goods sold at the colonial port of Philadelphia, it can be seen that Pennsylvania Dutch housewives enhanced their families' income by making numerous loaves of hearth-baked bread (the staff of life, body of Christ), sweet butter, and other foodstuffs that were exchanged or bartered for the necessities of life required to raise their families. In the Oley Valley and surrounding Kutztown area in Berks County, there are more than a few colonial farmsteads with outdoor bakeovens in which Dutch housewives baked bread to trade in various farm markets; they were used so

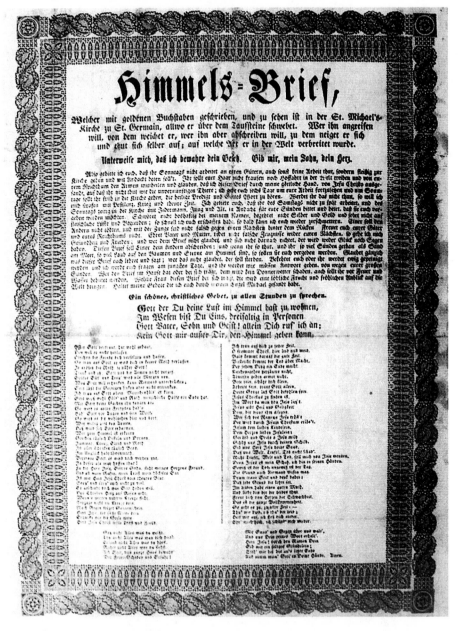

This rare Saint-Germain Himmelsbrief was printed by an anonymous Pennsylvania German press in Berks County (possibly for John George Hohman, a native peddler of Christian religious broadsides), circa 1836. It is not as elaborate as the 1811 Saint-Germain brief printed at Hellertown, Pennsylvania. It was found in a local German Bible and later duplicated for citizens at the Kutztown Folk Festival in the 1960s.

frequently that many of these brick arched crowns collapsed from overheating.[1]

Furthermore, yards and yards of homespun cloth were woven on looms to cover the huge 19th-century Conestoga wagons for the family's weekly trips to the port of Philadelphia, engaging in the early American textile industry. The colorful homes in the Dutch Country would be bare if it were not for the compulsive sewing and weaving skills of these farmwomen, who, when not doing farm chores, labored to provide necessary clothing and bedsteads. Dutchwomen were more interested in providing for the wholesome needs of their families than fashionable dress for themselves. In fact, many a Dutchman surprised his wife with expensive early American dishware to adorn their cupboards, as presentation pieces for these hard-working women who seemingly labored more than 24/7 a week.

As mentioned earlier, holy letters are another English descript known in the Pennsylvania Dutch dialect as "Himmelsbriefs." When I was a teenager and my mother remarried an old Dutchman (Victor Miller), he showed me his personal holy letter, which, according to Pennsylvania Dutch folk beliefs, will keep the holder safe from accidental death unless it is the Lord's will. He had carried it in his wallet, folded, since his time fighting in Japan during World War II, and he continued to carry it until his death in 1998. As was customary, his holy letter (which he often credited with having saved his life during a heavily bombed encounter in the war) was placed with him for the afterlife.

In some respects, the Reformation period of Europe's 16th-century Christendom was kept alive among the early ancestors of the rural Pennsylvania Dutch people via their patronage of the 18th- and 19th-century German presses in America. Besides German Bibles, catechisms, and religious tracts printed by pioneer German immigrants for their new American citizens, house blessings and letters from Heaven were published from Europe's historic medieval period.

Tradition says that the original heavenly letter was delivered by an angel (Gabriel, Michael) and was inscribed with gold ink, as a sign that it was indeed a communication from the Lord. Reprints of these "briefs" often stated where the letter was dropped from Heaven and the historic year when it appeared. The religious text of most Himmelsbriefs is a Christian one, warning all Christians to follow the straight and narrow path and to be devout in worship, also taking care of the poor and needy and not living a life of vanity and sin.

Whether the original Himmelsbrief was a revelation by an inspired penman from a Christian monastery, written with gilded lettering and left for

This particular Himmelsbrief measures 15¾" × 12¾" and is from Saint-Germain, France. It was printed in German in the 19th century, with the angel announcing its arrival, and was found among the local Pennsylvania Dutch farmers. This broadside is one of the rarer prints with a woodcut.

the people to discover, cannot be known for certain. Regardless, this beautiful golden text certainly made an everlasting impression, encouraging people to follow the Lord's teachings down through the ages. A human rights obeserver might suspect that the motive of a medieval heavenly letter may not have been solely religious, for all Himmelsbriefs warn that there should not be any work done on the Sabbath (Sunday), which is a day of rest. During the

Humble Christians may display a *Haus Segen* (house blessing), still printed in the native Pennsylvania Dutch language, that was created by an earlier generation to invoke God's Christian blessing on the entire family, similar to a Himmelsbrief.

Middle Ages, serfs and people serving certain lords and merchants were unjustly forced to work on Sunday to gain an economic edge over their competitors, violating Moses's second commandment (perhaps another motivation of the unknown pensman).

However, unique among various religious texts when brought to the

New World, the Himmelsbriefs were marketed by enterprising printers throughout the early American period, bringing God's protection to individuals and entire households. Although not expressly stated in these reprinted religious broadside copies, the common folk belief among the Pennsylvania Dutch was that if a person had a Himmelsbrief in his home or carried it with him, this Christian person would be protected from fire, flood, and pestilence, and he would not die unless it was the will of the Lord Himself. Some reprinted letters from Heaven were artistically printed with ornate borders framing the text or letter, believed to have been written by God and sent down to earth.

In the Pennsylvania Dutch community of Allentown, there was a great fire that consumed a large portion of town in 1848, because apprentices were forced to work for a tobacconist on Ascension Day, June 1 that year (May 10th in 2018), which was a religious holiday. However, this punishment was not the Lord's doing, but rather the work of a disgruntled laborer, according to the local newspaper.[2] The Sunday "Blue Laws" that once limited Pennsylvania's retail sales on the Sabbath were also fostered by this humanitarian Heaven-letter legacy.

Among the most uncommon local briefs are the St. Germain briefs (undated), found in France. One such early letter from Heaven was printed in German with a wood cut of an angel blowing a horn with a local printed typeface border. Its text most likely dates from an earlier 1800 Pennsylvania printing. Having lectured about charms and good omens, I was not surprised when a truck driver from Pittsburgh, Pennsylvania, showed me his small, personal Himmelsbrief, which he carried in his wallet. Engaged in a life-defying occupation of hauling steel, he felt more secure when carrying the Lord's letter with him for protection against the dangerous shifting of his steel load.

Since working under the lineage tree of the father of the American folklife studies movement, Dr. Alfred L. Shoemaker, I have collected a number of early printed Himmelsbrief broadsides in the Dutch Country, their popularity ranking next to itinerant printed German birth and baptismal fraktur broadsides of the time. They are usually found folded neatly in the large German Bibles with other sacred family papers. Perhaps no exhibit better illustrated the importance of this folk belief than that by Richard Machmer, a Pennsylvania Dutch scholar who gathered and examined a large collection of Pennsylvania German imprint broadsides, which were cataloged in a Berks County Historical Society special issue, showcasing this significant collection.

Of all the Pennsylvania Dutch sacred and secular broadsides that have been published, perhaps none is more unique than the one created by Reading printer Heinrich B. Sage, who printed a large copy of the 1776 Declaration of

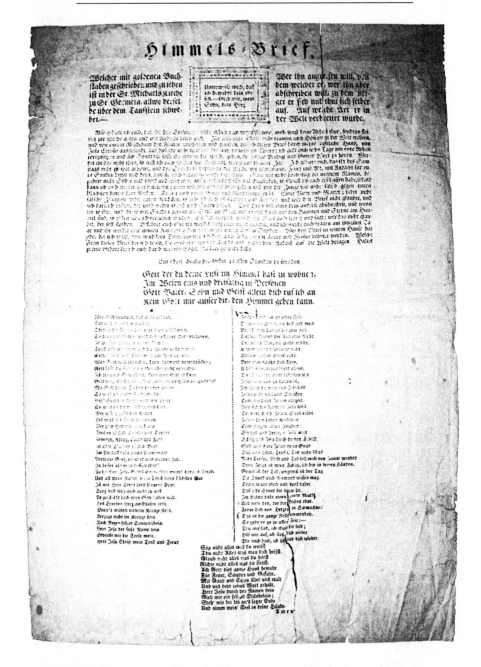

A 1783 Magdeburg Himmelsbrief in German, printed by the Pennsylvania German press in the early 19th century, would be hung in the family home in order to protect individuals from evil and house fire in the Dutch Country.

An outstanding collector of Pennsylvania Dutch fraktur art (like his colleague, Dr. Donald Shelley), Richard Machmer was also an authority on Berks County tall case clocks and many other antiques of the Pennsylvania Dutch Country. Dick arranged this extraordinary folk art exhibit for the Berks County Historical Society in 2001 to display local fraktur examples, which included briefs and other imprints falling under the umbrella of fraktur.

Independence in German in the early 1800s, on its 50th anniversary. Printed for all native-speaking Dutchmen to read and celebrate, it was complete with engravings for all thirteen original colonies. This 1826 broadside is in the collection of the Historical Society of Berks County (now Berks History Center)

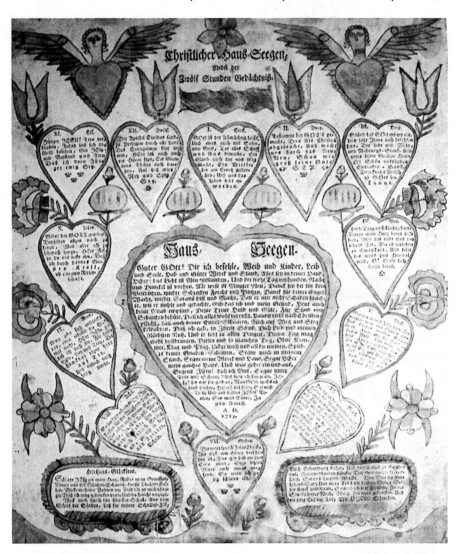

This rare 1785 fraktur *Haus Seegen* was done by Friedrich Speyer (1774–1801), an itinerant scrivener who sold his Pennsylvania German broadsides in Berks County. This particular format is similar to a German house blessing broadside printed at Augsburg, Germany, in the 18th century. Known as the Christian house blessing, it included a 12-hour religious reminder in the text through each additional heart.

and was indeed a commemorative memorial to all Berks Rhinelanders who had served under General George Washington to fight for our liberty and freedom.

Nowhere in our nation were there more diverse people from Europe who appreciated the right to "freedom of religion" that the new republic achieved. When John George Hohman, Berks County's famous compiler of sympathetic medicine and faith healing, arrived from Germany in 1802, he brought and reprinted the Grodoria Himmelsbrief to peddle and sell in order to pay off his indenture for his ship passage to America; after that time, he also printed a catechism for the Roman Catholic Church of the Holy Sacrament at Bally, Pennsylvania.[3]

The folk belief of the Lord's protection embodied in something physical among the Pennsylvania Dutch was so intense that Berks Countians created the following publications of these "letters from Heaven" after the United States officially entered World War I in 1917: The 1724 "Holstein Himmelsbrief" was printed in English at Oley, Pennsylvania, in 1917 by village printer Charles Bower; a German version was produced at Boyertown in 1918. The 1750 "Frauen Letter" found at Cologne, Germany, was reprinted in Reading by Reverend I.M. Beaver in 1917, as well as the "Magdeburg Brief" (circa 1918). The irony of Pennsylvania Dutch soldiers and European Germans carrying "Himmelsbriefs" for God's protection in both world wars was indeed an anomaly for these Rhineland descendants of early Christendom.

A prisoner of World War II in Germany, Dr. Alfred L. Shoemaker, is said to have come across a German child's nursery book titled *77 Nursery Rhymes for Our Little Ones*,[4] with sayings identical to those he had heard from his own German dialect–speaking grandmother in America. For a brief period in the war, he stated, he was emotionally transported back to Pennsylvania, where his immigrant ancestors had fled to avoid terrible European wars. Shoemaker, a pacifist working in army intelligence, was forced to carry a gun, but he kept it unloaded, according to his friends.

According to Rudolph Stube, the German authority on Germanic-type letters from Heaven, there are at least twenty such types found in countries from India to Iceland, some of which predate Christ's birth. Himmelsbriefs also circulated among other German and ethnic printers in America.[5] These religious reminders for Judeo-Christians were meant to help the less fortunate and needy, which inspired America's "corporate social conscious movement." The legend of the Lord's omnipotent power to reward faithful followers through these sacred letters had no small part in individuals seeking protection from mortal sickness or unnatural death itself.

In 1833, a German copy of the 1783 Magdeburg "Ein Brief" was printed by William Siegfried for his rural Pennsylvania Dutch Sunday School class

Ein Brief,

so von GOTT selbst geschrieben und zu Magdeburg niedergelassen worden ist.

Er war mit goldenen Buchstaben geschrieben und von GOTT durch einen Engel gesandt worden; wer ihn abschreiben will, dem soll man ihn geben, wer ihn verachtet, von dem weicht der HERR.

Wer am Sonntage arbeitet, der ist verflucht. Demnach gebiete ich, daß ihr am Sonntage nicht arbeitet, sondern andächtig in die Kirche gehet; aber euer Angesicht nicht schmücket; ihr sollt nicht fremdes Haar tragen und sollt nicht Hoffahrt treiben; von eurem Reichthum sollt ihr den Armen geben, reichlich mittheilen und glauben, daß dieser Brief mit meiner eigenen Hand geschrieben und von Christo selbsten ausgesandt sey, und daß ihr nicht thut wie das unvernünftige Vieh; ihr habt sechs Tage in der Woche, darin sollt ihr eure Arbeit verrichten, aber den siebenten (nämlich den Sonntag) sollt' ihr heiligen; werdet ihr das nicht thun, so will ich Krieg, Hunger, Pestilenz und Theuerung unter euch schicken und euch mit vielen Plagen strafen. Auch gebiete ich euch, einen Jeden, es sey wer es wolle, Jung und Alt, Klein und Groß, daß ihr am Samstag nicht spat arbeitet, sondern ihr sollt eure Sünden bereuen, auf daß sie euch mögen vergeben werden. Begehret auch nicht Silber oder Gold; treibet nicht Bosheit; meidet des Fleisches Lust und Begierden; denkt, daß ich gemacht habe und wieder zernichten kann. Freuet euch nicht wenn euer Nachbar arm ist, habt vielmehr Mitleiden mit ihm, so wird's euch wohl gehen. Ihr Kinder, ehret Vater und Mutter, so wird's euch wohl gehen auf Erden. Wer dieses nicht glaubt noch hält, der ist verdammt und verloren. Ich, JESUS, habe dies selbsten mit meiner eigenen Hand geschrieben, wer es widerspricht und lästert, derselbe Mensch soll keine Hülfe von mir zu erwarten haben; wer den Brief hat und ihn nicht offenbaret, der ist verflucht von der christlichen Kirche, und wenn eure Sünden noch so groß wären, sollen sie euch, wo ihr herzlich Reue und Leid habt, doch vergeben werden. Wer es nicht glaubet, der soll sterben und in der Hölle gepeinigt werden, und ich werde am jüngsten Tage fragen um eurer Sünden willen, da ihr mir denn antworten müsset. Und derjenige Mensch, so diesen Brief bei sich träget, oder in seinem Hause hat, dem wird kein Donnerwetter Schaden zufügen, er wird vor Feuer und Wasser sicher seyn; und wer ihn offenbaret vor den Menschenkindern, der wird seinen Lohn haben und fröhliches Abscheiden aus dieser Welt empfangen. Haltet meinen Befehl, den ich euch durch meinen Engel gesandt habe. Ich, wahrer Gott vom Himmels-Thron, Gottes und Marien Sohn. Amen.

Dieses ist geschehen zu Magdeburg, im Jahr 1783.

A 1783 Magdeburg Himmelsbrief copied in German and printed in Pennsylvania to protect soldiers in the War of 1812. It was intended to be folded and carried on one's person. A similar brief hung locally in the Maxatawny church in the 19th century, a longstanding Reformed church.

at Zion Union Church in Maxatawny, Pennsylvania. He was a deacon and elder of the Reformed congregation of this Berks County church. Dr. Don Yoder has featured this local brief in his *Pennsylvania German Broadside.* According to the late Dr. Yoder, "Letters from Heaven are not normally part of formal church religion, but our deep-seated Germanic roots embracing age old folk religion cannot be denied."[6]

Furthermore, angels delivering heavenly letters or adorning many folk art birth and baptismal broadsides were an integral part of Germanic Pennsylvania Dutch heritage from Europe. Antique dealer Robert Merritt Jr., who imported antiques from Europe for many years (to the delight of collectors), passed on European briefs in later years, lamenting that "the price was now too high." He was not talking about the exchange rate of the dollar bill but the fact that modern Europeans had finally realized that these items were very valuable, and they now will not part with these treasures. Having lost so many valuable artifacts in two world wars, Europeans now communicate with the American Folklife Institute concerning what German immigrants brought to America two and three centuries ago. Broadsides, rare books, furniture, and folk art still survive from the 17th, 18th, and 19th centuries and are admired by Americans and learned natives of the Pennsylvania Dutch Country.

Printed Broadside Documents Further Explained

A broadside was a document or notice printed on one side of a sheet of paper (this at a time when paper was a scarce commodity). It can be a religious or political text printed for the benefit of the reader—a communication worthy of being set up in Guttenberg's movable type, or else printed from a carved wooden block. "Importance" is associated with the text of early broadsides by the mere fact that they were considered vital enough to be printed in this form, usually with a border. Birth and death notices provided vital information, as did important moral ballads and religious teachings common in early America.

Most common among all broadsides were the printed fraktur birth and baptism certificates that were peddled by learned artists who would go from door to door to fill them out and decorate them for individuals who did not have a suitable announcement of their birth, as a remembrance. It was also customary for local Pennsylvania Dutch children to attach their illuminated broadside birth certificates to the undersides of the lids to their dower chests.

A great believer in the power of a Christian Himmelsbrief, Dr. Shoemaker was once presented with a Magdeburg heavenly letter printed on the back of an American dollar bill, which he carried in his wallet when traveling to Germany. He apologetically told the gift bearer later that he used it for an unexpected express train fare in Germany. Later, I came across one of these Magdeburg dollar imprints, but I never could find out how many other holy letter imprints were produced in the 1960s by two Pennsylvania Dutch village printers who stamped such on the backsides of U.S. dollar bills. On my maternal side, several members of the family kept handwritten Magdeburg briefs rolled up in milk bottles or placed in the attic (perhaps serving as protection for those hilltop homes that did not have lightning rods).[7]

World War I Letters of Protection for Soldiers

In 1917, during World War I, a holy letter was reprinted for Pennsylvania Dutch soldiers who were off at war by Charles Bower, the village printer of Oley, Pennsylvania. Copies of the traditional German 1724 Holstein letter from Heaven, which was a popular Christian amulet, would protect the bearer from being killed. Both Francis Rush and Bower's own son, James, carried copies of this holy letter when they went off to fight in World War I, and both returned home safe and sound to the Pennsylvania Dutch community of Oley. Mrs. Betty (Rush) Hoch kept her father's Holstein copy, which he had carried in the war, as a keepsake for many years. The second most popular type of holy letter carried in both world wars by local soldiers was the 1783 Magdeburg Himmelsbrief, which was copied both in the original German and in English to protect soldiers going to war from Berks County, Pennsylvania. Below is the English translation of the 1724 Holstein letter:

> *In the name of the Father, the Son and the Holy Ghost, as Christ stopped at Mt. Sian swords or guns shall stop. Whosoever carries this letter with him shall not be damaged through the enemies guns or weapons. God will give strength that he may not fear robbers or murderers, and guns, pistols, swords or muskets, shall be hurt through by the Cannon of Angel Michael in the name of the Father, the Son and the Holy Ghost, God be with you, and whosoever carries this letter shall be protected against all danger and who does not believe in it may copy it and tie it to the neck of a dog and shoot at him and they will see that this is true. Whosoever has this letter shall not be taken prisoner nor wounded by the enemy, Amen. As true as it is that Jesus Christ died and ascended into Heaven, and suffered on earth by the living God, the Father, the Son, the Holy Ghost. I pray in the name of Christ's blood that no ball shall hit you be it of gold, silver, lead or metal. God in Heaven may deliver you of all sins in the name of the Father, the Son and the Holy Ghost. This letter was found in Holstein 1724 where it fell from Heaven.*
>
> *It was written in golden letters and moved over the Babtrin of Magdaginery and when they tried to copy it, it moved away until 1791 that of everybody copy it and communicate it to the world. Then it is further written that whosoever works on Sunday he shall be*

condemned. Neither shall you work on Sunday but go to church and give the poor of your wealth for you shall not like the reasonless animals. I command you six days shall you work and on the seventh day listen to the Holy work of God. If you do not do so I will punish you that you shall not work too late on Saturday. Let you be rich or poor you shall pray for your sins that they may be forgiven, do not fear the intrigues of men and be sure as fast as I created you, that fast I can crush you. Also be not false, with tongue respect father and mother, do not bear false witness against your neighbor and I will give you good health and peace, but he who does not believe in it shall not have happiness nor blessings. If you do not convert yourself you certainly shall be punished at the day of judgment when you cannot account for your sins. Whosoever has this letter in the house no lightning shall strike it, and whosoever carries this shall bring forward fruit, keeping commandments which I have sent to you through my Angel in the name of my Son Jesus Christ, Amen.

Contemporary Holy Letters Still Carried Today

One June morning, staff members at the American Folklife Institute were invited to have breakfast with two of our contributing readers, David Henninger and Nancy (Seltzer) Heffner, at Jonelle's Restaurant on the Bowers-Lyons road, where many Pennsylvania Dutch natives congregate to enjoy good food and conversation. Since I had featured the folk legend of the Pennsylvania German Himmelsbrief in a recent issue of the *Kutztown Patriot*, including a follow-up about natives who carried these amulets of protection in later wars (including the Korean, Vietnam, and possibly Gulf War), attention was once again drawn to this popular folk religious belief. As a result, I had received a number of responses from local Pennsylvania Dutch people whose male relatives surely carried these heavenly letters to protect themselves from unnatural death.

David Henninger remembered being given such a traditional charm by his mother, who lived locally at Kempton, to protect him while serving in the nation's armed forces. Mr. Henninger's mother had also forwarded copies of the *Kutztown Patriot* newspaper to him for a number of years, wherever he traveled in his motor home, so he would not lose his connection to his humble Dutch roots. Through his many moves around the country, David still had retained a slight Dutch accent, which was apparent when he remarked that he missed the native Pennsylvania Dutch dialect columns once printed by local Vernon Kamp in the early *Patriot* editions.

Although David's original heavenly letter was given back to his mother, he managed to obtain another copy in English for the American Folklife archives, one very similar to the holy letter carried by Betty Hoch's father during World War I. David Henninger's mother kept her own heavenly letter hanging in her household for years after her son returned from war. Below is a letter I received from David, as well as an excerpt from my aforementioned column:

Ein Brief

so von

Gott selbsten geschrieben, und zu Magdeburg niedergelassen worden ist.

Er war mit goldenen Buchsta- durch einen Engel gesandt wor- den soll man ihn geben, wer ihn

ben geschrieben, und von Gott den; wer ihn abschreiben will, verachtet, von dem weichet

Der Herr.

Wer am Sonntag arbeitet, der ist verflucht. Demnach gebiete ich, daß ihr am Sonntag nicht arbeitet, sondern andächtig in die Kirche gehet; aber euer Angesicht nicht schmücket; ihr sollt nicht fremdes Haar tragen, und sollt nicht Hoffahrt treiben; von eurem Reichthum sollt ihr den Ar- men geben, reichlich mittheilen und glauben, daß dieser Brief mit meiner eigenen Hand geschrieben und von Christo selbsten ausgesandt sey, und daß ihr nicht thut wie das unvernünftige Vieh; ihr habt sechs Tage in der Woche, darinnen sollt ihr eure Arbeit verrichten: aber den siebenten (näm- lich den Sonntag) sollt ihr heiligen; werdet ihr das nicht thun, so will ich Krieg, Hunger, Pesti- lenz und Theurung unter euch schicken und euch mit vielen Plagen strafen. Auch gebiete ich euch, einem jeden, er sey wer er wolle, Jung und Alt, Klein und Groß, daß ihr am Samstag nie spät arbeitet, sondern ihr sollt eure Sünden bereuen, auf daß sie euch mögen vergeben werden. Be- gehret auch nicht Silber und Gold, treibet nicht Fleischeslust und Begierden; denket, daß ich euch gemacht habe und wieder zernichten kann.

Freuet euch nicht, wenn euer Nachbar arm ist,

habt vielmehr Mitleiden mit ihm, so wird es euch wohl gehen.

Ihr Kinder! ehret Vater und Mutter, so wird es euch wohl gehen auf Erden. Wer dies nicht glaubt und hält, der ist verdammt und verloren. Ich, Jesus, habe dieses selbsten mit meiner eige- nen Hand geschrieben, wer es widerspricht und lästert, derselbe Mensch soll keine Hülft von mir zu erwarten haben, wer den Brief hat und ihn nicht offenbaret, der ist verflucht von der christli- chen Kirche, und wenn eure Sünden noch so groß wären, sollen sie euch, wo ihr herzlich Reue und Leid habt, doch vergeben werden.

Wer es nicht glaubt, der soll sterben und in der Hölle gepeiniget werden, auch ich werfe am jüngsten Tage fragen um eure Sünden wenn da ihr mir dann antworten müsset.

Und derjenige Mensch, so diesen Brief bei sich trägt, oder in seinem Hause hat, dem wird kein Donnerwetter Schaden zufügen, er wird vor Feuer und Wasser sicher sein, und wer ihn offen- baret vor den Menschenkindern, der wird seinen Lohn haben, und fröhlich aus dieser Welt empfangen.

Haltet meinen Befehl, den ich euch durch meinen Engel gesandt habe, euer Gott vom Himmels-Thron, Gottes und Maria Sohn. Amen.

Dies ist geschehen zu Magdeburg im Jahr 1783.

Of the various Himmelsbriefs printed by the Philadelphia Germantown press for the Pennsylvania Dutch Country, this late 19th-century Magdeburg "Ein Brief" was quite elaborate and used as a Victorian wall piece—a prized example of Americana folk religion.

I read your article in *The Patriot* about Himmels Briefs. It brought back memories of me and my brother's military service time. My brother was two years older than I and enlisted in the Army. Just before he left for active duty in 1960 our mother gave him a letter to carry at all times to protect him. She told him it was a Heavenly letter.

In 1962 I enlisted in the Navy and also received the hand written letter from my mother. I did carry it with me for my whole tour of duty. I had totally forgotten about the letter until I read the article. My mother is now 88, still living in the Kempton area, and I called her and asked her where she got the letter. She told me she had it framed and hanging on the wall in the house. She also told me that she carries it with her all the time, maybe, that's why she will be 89 in April. Obviously my brother and I ended our military tours and returned home safely. I guess the letter helped after all.

I am retired and reside in Abingdon, Va., when not traveling in our motor home. We are currently "wintering" in Poteet, Texas. We will be making a trip to Kempton, PA in June and I will retrieve a copy of the letter from my mother. I was a native of Kempton until 1978 when I left and moved around a bit.

P.S. My mother gets a *Patriot* subscription mailed to me every year since I left Pennsylvania. Years ago Vernon Kamp, who was my Sunday school, teacher, used to write a column in the paper. One column was in Pennsylvania Dutch and the translation aside of it English. I am losing my ability to speak the Dutch language. I used his column to try to stay on top of it. Is there any chance that someone could reestablish the column or maybe, even reprint old issues? I think that would really help maintain and avoid the language from dying. Thanks.

My response:

Life is sacred and any family who suffers the loss of a loved one; or any woman who gives birth to a newborn child, will unequivocally agree how sacred a human life is in our Pennsylvania Dutch culture. Recently, I received a communication from David M. Henninger in regards to the PA Dutch practice of carrying a Holy Letter (Letter from Heaven), called in PA Dutch dialect, a "Himmels Brief." Mr. Henninger's mother had purchased him a subscription to the *Patriot* having moved out of Pennsylvania years ago to keep him acquainted with the area and his hometown of the Kempton area where his mother still resides.

Both he and his brother received a handwritten Holy Letter by his mother before going off in the service; he in 1962 for the Navy, and his brother in 1960 for the Army. This letter of God's protection was meant to keep them safe from any harm during their respective tours of duty, and they both did return home safely. His mother, 89 this month, has her Holy Letter framed on the wall of her home, as an amulet of protection and faith in the Lord. Himmelsbriefs were originally in German, and later translated into English, becoming Holy Letters today.

A PA Dutchman, Mr. Henninger recalls reading the German Dialect columns of Vernon Kamp with the translation in English right alongside of it. He suggests that we might reprint some of these columns to retain our native tongue at a time when the oldest living American veteran has died from World War I; it is ironic that our native Rhineland citizens went off to fight the Germans carrying the same Holy letters used for protection from the very same culture from which it was spawned.

Chapter Notes

Chapter 2

1. A scribe and well-read man, Hohman also could have been a "journeyman printer" moving from place to place seeking employment at shops that printed for the Pennsylvania Dutch and doing jobs for himself.

2. For further information on John George Hohman's life and writings, see the April 1948 issue of the *Historical Review of Berks County*.

Chapter 3

1. Built in 1743, the Roman Catholic Church of the Holy Sacrament had a German catechism printed for it by John George Hohman in 1819, the same year that he wrote *The Long Lost Friend*.

Chapter 4

1. For further reading, see Thomas R. Brendle and Claude W. Unger, "Folk Medicine of the Pennsylvania Germans," *Pennsylvania German Society* XLV (1931).

Chapter 6

1. Interviews with Richard H. Shaner about Freddie and Annie Bieber, 1997, 2003, 2006, 2015, 2017.

Chapter 8

1. This letter was reprinted from the *Pennsylvania Magazine*, volume 13 (1889), published by the Historical Society of Philadelphia.

Chapter 10

1. Peter G. Bertolet, *Fragments of the Past: Historical Sketches of Oley and Vicinity* (1860).

2. The American Folklife Society, which was entrusted by the owner, Richard Boyer, with operating the historic Keim houses and a portion of the estate for a museum and festival grounds in the 1970s, placed the buildings on the Historic National Register on May 1, 1974.

3. Richard Boyer, a descendant of Mahlon Boyer from Pine Grove, gifted the historic Keim buildings to the Historic Preservation Trust of Berks County in 1978, after the American Folklife Society decided it would no longer hold its folk festivals.

Chapter 11

1. Sociologically speaking, "culture shock" would have been twice as devastating for Betsy Keim once she realized that her sisters were gone and no one else could replace them. Betsy continued to use primitive household tools and folkways; the leap from habitual colonial ways to the automation of the 20th century was much too great for her to make. Yet her old German religion brought comfort in the form of a mysterious, all-powerful God, whom she knew could be trusted in his design for the earth.

Chapter 12

1. Edwin M. Fogel, *Beliefs and Superstitions of the Pennsylvania Germans* (Philadelphia: American Germanica Press, 1915).

Chapter 16

1. Wilbur H. Oda, "John George Hohman:

Man of Many Parts," *The Pennsylvania Dutchman* I, no. 16 (1949): 1.

Chapter 17

1. Allie Day (of Irish descent), whose mother possessed unusual healing abilities, often told Alma he needed to hug her, for he had not used his Powwowing ability much and had to pass his overload of healing power onto a member of the opposite sex. Allie Day's brother, Charlie, who also had lived near Fredericksville, was said to be a charming gentleman but was not as Dutchified (that is, acculturated to local Pennsylvania Dutch heritage) as Allie.

Chapter 22

1. Delinquent in not clipping his scovy ducks' wings, Harry E. Miller (1877–1936), whose farm was adjacent to the college campus, was often embarrassed when they flew with migratory ducks to perch atop the clock tower of Old Main. His farm, eventually acquired by the university under President Lawrence Stratton in 1972, was later converted into the Pennsylvania German Heritage Center by the Kutztown University Foundation. With the aid of the Pennsylvania Dutch Folk Culture Society at nearby Lenhartsville, founded by alumni members Russell and Florence Baver, the foundation operated the center and acquired the necessary assets of the Folk Culture Society for the museum.

Chapter 23

1. For an excellent study on Pennsylvania Dutch folk art and early Germanic fraktur designs, read Dr. Donald A. Shelley's *Fraktur Writings of the Pennsylvania Germans* (Allentown: Pennsylvania German Folklore Society, 1961).

2. It is possible that the builder of the 1801 Bieber homestead was a John Bieber (1748–1844), grandson of the immigrant George Bieber and recorded as living two miles east of town. As further documented, he was a prominent and generous citizen of Maxatawny Township.

3. In his 1886 *History of Berks County, Pennsylvania*, Morten L. Montgomery lists gristmills in the vicinity of the Snyder barn at Lenhartsville and speaks of the old Kistler mill as having a substantial stone house. Since old Route 143 cuts behind the Snyder barn across an adjacent waterway, it is possible that it was a subsequent farm-mill operation.

Chapter 24

1. Heber W. Youngken, *Pharmaceutical Botany* (Philadelphia: Blakiston, 1921).

2. John King, Harvey Wickes Felter, and John Uri Lloyd, *King's American Dispensatory* (Cincinnati: Ohio Valley Co., 1909), 431.

3. *Ibid.*, 286.

Chapter 25

1. Richard L.T. Orth is one of several Americana collectors in Berks County who has been fortunate enough to have amassed a fine collection of native Pennsylvania Dutch material culture, which is a part of his native ancestry.

2. Wilbur H. Oda, "The Himmelsbrief," *The Pennsylvania Dutchman* I, no. 21 (1949): 3.

Chapter 26

1. For a definitive explanation of heavenly letters, see Dr. Don Yoder, *The Pennsylvania German Broadside* (University Park, PA: Pennsylvania German Society, Pennsylvania State University Press, 2005).

2. Charles R. Roberts, *History of Lehigh County*, Volume I (Allentown, PA: Lehigh Publishing Company, 1914), 433.

3. Wilbur H. Oda, "John George Hohman: Man of Many Parts," *The Pennsylvania Dutchman* I, no. 16 (1949): 1.

4. Alfred L. Shoemaker, *Rhymes and Jingles of the Pennsylvania Dutch* (Lancaster, PA: Pennsylvania Dutch Folklore Center, Franklin & Marshall College, 1951).

5. Rudolph Stube, American Folklife Institute Archives.

6. Yoder, *The Pennsylvania German Broadside*, 216.

7. Conversations with Richard Shaner about Dr. Alfred L. Shoemaker's Pennsylvania folklife archives of the 1960s.

Bibliography

Bertolet, Peter G. *Fragments of the Past: Historical Sketches of Oley and Vicinity.* 1860.

Birmelin, John. "The Later Poems of John Birmelin." *Pennsylvania German Society* XVI (1951): 117–18.

Brendle, Thomas R., and Claude W. Unger. "Folk Medicine of the Pennsylvania Germans." *Pennsylvania German Society* XLV (1931).

Croll, Reverend P.C. *Annals of the Oley Valley in Berks County, PA.* Reading, PA: Reading Eagle Press, 1926.

Eshelman, John E. "The Keim Family of Lobachsville." *Historical Review of Berks County* XXI, no. 1 (October–December 1955).

Fogel, Edwin M. *Beliefs and Superstitions of the Pennsylvania Germans.* Philadelphia: American Germanica Press, 1915.

Graver, Lee. *Beacon on the Hill: A Centennial History of Kutztown State College.* Kutztown, PA: Kutztown State College, 1966.

"Heads of Families at the First Census of the United States in the Year 1790—Pennsylvania." Washington, DC, 1909. https://www2.census.gov/library/publications/decennial/1790/heads_of_families/pennsylvania/1790i-02.pdf.

Hollinshead, Benjamin M. "Mountain Mary." In "Pennsylfawnisch Deitsch Eck," *Allentown Call,* October 21, 1939.

King, John, Harvey Wickes Felter, and John Uri Lloyd. *King's American Dispensatory.* Cincinnati: Ohio Valley Co., 1909.

Montgomery, Morten L. *History of Berks County, Pennsylvania.* 1886.

Nutting, Wallace. *Pennsylvania Beautiful.* Eastern edition. New York: Bonanza Books, 1924.

Oda, Wilbur H. "The Himmelsbrief." *The Pennsylvania Dutchman* I, no. 21 (1949): 3.

_____. "John George Hohman: Man of Many Parts." *The Pennsylvania Dutchman* I, no. 16 (1949): 1.

Robacker, Earl F. *Pennsylvania German Literature, 1683–1942.* Philadelphia: University of Pennsylvania Press, 1943.

Roberts, Charles R. *History of Lehigh County.* Volume I. Allentown, PA: Lehigh Publishing Company, 1914.

Rupp, I. Daniel. *History of the Counties of Berks and Lebanon.* Lancaster, PA: G. Hills, 1844.

Shelley, Donald A. *Fraktur Writings of the Pennsylvania Germans.* Allentown: Pennsylvania German Folklore Society, 1961.

Shoemaker, Alfred L. *Pennsylvania Hex Marks.* Lancaster, PA: Pennsylvania Dutch Folklore Center, Franklin & Marshall College, 1950.

_____. *Rhymes and Jingles of the Pennsylvania Dutch.* Lancaster, PA: Pennsylvania Dutch Folklore Center, Franklin & Marshall College, 1951.

Strassburger, Ralph Beaver, and William John Hinke. *Pennsylvania German Pioneers.* Volumes I and II. Norristown, PA: Pennsylvania German Society, 1934.

Yoder, Don. *Discovering American Folklife.* Mechanicsburg, PA: Stackpole Books, 2001.

_____. "Kutztown and America." *Pennsylvania Folklife* XIV, no. 4 (1965).

_____. *The Pennsylvania German Broadside.* University Park, PA: Pennsylvania German Society, Pennsylvania State University Press, 2005.

Youngken, Heber W. *Pharmaceutical Botany.* Philadelphia: Blakiston, 1921.

Index

253